What people are saying about
From the Ganges to the Snake River

*Writing in first person, Majumdar tells of serene
Idaho—a place far from his native India . . . exam-
ining the landscape through an outsider's eyes and
reflecting on his experiences from India. ..."From
Ganges to the Snake River" may awaken memories
in the reader, leading him or her to realize how the
world changes but some things remain constant. . .*
—David Eggert,
Idaho Falls *Post Register*

*Majumdar's wittily agile and empathic percep-
tions embrace a true internationalist's view of two
vastly different worlds. His profound insights and
experiences in India and Idaho bring these worlds
together with spirit and clarity. The grand sweep of
mythology, history, and modern life of the Ganges
and Snake Rivers is brought into the reader's mind
and heart with the vivid and finely nuanced
accounts of this gifted writer.*
—Carl Eberl, Professor Emeritus,
City University of New York,
Conductor Laureate,
Sun Valley Summer Symphony.

*The continuous interweaving of the Indian cul-
ture with north American reality, the intelligent
shuttle between past and present, meticulously
observed details of everyday life, penetrating dialogue, a human warmth and a love of nature are but
a few features of Majumdar's literary work. So much
sincerity is hard to find in the troubled times of
commercialized modern literature.*
—Leon Torossian,
Editor, *Echo*, Vienna, Austria

From the Ganges
to the
Snake River

An East Indian
in the American West

Cover Photo of the Snake River by Robert Bower

From the Ganges
to the
Snake River

An East Indian
in the American West

Debu Majumdar

CAXTON PRESS
Caldwell, Idaho
2000

The stories and essays in this book, except for "Indians Across the Ocean,"
first appeared in their original form, as a joint publication by Rendezvous:
Journal of Arts and letters (Vol 33, No. 1) and the
Idaho State University Press.

Library of Congress Cataloging-in-Publication Data

Debu Majumdar —December 10, 1941
    From The Ganges to the Snake River: An East Indian in the American West/ Debu
    Majumdar
        p. cm.
    Includes bibliographical references and index.
    ISBN 0-87004-397-8 (pbk.)
    1. Majumdar, D. (Debu). 2. East Indian Americans—Idaho—Idaho
Falls—Biography. 3. Idaho Falls (Idaho)—Biography. 4. Idaho Falls
(Idaho)—Social life and customs. 5. Calcutta (India)—Biography. 6. Calcutta
(India)—Social life and customs.
    I. Title.

F754.I2 M35 2000
979.6'53--dc21
[B]
                                                                    00-020777

Lithographed and bound in the United States of America
CAXTON PRESS
Caldwell, Idaho
165703

To my sister, Dr. Nilima Sarkar, a true scientist who will probably never find any time to read this collection.

TABLE OF CONTENTS

Photographs

Photos by Robert Bower
Photo of Benaras, the Holy City of the Ganges, by Jarmila Pech.

FOREWARD

By Dante Cantrill

The practice of viewing ourselves through the eyes of others has a tradition in American letters that is almost as old as the country itself. This is merely to say that, nationally as well as individually, the image we form of ourselves is influenced by the ways other people describe us.

Since the early nineteenth century, when we began to look through the words of Alexis de Tocqueville to help us interpret our experiment in democracy, American readers have repeatedly used the verbal expressions that outsiders have rendered us by to form ideas and feelings about our customs, beliefs, even the very climate and land. These literary mirrors help us measure ourselves against the ideals we think we project through our actions. If we find shortcomings in the comparison, we can usually rationalize by saying that the observer just didn't understand the way things really work from the inside; but occasionally we come across a piece that puts together both perspectives.

A few years ago, Bill Bryson, a native Iowan who moved to London for several years, returned to tour the United States and report on what he saw; the result, *The Lost Continent*, gives the viewpoint of someone with the understanding of a local and the fascination of a foreigner. This synthesis is particularly interesting because the realities of any place and its people can best be described by those who can get beyond the externals to see the systems as they operate, as only insiders can do.

Of course, Americans are not the only resident-subjects in the travel-and-report literature that abounds. In fact, during the twentieth century, our writers turned the tables by multiples, with accounts of other places, other cultures that are among the most popular literary works today. From Nepal to Tuscany, virtually no region in the world is now free from such scrutiny for exotica that might interest us. Ultimately, what is behind this is the fundamental drive to satisfy our curiosity, to find interesting differences, to know more about the world. And, by way of that, to know more about ourselves. When Margaret Mead published her landmark book, *Coming of Age in Samoa*, in 1928, she pointed out that we can benefit in our struggle to create a better society by learning how other societies do things in comparable situations. She traveled to old, traditional cultures in the South Pacific to make a comparison against her own young and rapidly changing one.

A great irony about Mead's study is that although the cultures she visited were long-settled and well-developed, they served her need for a "primitive" culture: one that she thought would demonstrate a simpler, more basic lifestyle than hers. It was a sort of return to "nature" to provide an alternative to our technologically customized "civilization." In fact, as we look into it, we will find that this search for a more natural place by which to measure one's more civilized culture has very often been the underlying attitude, even the conscious driving force, for literature about others—the history of literature is dotted with such.

Sometimes, as in Charles Dickens' writings about his journey to America, the report conveys sarcasm to the point of disgust, but in most instances the authorial attitude is sympathetic, perhaps admiring, and good-willed, even if sometimes patronizing. This kind of writing does not have to be taken as a sign of colonialist mentality, as some are quick to suspect these days; we simply want to find something other, something different, because that is how we learn more about who and what we are.

It is interesting, though, how much twentieth-century American writing about other people—many living in much older cultures—inverted this relationship of "natural" versus "civilized." Travelers have gone from here to all parts of Europe, Asia, Africa, South America, and the many islands between in search of a more primitive world to describe. There is a romantic quality to the adventure: looking for a more pure, benevolent, wise, serene, and healthy world, one not gripped with a fever for money, violence, pollution, and technology. Energized by a reaction against a sense of decadence here, journalists and ethnographers, missionaries, nurses, and scientists have been joined by dilettante settlers and even retirees from the "First" world in their search for the simpler life.

And so it is amusing and not inappropriate to find ourselves inspected in just this same way by someone from the outside. Let's face it, after all: without the inclusion of Native Americans, we in America are a much younger society than most. We are, at least technically, the barbarians. In unprecedented ways, the more "civilized" people from the older world, now technologically informed, can visit us and compare their lives with ours. We are moving steadily and quickly to become a global community in our time, and most of the time America is the "nature" in the equation. But this is a good thing for the world, whichever side we symbolize. We can all now see more readily how others live, learn what they think, answer their questions and question their answers.

I became acquainted with the author of this series of engaging essays a few years ago, when he audited a course in contemporary nonfiction that I was teaching on the Idaho Falls campus of Idaho State University. Halfway through the course, after listening to our talk about ways to apply aesthetic consideration to what is sometimes called the "prose of fact," Debu one day modestly handed me a short piece he had written and asked me just to read it. I did, and I told him later that I found it rather slight but charming and pleasant to read. It was about his experience of an Idaho winter, his first, and though it seemed to lack the heaviness that is characteristic of much work in this genre today, a heaviness that might come from much detail or clever language or narrative self-consciousness, nevertheless it was refreshing because of its honesty and directness, as well as its simplicity. I complimented him sincerely and wished him well. A second essay appeared in my hands the next day.

So the process began, one essay after another, sometimes soon, sometimes with delay and encouragement: Debu, now settled for several years in Idaho, appeared to discover, in the act of writing about his new home, a range of experiences and emotions that involved more than a purely objective account of the physical features of this "exotic" frontier. As he moved from one topic to another, as he realized that ideas he had long stored up were legitimate subjects for writing, he seemed to grow into the understanding of what essays are all about: they are efforts to understand the world by talking about it. And as he continued to revise his descriptions of various aspects of his new life in Idaho, his work took on more profoundly interesting dimensions.

The entire series started with disparate, impressionistic accounts of normal events in Idaho Falls, simple portraits of ordinary daily life; then they gradually acquired, in assemblage, metaphoric depth as they uncovered a deeper sense of possibilities in making the connections in our global community. Fortunately, Debu's writing does not suffer from this increasing sense of meaning behind the descriptions. He manages to keep his narrative viewpoint consistently "innocent," to let us see clearly. And by bringing the old world—which is new to most of us—to bear on this new world of ours, he helps us think again about the ways our lives are often aged by routine and presumption.

To me, the most delightful aspect of Debu Majumdar's attempt to describe our Southeast Idaho culture is that he is an Indian American. For too long, we more recently immigrated Americans have lived contentedly in a land long ago settled by people we named "Indians" and then set aside as outsiders. The double meaning of the word "Indian" lends a resonance, an ironic vibrancy, to this Indian's portrait of a land and culture that still bears the raw features of the primitive. This Indian comes from a much older world whose roots are the same as those of Euro- and Asian-Americans; he is one of these. But, as the name suggests, his ancestors are also the ancestors of our American Indians; he is one of these, too. If anyone has trouble following the genealogy, he can at least understand the symbolism. Debu's Indianness confuses the denotation of "Indian," and his often-professed role of outsider in this book suddenly takes on a new, startling dimension. Indians, on both sides of us, have us surrounded: we are being watched and we see ourselves as we are.

Robert Bower

Chapter One
FIRST IDAHO WINTER

I clearly remember the day I first arrived in Idaho Falls from New York, the day after Thanksgiving in 1980. It was a crystal clear day. The plane flew over long stretches of mountains and lava fields, and I remember seeing clusters of human habitation separated by wide open fields below, all connected by one narrow black road. The drive from the airport reminded me of the little mining towns I had seen in Colorado. "Oh boy," I thought, "where am I taking myself to?"

On December 12, I woke up and found everything white, and still snowing. More than a foot of snow on the roofs of buildings! Looking from our bedroom window in the West 15th Street apartment, I was certain there had been a blizzard through the night, with snowfall the likes of which we had seen only once in several years on Long Island. I rushed to the front door to get a clear view of the snowy landscape, but couldn't open it against the pile of snow. I woke up everyone and shouted with joy, "Snow day today—no school, no work!"

Through clutter of unopened boxes, the playpen and chairs, I threaded my way to the kitchen and started hot water for tea. My wife and two children came down the stairs, bubbling with happiness: "Daddy doesn't have to go to work today." Had the TV been working we would have known about this storm, but now we all looked outside with amazement; the beauty of the snow had covered the otherwise drab neighborhood. We had heard of Idaho winters, but hadn't expected this, especially at the beginning of December.

"Until they clear the roads everything must stop in this town," I told myself. No plows had come to clear the road, and no car drove by our apartment. I worked diligently and got the front door open and spoke to my wife, "Let's go out and see how bad the situation is."

Along the road to South Boulevard there were no people. Snow-covered pickup trucks in driveways stood as symbols of the stand-still town. The smell of burning wood filled the air. Black-gray smoke rose almost straight up from top of chimneys, and the neighborhood looked stationary and as picturesque as a painting by Grandma Moses.

A man, without gloves, was shoveling his driveway, and I wondered how he was going to drive on the road even if he did clear his driveway.

"When are they going to clear the roads?" I asked the man.

"It may be a week before they come to this street," he said, and looked at me as if I should know that. "We'll be lucky if they clear the main roads today."

A few cars were running on South Boulevard. The road was full of snow, but that didn't stop them. "There must be many accidents on this road," I thought. But I couldn't see any cars stranded; the few cars on the road had been parked last night, before the snow. We walked toward 17th Street and Tautphaus Park. We passed a few children playing at Hawthorne Elementary School playground. An older woman was with them. "Was she the teacher?" I wondered.

There were more cars on 17th Street, going both ways at rather high speeds. I hoped they were good drivers. "No one would drive in these conditions on Long Island," I told my wife. Why drive at all? Nothing could be open today!

We walked further south along South Boulevard, the wealthy neighborhood of Idaho Falls. Tall trees gracefully draped with snow stood next to driveways of big houses. Here the street was also lined with trees, as a boulevard should be. In contrast, the row of houses on 17th Street, which we had just left, looked like small summer cottages at the far end of Long Island.

We passed by the hospital. It looked lively. "I'm glad they can keep the hospital functioning," I thought. Opposite the hospital, the park was white and beautiful; the row of pines at the end dazzled with snow sculpture. The round fountain in the middle stood out like a grand wedding cake. But there was no one at the park, no children playing in the snow. The mothers must have kept them in their warm homes on such a day.

It was then that I looked toward the southeast end and saw the most wondrous sight in Idaho Falls—a row of sparkling white mountains against the sky. They rose like the Himalayan ranges one sees from far away. I remembered my first experience of the Himalayas from my aunt's house in the planes of Siliguri, below Darjeeling. I stood and gazed at them for a long time: "What a beautiful place, and we are going to live here."

We returned to our apartment, but I suddenly decided that I would walk in the other direction to my office on Second Street to see how bad conditions were there. "I shall be back soon," I told my family.

The road conditions were worse along the low-numbered streets until I reached Holmes Avenue. Traffic on this road was similar to that of 17th Street, with a fair number of cars going faster than I thought safe.

When I reached our office parking lot there were piles of snow on it, but there were also cars parked there. Some of these seemed to have a ton of snow on top of them. I was surprised to see so many cars in the parking lot. Since I worked for the federal government, I knew the security people would be there, and I thought I'd go inside and say hello to them.

As I entered the building I saw the guards in the lobby, chatting as usual. The building was warm, and I saw my co-worker, Armando, coming down the stairs.

"Hey! What are you doing here today?" I shouted at him.

He looked at me puzzled. "Why? Aren't you at work?"

"What? Isn't it a snow day today?"

"Heavens," he said. "This is nothing! Wait till January, then you'll see snow."

Flabbergasted, I went upstairs and found everyone at their desks—a most normal day at the office.

Chapter Two
IDAHO TROUT

The first time I received a call from Idaho I was very surprised! It was for a position with the government, but I hadn't applied for a job in Idaho. In fact Idaho did not exist in my mind; one might as well think of Saskatchewan. So my spontaneous reaction was "Thanks, but no thanks," and I hung up. For someone who came to this country from India, Idaho has a connotation of the frozen North Pole. I chuckled and told my wife, Catherine, about the call from the federal government.

"You know, Idaho has its own beauty," she said. "Perhaps you should be a little more open-minded." Coming from a woman born and brought up in New York, the response was a surprise.

"So, tell me what is good there beside potatoes?"

"What about trout? You hardly find freshwater fish here."

That was intriguing. I grew up in Calcutta eating a small piece of fish floating in a soupy curry sauce with rice for both lunch and dinner. If one asked for more, there was none, because each piece was already counted for every member of the family. So we learned to savor its flavor in the curried rice. Going to a supermarket and being able to buy fresh fish would be like going to heaven for a Bengali. "Hmm. Fresh trout."

Destiny looms over our lives, and a few months later on a November day in 1980, I flew to Idaho Falls and my family followed a few weeks later. It was not the trout that helped me make my decision. That came from an unexpected corner.

Catherine's father told me that he refused to go to New Jersey in 1949 when he was offered a big territory for his sporting goods business. "Who goes to the hinterland?" he told me, "I vehemently refused, and stayed on Long Island." He looked far outside through the bay window in our living room and, although he was retired for some time, I could see regret in his face. Indeed New Jersey flourished in the next two decades and made the man who accepted the job very rich. It was not the money that bothered my father-in-law (he did quite well in his life), but the failure to accept the challenge and go to an uncharted territory that haunted him most. "You have come all the way from India. What's the difference to you between New York and Idaho?"

As soon as we settled, actually the second day after my family's arrival in Idaho Falls, I went to the biggest Safeway in the area, and looked for trout. There was none. I carefully searched the aisles again, but there was no trout anywhere. Puzzled, I went to the manager and asked where he kept trout.

"You want to buy trout?" The manager looked at me sympathetically. "They are not sold in supermarkets. You can buy other frozen fish here."

"No trout in this store?" I was so astounded. "Is there another store that sells trout?"

"You can't buy trout. It's free. You have to catch it." He smiled and patted my shoulder, "Go buy a fishing rod."

It was a blow to my dream—no fresh trout curry for lunch or dinner. "How strange. It is free, but I have to catch it."

At the office my colleagues comforted me. They told me many stories of trout fishing, how they caught big trout in many streams. The mere mention of trout fishing brought several more to my office. "It's so easy," they all assured me. "It's fun, you'll see."

"We'll get some fish for you next season," Dennis told me.

The summer came and I bought a fishing rod, a Mitchell reel, lead sinkers, forty-pound nylon line, and a few shiny metal lures. I was ready, but my two sons were more ready

Robert Bower

than I. They used the hobby horse stick and practiced fishing in the small living room of our apartment. They jumped up and down and told us, "We'll catch big fish." I loved watching their excited, happy faces. "This is what Idaho is all about," I thought. They would grow up loving what nature offered here.

I bought a detailed map of the area and looked for streams and lakes where we could go for fishing, but everything was far away—one would have to drive miles to go there. I consulted my colleagues at the office. They all pored over the maps and traded fish stories, but no one told me where to go.

When I asked directly, "Well, suggest to me a place I can try out this weekend," they talked among themselves. "Hmm, he can try the Buffalo River, that's good." Someone said, "Perhaps Silver Creek. What do you think?" Another said, "That's good but the current is fast now, try out Indian Creek." And they all dispersed.

I looked at the map. The Buffalo River was fifty miles away. "Do I have to drive that far to go fishing?" Silver Creek was nearby, but I found the name in several areas. Was it a common name for several streams? How do I get to Silver Creek for fishing? Was there a public place where people go for fishing? I bought a fishing license, but did I need permission from the landowner to fish from his property?

Willis, my coworker, told me, "Go to Birch Creek or the Camas Creek in the Mud Lake area. It is very easy. Drive north, and when you see a stream, park the car and fish."

So, the next Saturday, I took my family out for fishing, and drove north along Route 15. "We'll have fish curry for dinner tonight."

In ten minutes we left Idaho Falls behind and passed by green fields, acres after acres, and mountains showed up in the distance. We gazed at the mountains, white snow still on their peaks, and exclaimed, "What a beautiful country!" After about half an hour of driving through side roads, we saw a stream. Willow, birch and aspen trees grew along the banks, and its water looked silvery—rippling through pasture land. It was very pretty to watch the stream. "Was this the creek I'm supposed to fish?" I wondered. "But how do I get there? Through the farms?" Fences bordered the lands and occasionally one or two horses roamed in the fields.

I couldn't see any path to the stream, and no place to park. Finally, in desperation, I parked the car on the shoulder of the narrow road. We walked along the road with my fishing gear but found no path to the stream. We found an open field and walked across it. There was no other way to reach the water. The few cows grazing nearby looked at us once and went back to grazing: "Strange humans. Don't know what they are doing."

I hooked a small lure to my rod, the one the store owner told me would be good for catching trout. The stream was clear, I could see its bottom very clearly, but the flow was fast. "Are there trout in this stream?" I cast my line and waited. My older son went to the water and called for the fish. He ran back and forth between the stream and his mother telling her how it was proceeding. My other son went straight into the water and wanted to catch a fish with his hands.

While my two sons talked, ran around, and cheered me on, I tried over and over again to cast my line at different parts of the stream, but got nowhere, no bite. "How long do I wait with the line?" I asked myself.

Time passed by. Catherine sat quietly and read a book. But she could not concentrate because our two sons were running back and forth and telling her what they were finding in the stream. "Daddy, when are you going to catch a fish?" my older son asked several times.

I questioned if one could fish with young children around. But how could I go fishing without taking them along?

The surrounding was uniquely beautiful—my family was there and no one else under the wide blue sky. The few trees along the stream provided shade for us, and the fields around were lush green. Distant mountains stood still in the sky. What a contrast to New York. Then I wondered, "Have we trespassed on someone's property?"

When I was totally frustrated, and the children disappointed, two teenagers came along walking in the stream with fishing rods in their hands. They had several small trout in a basket. They threw the lines in the same spot I was fishing and little trout appeared magically and bit their hooks. Suddenly I could see many trout in the water. They were small and shiny. The two boys caught several and ran along the river. They were having such fun. All this happened in a few minutes and they were gone, and we were back to the same place.

"How come they caught fish and I don't get a bite?" I asked myself.

We returned home empty-handed.

Willis confided in me: "Fishing locations are secrets; no one will tell you their favorite spots!"

"But there is so much trout in Idaho?"

"It is an enigma. You'll discover it yourself."

"Do you eat fish?" I asked.

"Oh, no. I hate fish."

"Why do you fish then?"

"Why? It is to get away. It is wonderful to be alone and fishing. I take a six pack, some sandwiches and snacks, and spend the whole day fishing. It's great."

"You don't care what you bring back?"

"No. I release them."

Then he told me to go to the Roberts Bird Sanctuary. "It's close by and you will catch some there."

Undaunted with the last experience, we ventured out to Roberts. It was a small town on Route 15, but we couldn't see a sign for the sanctuary and ended up in the town. It was Sunday and no one was around. A bar stood out at the center, which surprised me: "A bar in the middle of a Mormon town?"

I saw a man feeding his horse and asked, "Is there a fishing place here?"

"What? Fishing? No fishing here."

"How do I go to the bird sanctuary?"

"That's easy."

He gave me directions. I was pleased when a nice road led us to the place—a wilderness with plants, mostly cattails, grown all over the area. We searched for a fishing creek but found water in something that looked like a canal in between the cattails. No one was in sight. Was this the place Willis had mentioned?

Morning sun cast its warm rays on the plants, and I saw birds scooping in and out of the canals. Lots of different birds: yellow warblers, hummingbirds, redwing black birds, sandhill cranes, killdeers, and Western tanagers. They must be diving for insects. Fish must also be there. I took out my rod. I could not go to where the birds were feeding and settled for the near-by water. I threw my line and it immediately got stuck in a cattail on the other side. I pulled the rod, swung it this way and that, but it remained stuck. Finally, Catherine said, "Cut it and let go."

Next time I was careful. The children ran around, and finally went away with their mother to another spot to watch the butterflies. "Call us, Daddy, when you get a bite."

"Good. I can now fish in peace."

But no fish came to my hook. Worse, my line got caught again and I lost another lure. Another struggle. I looked at the far end toward the mountains. What intensely blue skies. Why couldn't I just enjoy the day and forget everything else?

On Monday at the office, Dennis was beaming with pride. Sunday, he had caught a twenty-inch trout at Ririe Lake. Our secretary, Pat, said she had also caught a big one last year from the lake. Dennis advised me to go to the lake. "It's easier to fish from the lake."

Finally, someone had revealed a secret location! I bought a few more lures, and rushed to Ririe Lake the next Saturday. It was straight forward to go there for a change. We took Route 26 going east and saw a sign for the reservoir a few miles before Heise. The lake looked big, but calm. It was not in a scenic place—no interesting mountain loomed in the distance and no panoramic view came into sight. Instead it was brown all around. The lake was a reservoir in a large hole in the middle of several hills. A few boats stood still in the calm water. When we walked close to the lake, I saw only two men fishing from the shore.

One man shouted at us, "Watch out. There are rattlesnakes here."

"Rattlesnakes, you say?" I was shocked.

"Yes. One man was bitten yesterday."

Catherine stopped, and held our boys close to her. "Oh, brother!" she said, and was ready to return.

"Let me try once," I told her. "Then we'll go back."

We walked slowly and very carefully. We saw a single man fly-fishing at one corner. What a desolate, but striking picture, it was. How wonderfully the line swung in the air before falling on water. We gazed at the man. The line went up in the air so gracefully, made a loopy curve and gently came down to the water as if to kiss it, and lay on the surface for a fish to be fooled by the colorful lure. It was indeed an art. One could watch how the man was throwing the line for hours. It appeared to me that he was fishing so single-mindedly—nothing else existed beside his rod, the line, and the fish. A great game he was playing alone and having fun even if he didn't catch any. "Was this why people talk about fishing?" I wondered.

I cast a few times but got no bite. The line fell on the water lifeless and only drifted with the current. A motor boat zipped by, sending waves to the shore. I doubted that I was at the right place for my kind of fishing.

At the office I asked Dennis which part of the shore he was fishing from.

"Shore? I don't fish from the shore. It's too hard. I have a boat. I go to the middle and fish where there is no one."

He told me that some people do catch fish from the shore. "You have to practice. You will learn."

Then he said, "Have you tried the Snake River? Go there after work, spend a few hours. You may catch some. In fact you may get a big one from the river."

Wow! The river was next to our apartment. "Why didn't I think of that before?"

The Snake River goes through the heart of Idaho Falls, and Memorial Drive by the river had become my favorite road to come home from work—the river on the right and distant unnamed mountains on the far southeast, the most scenic place in Idaho Falls. Small Keefer Island, with an old cabin standing as a symbol of the early settlers, sits out in mid-stream. The tall Mormon Temple with its angel on the spire rises gloriously on one side, and ducks and Canadian geese make their home on the other bank. Construction work was going on for the Broadway Bridge, and I decided that I should get away from the center and go south of the 17th Street Bridge. There is an island in the middle there and water flows in uniform patterns on its two sides. I had not seen people fishing from this area. This should be an ideal place. When I went there alone, however, someone was already fishing, and he had caught a large fish.

"What's biting?" I asked.

He showed me a spinner with yellow and red dots, but I didn't have that. I tied a different lure, cast a line some distance away from him, and opened a can of beer. This part of the town was desolate—a concrete mix factory stood on the opposite bank. Streams of cars passed by on the bridge over the river. The noteworthy thing was the water and I watched how it was moving. As my line drifted, I cast again, and again. Soon I was absorbed in doing that. I didn't care that no fish were biting. It was fun to throw the line and watch it fall and drift in the water. An hour passed by. The crimson rays of the sun dimmed, and I could hear birds settling in a nearby tree. The traffic had become slow on the bridge and headlights were on. I collected my tackle-box—it was time to go home.

July came and I hadn't caught a fish. I had stopped talking about fishing in the office. Out of the blue, one day, my boss, George, asked me, "Are you ready for an experience?"

I didn't know what was in his mind, and looked up. He winked and said, "I'll take you out fishing, if you want to."

I was elated because he was a great fisherman. Stories about him abound in the office.

He closed the door, stared at me for a few seconds, and said, "You have to promise that you won't tell anyone about my fishing place. It's a secret. I'll kill you if you tell anyone."

I had stopped being surprised when it was about fishing. I said, "Sure. I won't tell anybody. Besides, I am still new, I wouldn't know where we go anyway. You are safe."

One afternoon we went fishing straight from work. He came prepared; he had everything in his truck: his clothes, the cool beer, worms, snacks, everything. Before we started, he reminded me that I must not tell anyone where we were going.

We went to Bone Road, and continued driving for what seemed like hours to me. We went by many hills; soon I was totally lost. We passed by an isolated, dilapidated outhouse. Finally he pulled the truck on top of a hill and parked. He pointed down below and stated, "That's Willow Creek." I saw with horror that if he hadn't put on the brakes just when he did, it could have been a disaster—a steep downhill below, no road, only boulders scattered all over.

He looked around, and said, "We'll have good fishing. First I have to take a leak."

We went down the hill and came to a creek with bushes on both sides. The sun could set in an hour.

"This is the time the fish will have their last bite," he told me in a low voice. His mood was changing, and I thought he was transforming to a fisherman. He got down in the middle of the stream and waded through the water. I followed him: "I must get in to catch fish. So be it."

He opened a can and said, "Worms are the best for brook trout." I put a worm through my hook; I was disgusted, as its soft body wiggled and protested.

"Don't take that long to hook a worm," George whispered to me. "Just do it."

I threw my line and it went straight to the other side and caught a bush. "Oh, shit," he shouted. I struggled to free the line. Finally he untangled the line and went ahead of me.

It was late, and the shadows in the canyon made it darker. I cast a line. I proceeded in the direction of George. The river took a bend, and I could neither see nor hear him. Fishing in such a stream down in the canyon was new to me—especially being alone. Sunshine lit up a small portion of the eastern canyon wall, and the stream made a gentle, soothing sound as it flowed on its rocky bed.

I looked back and the darkness had a dense, almost solid quality to it. Suddenly a thought came to me: what if a bear or a wild animal came over? George had moved ahead of me. A chill ran down my spine. It was the spirit of adventure I didn't have. "I'm really a city boy," I told myself. Like he parked the car, right at the edge of the hill. He could have parked a little behind, but there was no challenge there. People came out alone in these wild places, purposely. Strange! What would happen if there was car trouble, and it wouldn't start? What if bad guys surprised us? Could bears be around in this area? I had heard of many horrible incidents that happened to people in the wilderness.

I cast a line and told myself, "I'm here and nothing I can do about it now."

Soon, however, those thoughts vanished and I immersed myself in the quiet beauty of the stream and wondered how many New Yorkers had a chance to experience this? I remembered this time of the day is called "Godhuli Lagna" in India—the time when cows come home from fields and raise a cloud of dust in their path. This is an auspicious moment between day and night, a quiet time, a time to meditate.

A village in India came to my vision: I could hear the chime of bells hanging from necks of returning cows; mothers calling their young ones to come home; and birds noisily settling in large trees. Soon lights were lit in houses, and crickets started their droning concert. If it was rainy season, frogs would join in. Otherwise, quietness fell on the village.

My line suddenly became stiff, and I pulled. A fluttering sound in the stream. I shouted, "George, George, I think I caught something."

George was just at the bend, and came over. It was a small trout, only five inches, a black and silvery thing, which tried to free itself from my palm. I looked at the beautiful brook trout. Is this why people fish—to feel a live fish in his hand, experience the last few moments of nature's creation?

"Do you want to keep it?" George's question pulled me back from my stray thoughts.

"Sure. It would be fun to take home something."

We put the fish in a small bag. He went ahead again.

Soon I caught another, a small trout. And then another. I didn't call George anymore.

It was not a good day for George, however. I yelled at him, "George, how are you doing?"

"I got a few, but they are very small. I released them."

It was getting dark; we decided to quit and climbed up the mountain. "At least you got one. Isn't that great?"

"Yes. It's my first trout."

I wondered if fishing was pure luck. I didn't know what I did, but I caught five.

Fishing seemed so difficult. Why couldn't someone teach me how to fish easily? I figured out what I would have to do to catch trout for my fish curry. I would have to buy a heavy-duty four-wheel-drive car that could run on mountain terrains for the unexplored streams, or I should buy a boat and fish from lakes. Most important, however, was the time—time away from home, from my family. Why couldn't I just buy fish as I could in New York?

In August, Catherine told me she had met a friend, whose husband, Ron, was a fisherman.

"What do you mean by a fisherman? Is that his profession?"

"No. He works for a printing press. My friend said he lives to fish. He would go fishing every day if he could. When Ron heard that a Bengali fish-eating man was starving, he said he would take you out for fishing."

Truly we were in Idaho for almost ten months and had not had a decent fish curry. At this rate I would soon forget my childhood memories.

So, I called Ron up immediately, and he was very kind. He said, "I cannot guarantee you a catch, but I'd be happy to go fishing with you."

Ron was about fifty years old, a local man with a round reddish face and big shoulders. He didn't talk much as he drove his beaten-up truck through Swan Valley.

"You know I eat fish, but I don't go fishing for that."

"Really?"

"I love to be near a stream when nobody is around me."

We went by the Palisades Reservoir, and then by several smaller roads; he opened a couple of gates to follow a dirt road. After about an hour we came to a meadow and he parked the car. We walked through a lightly trodden path with bushes all around us. We pushed aside the branches and eventually emerged next to a stream. "That's Moose Creek," he told me.

It was a flat land with an aspen forest interspersed with pines at the far end. A panoramic view was in front of us. The Wyoming mountains from the Jackson Hole side shot up majestically in the sky. The stream, only about twenty feet wide, was rather fast. A herd of cows grazed nearby. What a silent picture of the wide blue sky, the distant mountains, and the green meadow. There couldn't be any place more beautiful than this, I thought.

Ron took out a few finger-size live fish from a small basket. "These are minnows," he told me and gave me a wry smile, "The Fish and Game people don't like us to fish with minnows, but you can catch big fish with them."

He hooked one and moved to the stream. I took out my rod and a lure.

I cast my line as usual. I saw that Ron went away from the place. The lure sank with no action, but I had stopped being anxious. I learned that one cannot expect to get a bite each time a lure was led. "It'll happen," I told myself. The day was beautiful and warm, and I kept on casting—it would bite the next time, I was sure.

I took a break and went to visit Ron. Just then he caught a big one and was struggling to get it in. I rushed with the net. "Wow!" I shouted, "It's a large rainbow trout!" What a wonderful sight it was to see the pink fish come out of water.

"Must be fifteen inches," Ron said, and showed me he had another in his basket.

"You are great," I said, "may I fish next to you?"

"Certainly. And here, use one of my minnows."

I cast my line with a minnow, and saw the little fish flutter in the stream, but no fish bit it. Ron caught another—at the same place. A strange thing had happened to me over the last two months; I was not envious of him. I felt great joy in his success.

"How do you do it, Ron? Please tell me."

"Just relax and keep trying. Don't let the fish know you are nervous. Let go of yourself and enjoy. It will come."

Perhaps he was right. I went to another spot to try myself. I have failed so many times; so what if I go home again without any fish? Wasn't I happy to be here? Wasn't it great to see him catch such a big trout?

Vivid colors of the scenery became more intense to me: the sky was bluer, the fields greener, and the mountain tops whiter than before. What a wonderful day. I was glad that I took the job and came over to Idaho. I had no urge that I must have success in fishing. It was okay if I didn't catch a fish.

My whole reason for fishing was to eat fish curry, but suddenly I felt that was very short-sighted. To be here was a much more pleasant experience. There was greater joy in fishing.

I hooked a new minnow and threw the line out. "Look at the water, how lively it is," I said and watched how the little minnow was moving in the fast stream. The water was so clear, I could see the stones at the bottom of the Creek. Soon I saw a large fish swimming over and it went after the minnow. I was amazed I could see it so clearly. The fish gobbled the minnow just when I pulled back on the line. My rod bent like a rainbow, and I felt a strong pressure in my hand. "Oh yes. I feel it. I feel the struggle of a great force." A large pink trout jumped out of the water and made a splash. I let go of the line and then I reeled and reeled it in. "Oh God. I have a big trout. I did it. I did it." I pulled it up in the net. What a lively creature, at least a twelve-inch trout. What two beautiful pink stripes on the sides, what colorful mottled skin! I held it in my arms against my breast. And then I took it over to Ron.

Ron was very pleased with my success. "Now you are a fisherman," he proclaimed. "With a little more practice you can have fish curry every day."

The fish squirmed in my hand, and I gazed at the various colors of light being reflected by its body. What a beautiful creation of nature. For a moment I forgot the purpose of my fishing.

On our drive back Ron said, "I didn't tell you minnows are illegal for fishing. There is a severe fine for using live baits."

"Really?"

"Yes. I took a chance to make sure you would catch a big one and get the thrill of fishing."

"Wow!" I looked at him with astonishment, but didn't know what to say.

"Minnows are not good for the streams. They multiply too fast. Practice with worms. They are as good as minnows when you get the hang of it."

When we returned home, he asked me to take all the fish we caught—five fish. I was bubbling with my new experience, and was grateful to him, but I didn't want to take his fish. "You caught most of these. Don't you want to take home a few?"

With a glint in his eyes he replied, "It's not the fish I'm after," and started his truck.

I wondered if one becomes a fisherman only by letting go of ego; that's when one starts to appreciate the beauty of fishing; it's not the catching, but time spent. It is meditation. When we learn this meditation, fish come automatically. The fish curry would have to be a by-product, not the reason for fishing.

Chapter Three
FOURTH OF JULY

In the summer of 1981 we moved into our new house. The pitch road stopped at the end of our driveway, and beyond that was a field that no one had planted for the last few years. Cows mooed from this field and at dawn we could hear a variety of birds from nearby trees; a particular owl hooted regularly in the morning and in the evening. What a country atmosphere, although we live in a town, one with 45,000 people. Another such town, fifty miles south of us, is Pocatello, but no other big towns in the north, east, or west. The best known place in this area, Jackson Hole, is ninety miles away.

Near the end of June one day we heard a loud noise just after dinner, a sound like a small bomb blast, and we went out to the front. No signs of commotion could be seen or heard from any corner. A girl was riding her bicycle, unconcerned. The evening was upon us, only a few remnant lavender tints in the sky. Then we heard another blast.

Our oldest son loved the sound and shrieked, "Fireworks."

"Fourth of July," Catherine murmured.

"Such huge blasts! These must be good size M-80s," I talked to myself. "Are they selling these in stores in Idaho Falls?"

Fireworks didn't bother me. I had made those myself when I was young, but these were more than simple fireworks.

"Daddy, when do we get fireworks?" my younger son asked, holding his brother's hand.

"Fourth of July is far away," I told them. I was not ready for fireworks.

At the office, Dennis said, "They have started earlier this year."

Willis agreed, and I thought it was a chance to question local experts. "I see so many trailers selling fireworks; do they sell M-80s?"

"For good fireworks you have to go to Wyoming," Dennis said. "It's only an hour's drive. There you can buy anything you want."

I was surprised. "People would drive fifty miles to buy fireworks?"

"Sure," Dennis said. "When I was young, we bought fireworks from the Indian reservation. Now people go to Alpine Junction."

"It's a family town," Willis interjected. "Lots of children in each family. They love fireworks. Wait for a few more days; you'll see."

"I know someone who uses bottle rockets for coyotes," Dennis commented.

I had no clue what Dennis was talking about.

"Coyotes are bold in farming country," he explained. "They often stand near a fence to steal a chicken or something. When dogs carry on continuously you can see the coyotes. Specially, the brazen ones. You can't shoot them in the dark. What my friend does is light a bottle rocket, and off they go."

"What a solution!" I exclaimed.

Farm life was certainly different in Idaho. Fireworks, especially those that go up in the sky, were dying fast in crowded cities for obvious safety reasons, but here they have found a use for them. And why not? My curiosity was piqued. "Are there any other unique things, Dennis, at this time?"

"In some areas," Dennis said, "you can still see a grease-piggy contest. They grease a baby pig and let the kids catch it. It's a lot of fun, especially when the winner takes the piggy home."

The smile of a happy memory glowed on Dennis's round face. Clearly, he had participated in such contests with delight. I wondered if it was Dennis, or life in Idaho, that revolved around farm animals.

Next Saturday we drove to Alpine Junction in Wyoming, partly because of my own inquisitiveness. It was beyond the "square ice cream" store in Swan Valley and beyond the Palisades Reservoir—not a "never mind" little drive I was led to believe at the office. Perhaps it was so for them, but it took me over an hour to find a sign for the fireworks stores. The place was desolate: a gas station, one motel, a small store selling sundry items, and a few houses. Three fireworks trailers stood out prominently. Inside, the trailers were packed with fireworks—cartons piled up on the floor—only a narrow passage to walk through.

"Roman candles, Daddy, that's what we want," my older son told me.

I saw packets of M-80s and cherry bombs. My two sons gazed around and touched the packets with wonder. Fireworks spouted all around us. Boxes of fountains, pinwheels, bottle rockets, crackers, and long sparklers. Their pictures and colors took me to another world.

I saw a boy in a village on the outskirt of Calcutta walking through fields in search of dried eggplant stems. He would burn the branches to make charcoal. Light charcoal makes the best fireworks. Very few knew this secret—light charcoal powder makes the sparks fly high up. They also make fountains look full. One mixes the charcoal with finely ground sulphur, sodium nitrate salt, iron filings and fine aluminum chips. The aluminum chips produce the beautiful blue flowers that shoot out occasionally from the fountain. The recipe for this mixture was a secret. Different boys had different recipes and they would not easily share it with anyone else. We filled palm-size round clay pots with the mixture, tightly pressing each layer with the thumb. These pots were sold for this purpose only during this time. The small pots were finally sealed with clay at the bottom. One lights these from a small hole on the other side. Dried well in the sun, these shoot up to almost two stories high and make a ten-foot wide show.

Then the fireworks night comes, an auspicious New Moon night, the night of the worship of Goddess Kali. The darkest night of the year, and all houses are lighted with little earthen oil lamps on each door, each window, and around the roof. Silhouettes of houses glow in the dark, an ideal setting for fireworks. Fiery sparks cover the rest of space—the roads, the fields, and the sky. Light and sound everywhere, and a boy dancing in a trance.

"Daddy, Mommy wants to go home," my son pulled my hand.

Oh, yes. My house was in Idaho Falls, not in Calcutta. This place was spooky. We bought fireworks and headed home.

"Did you know that Utah hasn't had fireworks since 1943?" Catherine told me on our way home. "Only sparklers are allowed. This year they almost got a fireworks bill approved, but the governor vetoed it."

"How do you know all this?" I was surprised she was interested in this kind of off-beat news from Utah.

"I read in the paper," she told me. "You can buy fireworks in Utah this year, after no fireworks for thirty-eight years. The fireworks companies got smart and reinterpreted the definition of sparklers. Anything that gives off a spark! So they are now selling ground fireworks—cones, fountains and others."

"Interesting, how business people will find a way to make money." I chuckled to myself.

The West was perhaps the last resort for fireworks.

Palisades Reservoir was soon visible on our left—the long, winding body of water looked graceful, surrounded by green hills. Water seemed to float along the bends of the hills. Who would believe it was man-made? So natural in this place, so Idaho-like. It was actually a part of the Snake River, the South Fork, that passed through the narrow valley, now turned into a lake for hydropower and for water-control. The road went by its entire length and we gazed at the serene view from the high road.

The vast wilderness of pine trees, however, reminded me that a forest fire could ruin this beauty. How could one light fireworks in this area?

In the evening, armed with a large shopping bag of fireworks, my sons and I went to the open field near our house. The cows that mooed during the day had already gone home. We were ready to have some fun. I took out a plastic bottle and lighted a Roman Candle from it. However, as soon as the sparks started to fly, the bottle fell and the Roman Candle went straight to a bush. I watched with horror the sparks and smoke that came out of the little shaggy mass.

With courage I put rocks around the bottle, and lit another. This time it went nicely up in the sky. A nice display of color. But the next one bent and moved toward the neighborhood. My heart sank.

"Oh God. Let it not fall on a roof."

I imagined a headline in the *Post Register*: Federal Government Employee Started Fire in Rose Neilson Subdivision—Illegal Fireworks Involved.

My children cheered, "That was great, Daddy. Let's do another."

But I gaped at the roofs in the neighborhood. They were mostly made of shingles, not flat concrete roofs as in Calcutta. They could easily catch fire. I decided I needed a better place to light these fireworks.

"We have so many, Daddy!"

They both clamored for more, but I couldn't bring myself to light another rocket.

"Why don't you take them to the sand dunes?" Catherine suggested the next day.

My two sons' faces brightened up. Yes. The perfect solution.

Light stays up late in this area, but my sons were eager. They lighted their fireworks in the driveway even though the sun could still be seen at the horizon—the tanks marched, black snakes emerged, and colorful smoke covered the driveway. Finally, it was dark enough to go to the sand dunes.

People came to the sand dunes to ride horses, boys and girls slid down the sand hills with thrills and shrieks, and older kids brought drinks. But at this hour of dusk it was disquietingly quiet—no one around except for two men in an old car at one end. We marched up the hill. It was a long journey to the top, and when we reached there, a new view of Idaho Falls came to us: a light here and a light there, the picture of a thinly populated town getting ready to fall asleep. There were several other sand hills next to this big one, but no houses or trailers nearby. An ideal place to shoot fireworks.

I lit a bottle rocket, and it went up smoothly. I lit several others. The Roman candles displayed wonderful colors in the sky. My two sons took off their shoes and ran around. They chased each other while I lit the fireworks. They were happy we came for fireworks, but playing was equally fun. I lit away several more rockets. Then I saw headlights of a car coming toward the hill and stopping at the bottom. My heart stopped for a moment. "Is that a police car?" Had someone complained?

But police cars would have red and yellow lights on top. A chilling thought came to me; I was alone on top of a hill with two very young boys, and no one could hear our cry for help. I was not sure what there was to be afraid of, yet I was unsettled. It was the city upbringing that couldn't stand a lone adventure. I needed a crowd around me to feel comfortable, safe. Several boys got out of the car and went away in a different direction.

I remembered, Willis told me, what young boys did with Roman Candles. They lit those inside the Seventeen Mile Cave on Route 20. This was known to be a hiding place for horse thieves in the old days. The boys played games in the long, dark cave. Each boy would have a pipe to shoot Roman Candles to each other. "Imagine a bright light coming toward you in the pitch darkness of the cave?" Sometimes they would light several and shoot in succession guessing the direction of an opponent. "You must duck and shoot back."

"Isn't it dangerous in the cave, when you can't see anything?" I asked.

Willis only looked at me and I understood his unspoken words, "Can there be any excitement when there is no danger?"

The sand dunes were quiet, a large empty space under the sky, not like the cave. My children had no fear—they were happily running around the sand.

I lit a few more rockets, but my heart was not there anymore. The child had escaped.

"Can a city boy make it in Idaho?" I asked myself.

Over the last few months I had come to know Willis. Fifty-three years old, white curly hair, and white beard surrounding a happy round face. Willis was different. A doctorate from Berkeley in nuclear engineering, but he had no pompousness about his education. What amazed me most was that Willis spent long hours at local cowboy bars playing pool with men who had never gone to college; many had not even finished high school. "They call me Doc," Willis said with a smile.

On Friday, July 3, Willis asked me, "Why don't you come over to my place in the morning? I'll take you to Bernie's to start the celebration."

"Who's Bernie?"

"An old lady, a friend."

"Where do you go to see fireworks?" I asked Willis.

"We rent a room at the Westbank."

"In a hotel?"

"We'll have a party—lots of food and drink. Hard liquor, you know. And we'll watch fireworks from the balcony. It's fun that way."

I couldn't understand how, in this wide open country, Willis preferred to watch the Fourth of July fireworks from a balcony on the top floor of a hotel?

When we went to Bernie's house, I didn't know what to expect. She was sixty-five years old and dressed in a long white skirt with red and blue flowers, a white top with frills, and a colorful vest, reminding me of the colonial times. "I'm glad you could come to our Independence Day celebration," she told me. Several people from the neighborhood were already in her house. They knew each other. I was the only newcomer.

"Are we ready?" Willis asked her.

We formed a line: Bernie at the head with a flute in her hand, and others with different instruments—several kazoos, an oboe, a little child's drum, and some with pots and pans. Willis gave me a metal gong from the top of her display case.

We followed her to the outside like a band of children.

The procession went to the backyard, and started to play *America the Beautiful*, all marching behind Bernie. The pots and pans joined in the music. As we strolled outside, it became a fun procession. Several marched with distinct body gestures, some purposely waddling. The music was not in unison and the marchers were not together, either. But gaiety was apparent. Soon my hand started to beat the gong and I happily marched behind Willis.

We went by a little path through her garden, by the flower bushes and the trees. All knew it was frolic—"march any way your heart desires." The tune changed to *Battle Hymn of the Republic*. And we went out of the garden and around the house. By the time the little march was over, I realized it was an Independence Day celebration of their own. My stuffiness finally melted in the joy of the occasion. Bernie's husband had passed away eight years ago, but she still followed what they did together on the Fourth of July—a little parade in their own backyard.

Inside, a hearty breakfast was waiting. Bernie had baked for several nights to prepare for this occasion. Some guests also brought homemade goodies. Willis stood out prominently among all: he wore a specially wide stars and stripes tie—bright red, blue, and white, and a white top hat. This was his singular outfit for the Fourth of July, and he obviously enjoyed wearing it for the occasion. I wished I had something special to wear instead of the regular office clothes I was wearing. Willis was so cheerful. I wondered with some sadness if I could ever experience the true feelings of the day as these people did; perhaps they couldn't be generated unless one was born here.

I remembered the Independence Day in India, August 15, but felt that it was very sterile. As a young boy, I participated in marches, and heard lots of speeches by politicians during the day, but there was not much else for a boy to do. It was the same for the grownups. The struggle to survive was so overwhelming in India that people could not afford the luxury of nostalgia. That is also the way it is in the big cities of the

United States. The Fourth of July is a day off to rest and catch up on work needed to be done. The feeling of these people in this little parade in Idaho, a homegrown family tradition, cannot be reproduced anywhere else.

In my time in the fifties in India, Independence Day celebrations were primarily a celebration of the very recent freedom from British Rule. It was a day of remembrance for those who gave their lives and praise for those who fought against the British. A joyous day, and many, who could afford to buy one, raised flags on their houses. It was also a day for the politicians to earn credit with the public by making patriotic speeches and reminding people how they had personally suffered to win India's freedom. In the U.S., after 200 years of freedom, it has become a celebration by individuals for the freedom they have. A personal celebration rather than a public one, focused on the individual blessings and joy.

I remembered how, as a young boy, I had proudly gotten up and rushed to my school to join the "march" early in the morning. We paraded through the streets with older boys holding the tri-color flag of India in the front, and occasionally shouting, "Jindabad (long live India)." Then I returned home, hungry, and had nothing to do the rest of the day. No bar-B-Q at home and no block parties; no parades with beautiful floats, and no fireworks. Nor there would be the big, colorful tents that popped up everywhere during the religious puja festival in the fall. Independence Day observance took a backseat to puja celebrations, when each neighborhood vibrated with pride and joy.

Where I grew up people organized evening entertainment programs for Independence Day celebrations—we called them "functions." A small outdoor stage would be erected in an open field, and when the microphone sounded, people automatically gathered around. As usual, speeches were made first, loud and long. Often the local boys performed gymnastics and demonstrated martial art techniques. These were something left over from the pre-independence days, when all boys were urged to be physically and morally strong. The interest in the martial arts started, I thought, with the idea of fighting the British. The Tommys must be repulsed, and since we were smaller and didn't have their firepower, we needed martial arts to fight them. It is not well understood by outsiders that the British didn't leave India because of Gandhi alone. There was a large violent component responsible for India's liberation. The display of martial arts exercises were symbolic of that spirit. After the speeches and the youth programs, the songs and dances began; these were the real reason people attended the "function."

The rainy season came to its end at the time of the Independence Day. The temperature dropped down from the high marks of tropical summer, and the skies were blue again. It was nice to sit on the grass with friends and listen to the live songs accompanied by only a harmonium and two tablas. Young full-bodied girls danced in shiny costumes, while bright lights focused on the stage. These colorful lights rotating on the dancers in the pitch-dark-night under a star-lit sky brought the finale to the Independence Day celebration.

The Fourth of July Parade started at 10 a.m. South Boulevard was lined up with families, especially those with young children. In several places in the Tautphaus Park area, where we were, people had cordoned off the front of their houses with chairs for private parties. Many brought chairs to sit on the strip of grass next to the road. The astonishing thing was that we recognized so many. Neighbors and people from work, all seemed to be there.

A young boy distributed little flags for people to wave during the parade. The same group probably planted the flags on lawns in our neighborhood, so unusual from my New York experience.

Many roamed lazily along the sidewalk, socializing. Several kids—boys and girls—ran up and down the street selling candies, cold drinks, and crushed ice. Large umbrellas and colorful tents in the Park invited all to spend the afternoon there. The orange rays of the sun made the scene more cheerful. A cool breeze came from the southwest.

We watched the parade for a while standing at the corner of Hartert and South Boulevard and then moved on from one spot to another, slowly marching up north from where the procession was coming. People were more scattered beyond 17th Street. They were there not just to see the parade, it was a big party. Why to stay still in one place?

A four-year-old boy pointed to the far end, "Mommy, horsey," and soon a procession of horses came by. Men and women rode healthy horses and simply went by nodding to many they knew.

Then came a sound as if ten lawnmowers were working at the same time, and everyone looked down the street with pleasure. The Shriners were riding go-carts; sitting low on the ground, they went in and out, and round and round. Old people with their Shriners red uniforms and caps were having such great fun; we each wished we had a go-cart. They totally broke the age barrier.

A large truck came with many people—a whole family. The sign said, "Ward 23." "It's from the Mormon Church," Catherine told me.

"But there was another big truck for the LDS."

"Right. Wards are places where they meet. It's like the neighborhood community center."

"Why religious organizations marching on Fourth of July?"

"Ssssh. People will hear you. This is how they do things here."

I still wondered what religion had to do with the Fourth of July. It's true that the pilgrims came here for religious freedom, but if all churches showed their patriotic feelings in the form of trucks carrying their members, won't it lose its effect? Imagine a Hindu or a Buddhist truck in the parade singing "Om Shanti" or "Om Mani Padme Hum." Would people like it if the Hare Krishna Society had a float here? Patriots come from all religions. I preferred a separation—to draw a clear line—between church and state in public affairs.

I expected to see large beautiful floats in the parade, but none were there. The one that came close to a decent one was the float by the Freeman Institute with a constitutional theme. It had a replica of the Independence Hall and a big sign, "We the People."

The parade was essentially a procession of dignitaries and politicians, cars, trucks, farm equipment, horses, fire trucks, local businesses, and high school clubs. It was not glamorous, but rather homey. Clearly, the people didn't spend weeks preparing for the parade, and no one was barred from participation. However, the extra element of informality, the coziness between the paraders and the watchers, drew my attention. I loved listening to young paraders' voices: Hi, Dad, Hi, Mom, Hi, guys.

When the Iona Posse was passing, Catherine said, "Did you know that five men were recently charged for stealing horses?"

"Really? That's not just for Western movies?"

"They rounded up wild horses from public lands in Custer County, but police caught them in Mackay. The funny thing, they were acquitted of state grand larceny charges because it was not a felony under state laws. The district judge at Blackfoot ruled that the horses were wild and hence could not have been stolen."

"So, who got the horses?"

"That's not the end of the story. They are now charged by the Assistant U.S. Attorney in Boise for removing wild horses from public lands without a permit."

A truck with a replica of a humongous potato went by. More horses came, followed by a truck sweeping the street.

We met Nick Chaffin, our son's teacher, and his family sitting on the side. After exchanging greetings, I asked what his plans were for the day.

"No big plans. We take it easy and enjoy the day. My father is in the parade. He loves to be with his buddies from the Navy. We're here to see him. Then we'll go to the park and join in the picnic. Move around. See the fireworks. That's all."

Truly, what else was there to do on the Fourth of July?

The marching band from Idaho Falls High School came on. Young boys and girls in uniform were doing their best. They played *Stars and Stripes Forever*. This was the highlight of their practices, and anyone who knew them greeted them warmly—grandparents, neighbors and all.

The parade ended at about 1 p.m., and we walked back along with others to our car, a mere three blocks. This was my first Fourth of July parade west of the Mississippi. There was certainly a different flavor here. The paraders' pride was not in the beauty of their floats, but there was something unusual that dawned on me. They were simply parading who they were and what they did. And the message came across very clearly; they didn't have to decorate a float beyond their means to show how beautiful a float they could build. What people enjoyed here were not the floats, but their friends or sons and daughters or colleagues or neighbors in the parade. It was like going to the local high school play.

The weather on this day was exceptional, a perfect eighty-five degrees and not a speck of cloud in the sky. Lying down on the couch I told Catherine, "We can go to Tautphaus Park to watch the youth-activities, take advantage of the free swimming today, or go for a ride to Jackson Hole."

"Drive on the Fourth of July?" Catherine exclaimed. "You want to add our names to the statistics? Seventy had already died as of yesterday."

"We haven't gone out for a drive for a long time. The day is so gorgeous."

"Remember? We went to visit your friend in Queens and we spent an additional hour each way on the Long Island Expressway."

"I know, but I wonder what people in the country do today. How bad could the traffic be?"

Since we had no plans for the afternoon, we ventured out with timorous hearts toward Jackson Hole. As we came out of the town to Route 26, and proceeded east, we noticed a most astounding thing: there was no car in front of or behind us. We looked at each other. Where were those Fourth of July cars we were so worried about?

"Is anything wrong?"

I turned on the radio. Then I broke out into hearty, spontaneous laughter. "We are in Idaho, not New York."

The road went straight toward the hills and the sky beyond. Green potato fields spread, acres after acres, on both sides of the road, and how uniform the long rows were. From one angle it was a vast green field; then, another angle would reveal long rows. Row after row, how clean and straight they were. In some fields beautiful mists hovered over geometric designs of sprays from the sprinkler system. In the distance one or two homes could be seen. Occasionally, a few structures or buildings showed up near the road.

Grass grew on roofs of the silos. These potato cellars, triangular in cross-section, and usually seventy-five feet or more long and about a story high, had soil on the outside to keep light out and the potatoes cool. Such storage silos are absent in the East.

The news came on:

"The 205th anniversary is going in full swing all over the country, although rain and thunderstorms have tempered the celebrations in part of the Midwest and the upper Mississippi River Valley. Senate Majority Leader Howard Baker visited the Knoxville Zoo to adopt a three-year-old elephant from Africa and named him the Little Diamond. President Reagan is spending a quiet day in the White House . . . San Diego still brewing over the controversy for selection of the Retired Navy Commander Lloyd Butcher as Grand Marshal of the Fourth of July parade. He was the skipper of USS Pueblo when it was captured by North Korea in 1968 . . ."

There was nothing from Idaho in the national news.

The horizon looked far away. Were we the only humans here? The whole area stood still—the green fields, the sky, the distant hills, and this black road—and no sign of any human activity anywhere. A predominant silence. A few birds flew here and there, and the hawks sat on tall telephone posts waiting for their prey.

A perfect, lazy afternoon. No worries and nothing must be done.

When we reached Swan Valley, we felt the scenery would continue for miles, and we wouldn't know what the farmers do today from this road. We turned around.

Late in the afternoon Larry called, asking if I wanted to go to the Independence Day Rodeo at Sandy Downs. Larry and his family loved horses.

I was tired and wondered why a rodeo on the Fourth of July? The whole thing probably started as an outlet for the cowboys during their long cattle drives, a sport to show their skills and to have some fun. But the cattle drives are gone, and movie theaters are in. Still, the spirit of the rodeo has survived in the West. Perhaps fathers of many were cowboys and managed ranches and have imparted this old West zest in them. Thinking objectively, however, I questioned whether it is any different from chasing a small round ball in an open field. Playing in a rodeo is much riskier. How do you develop the courage and the skills to face an angry beast? The desire to go to a rodeo on the Fourth of July, however, must be in one's blood, acquired over a century of Western traditions.

"It'll be a great show," Larry explained. "Good competition. A hundred cowboys will be there, and a 'mutton busting' event. It's lots of fun."

"Mutton busting?"

"For young kids. They ride sheep instead of horses."

I had no interest in seeing a kid being dumped by a big sheep, or a man thrown out or kicked by a distraught horse. I had seen a rodeo recently and didn't understand its charm. It was a challenge for the cowboys, but its subtleties escaped me. It was a test for me, could one live in the West without appreciating rodeos?

"They'll have a bull riding competition," Larry went on, "you don't want to miss it."

The thrill of seeing if a bull could gore its impudent rider did not fascinate me either. The heart of the West contains these challenges of mastering wild animals, but an appreciation of this Western heritage was not within me. However, Larry's enthusiasm convinced me that I underestimated the importance of the rodeo; it is an intimate part of this culture and therefore natural for the Fourth of July celebration.

"Larry, thanks, but I have to help Catherine before the fireworks."

After I hung up, the picture of a young cowgirl came to my vision: long, milky white, pointed boots with beautiful design-work, a Western dress with intricate work on the back—frills hanging over her healthy bosom—and long golden-yellow hair falling out beneath her black hat. How lively she was with her sparkling eyes and contagious smile. She was not the only one at the rodeo. Several other women, dressed in similar Western outfits, strolled the arena with their men, also uniquely dressed in tight jeans, large belt buckles, Western shirts, bolo ties, cowboy boots, and hats. This was the part I had enjoyed most, seeing a counterpart of princely ballroom scenes. The brown, dry, beastly arena with raw corral fences was subdued by the elegance of these young men and women.

Still, I couldn't help but wonder how ludicrous the idea of a dusty rodeo on the Fourth would seem in New York.

As evening fell we packed our family and went to Freeman Park. We passed by the small Keefer's Island on the Snake River, from where they would shoot the fireworks. Many had camped on the east bank of the river near the Mormon Temple and on the little parks next to the road. Kids were lighting sparklers and throwing them into the river. Some dads also joined them. Mothers sat with baskets and comforters on the lawn. Little boys and girls ran around their mothers, their innocent, shrill voices sounding so cheerful. An impeccable scene of an old-style, happy family get-together.

I visualized such small gatherings in the wide open ground in the center of Calcutta near the Ganges River. But my family was never there. My childhood was a happy one just like these kids in the park, but in a different way in a very different culture. I couldn't imagine my mother sitting on a blanket in a park, doling out food and drinks, and father playing ball with us or lighting sparklers. That was not in the culture of my upbringing. Happiness was simply growing up in a pleasant, untroubled, care-free atmosphere. My memory of my father was primarily of a man confined in the house for his heart-ailment. How could we even think of going out on picnics? He was the provider and the protector, and mother the feeder and keeper of our health. Everything else was hidden, implied, and never expressed.

Freeman Park was littered with people. Perpendicular to the entrance of the vast, wavy ground stood a row of robust willow trees along the Willow Creek. Cottonwood trees lined the edge of the park at the bottom around the fast-flowing Snake River. Many came earlier and spent the day at the park. Spanish-speaking groups occupied the main part of the hill, where there was more space to play. The swings were also there for children. It was getting dark, but boys were still playing ball and running around. It appeared to me the Mexican contingent was the most fun-loving group; they obviously enjoyed the outdoors, and the camaraderie of these people came through very well.

Music came from many directions—diverse rhythms, songs, and decibels—each to one's taste. We made our way skirting many small groups and walked down to the river, but good positions between the large poplars were already taken. We spread our blanket on the grassy slope.

There were many places in the city to watch the fireworks, especially along the Snake River, but the whole town seemed to be here. Contrary to my previous experience it was an arch-ipelago—each group doing their own thing, but all a part of a big scheme. Isolated events were not isolated, but deliberately planned as part of a well-choreographed scene.

An afternoon image of New York City's Central Park came to mind: various groups playing, from soccer to frisbee, people sitting and standing in groups, dogs on leashes, and pigeons eating around benches near trees. The backdrop of the sky-scrapers was missing, but the human activities and the liveli-ness in Freeman Park were no different.

I remembered how we once stood near the dock in Bellport, Long Island, and watched the fireworks. The waves, barely visible in the muted darkness, lapped on the shore and the baywater sounded stronger than usual. Rows of boats lay still, lined near the shore, and many scattered in the bay. Lights from the boats, a little distance away, showed their presence, creating a romantic backdrop. The colorful sailboats had stopped and sounds of motor boats had vanished. The horizon appeared far-reaching and the sky wide open. Catherine and another mother held babies in their arms. A man stared in the water holding a rope for the crabs. People lingered here and there waiting for the darkness to fall in. Conversations floated in and out. All waiting in exciting anticipation.

Then suddenly the fireworks started from the end of the pier. The sky filled with sparkles. In the vast dark expanse a great show of color and sound continued in the sky. Little lights from far away houses from the opposite shores and the big boats in the bay made their presence known occasionally in between the fireworks. We were absorbed and watched in silence. We were the observers and not a part of anything special, but that was the way life was in New York.

Idaho Falls appeared less mysterious and less exciting. But there was comfort in sitting on the grass with everyone else, watching the kids running around and blending in the final event of the day.

Two bright stars showed up in the sky. The first firework shot up, and the family next to us started a tape—loudly, for all to share. "Oh say can you see by the dawn's early light?" A large neon-blue round ball shot out magenta color sparks filling the sky.

A wave of "Oh's" rose from all around. Then another large ball and a rapid succession of bursts in the sky silenced everything else. A pause, and the fireworks started again.

Sitting on the green grass with the Snake River a few feet from us, I wandered off to all the places I had been on the Fourth of July, from Philadelphia to Long Island to Syracuse to Ann Arbor. First time I saw the Fourth of July fireworks in Philadelphia, I was overwhelmed as I felt it was like what I had envisioned a Mogul emperor's celebration would look like. I had seen neither an emperor nor his extravagant celebrations. One only hears about these fireworks in India. What a fortunate thing here for all to see the stunning fireworks and enjoy.

Far away from the two coasts and the big cities, I had a serene feeling, not received in past celebrations. What struck me was the simplicity of life here. This celebration was not to prove a point or outdo others, but to let go and celebrate the freedom we have. Like the parade in Bernie's house. A commemoration of their own—a simple celebration away from the tense, busy lives that rule urban dwellers.

Coming here was a break, a breath of fresh air.

The sky filled with a large ball of sparkles. Two small sea-green balls shot out from the middle and exploded. A chorus of "Ohh" came from around. Then, a hush before the next one. In the darkness, I watched the silhouettes of the little groups in the park, and a song kept on ringing in my head:

Oh, beautiful, for spacious skies, for amber waves of
 grain,
For purple mountain majesties above the fruited
 plain!
America, America! God shed His grace on thee,
And crown thy good with brotherhood from sea to
 shining sea.

Chapter Four
TIGER HUNT

Grandpa, did you know that people in India put masks on the back of their heads so tigers won't attack them?" DeeDee said as she sat on the edge of her grandfather's lawn chair. Eleven-year-old DeeDee was reading about India for a class project.

"All Indians don't do that," Grandpa told her, "they do that only in the Sundar-ban area because so many man-eating tigers are there."

Her younger brother Raja was playing soldier on the deck and asked, "Grandpa, did you hunt tigers when you were in India?"

Grandpa moved his head toward Raja, a fair-skinned boy, who was always active and who often reminded him of the days he himself was a kid. Grandpa had come to America forty years ago with his wife and a lanky, brown son. His son, Raja's father, was now a doctor and had only a faint memory of his childhood in India. These two grandchildren, born in New York and living in Idaho, had no idea of life in India.

"Oh, yes," he replied, and a playful smile crossed his face. "I shot one, but that was long ago."

Raja came over with his GI Joe figure. "Please, Grandpa, tell me. Was it very scary?"

DeeDee rolled her eyes, and said, "You don't have a gun, and we've never seen you go hunting. Were you a hunter in India?"

Grandpa wished he could take them to his village and back to the time when he was a young boy. He could run around with them the same way he did in his childhood when he played with home-made toys.

"It was a long time ago," he told them as if he were telling them a tale. "We lived in a small village thirty miles south of Calcutta. The Sundar-bans are fifty miles farther away. So, tigers didn't usually come to our village. Once every few years, a tiger would come and kill a goat or a cow. It came very quietly in the early morning, and with one strike, it killed an animal. The tiger would drag it to the end of the village and eat it there. People would then beat large drums continuously for seven to ten days to scare the tiger away, and no tiger would come for a long time."

"Then, how did you shoot one?" Raja inquired.

"That's what I am going to tell you. I didn't want to shoot a tiger; they were too big for me. I wanted to shoot birds."

"You had a gun in India?" DeeDee asked. Her head with long black hair bent forward, two sharp eyes looking at him skeptically.

"I made my own gun," Grandpa started again. "I wanted to shoot a crane. In the early morning they came near a marshland at the end of our village. I loved to watch how they stood so quietly on one leg—their white feathers shining in the middle of tall green grasses. I wanted to capture one, but you can't capture them. They are very smart. So, I wanted to shoot and bring one home. That's the story I'll tell you.

"I was in seventh grade then. I decided to make a sling-shot, but I didn't tell anyone. My mother would be very angry, you know, because she believed sling-shots cause accidents. First I needed a Y-shaped tree branch for the sling-shot. I searched in many trees, but most branches break easily. The mango and leechee trees are big but not strong. Finally, I climbed a large guava tree in our own backyard, and cut out a branch that would make a strong Y, and that was just the right size for my hand. I carved the wood with my knife and kept it hidden under my bed.

"I needed three more things: a strong elastic band, a piece of leather, and little hard objects to shoot with. A piece of leather was easy to get from an old sandal, and I cut out an elastic band from the rubber bladder of a soccer ball. I tied two ends of the elastic band to the two sticks of the Y and tied the leather piece in the middle. That was my gun, the sling-shot. I tried it out with small stones and it worked fine, but my aim wasn't very good.

"Now I needed shooting things, missiles, for bird hunting. You can't hunt birds with little rocks, you know. So, I collected clay from the bottom of a pond. With the clay I made small round balls of different sizes. You know why? I'll use the big balls for big animals, and the little ones for the birds. You can't shoot all animals with the same size balls. It wouldn't work right! I dried the balls in the sun for several days. Then I created a large fire in a field behind our house and burned all those balls until they were glowing red. I covered the fire up with soil and went home. The next day I collected the balls; they were hard as rocks and perfect for hunting."

"Grandpa, can I make them?" Raja asked, holding the GI Joe figure like a sling-shot ready to shoot at a bird in the backyard.

"Oh no. You live in a city. It'll be dangerous to hunt in the city. Too many people."

"You had so much fun. We have nothing." Raja grumbled.

"Tell us, did you shoot a crane?" DeeDee asked with interest.

"Oh, back to the story. My school ended in early December. That's when all the exams are over and schools close in India. I was waiting for this day. I got up very early in the morning, grabbed my slingshot and went out of the house. I quickly walked to the edge of the village along a narrow path through the rice fields. I was alone and a little scared. The morning sun was not up yet. I tried out one ball, and it did go a long way. I found my aim was excellent. It had improved with practice.

"When I neared the marshland I saw only two or three cranes, but they were beyond my range. I slowed down and moved quietly so the cranes wouldn't fly away. In the early winter there was always a fog in that area. That made it mysterious and adventurous for me. I felt I was truly a hunter in a lonely place. I wanted to surprise everyone by bringing a crane home. I also wanted to show they really had two legs!

"Suddenly a few cranes flew over and landed near me. I crouched down, and watched them intently. They looked so beautiful standing on one leg. I thought this was my chance and I mustn't make a mistake! In my excitement I took a large ball and pulled the elastic of my sling-shot. I aimed at a crane through the tall grasses for a long time. Then, I saw the white crane move, and a faint orange-yellow color came to my view. The orange color confused me and I quickly let go of the shot. I saw the large orange color rise in the air and fall with a roar. I was frightened, not knowing what I shot.

"I heard several people running through the tall grass. They were not from our village. Someone shouted, 'We got him.'

"I crept forward. I didn't have to go far. I saw the orange thing lying on the grass—a big Royal Bengal tiger. Almost eight feet long."

Grandpa looked out at the pine trees in the backyard, as if he could still see a tiger lying on a marshland in India.

"Did you really shoot the tiger?" DeeDee inquired in a soft voice, touching Grandpa's arm with admiration.

Grandpa smiled. "It must be. What do you think?"

"I'm glad you killed the tiger," Raja said, "one day I'll go tiger hunting in India."

"When you're ready, I'll go with you," Grandpa said with a glint in his eyes. His white hair fluttered in the breeze.

Chapter Five
HUNTING

I fell in love with Jim Corbett in 1990 when I read for the first time *The Man-eating Leopard of Rudraprayag* (first published in 1948, his second book), and immediately understood why the game sanctuary in Kumaon, India, was renamed the Corbett National Park. It was his genuine caring for the people and the wildlife of the region that earned him the honor.

From 1918 to 1926 the leopard was an elusive terror over a 500-square-mile area of the Himalayan hills in Garhwal with 50,000 inhabitants and 60,000 pilgrims that passed by annually. Corbett struggled hard for over a year to track the leopard and kill it, but failed repeatedly. The day he succeeded, the villagers from miles away brought flowers to him in the fashion of an offering to God. Soon a huge hill of flower petals stood in front of Corbett's feet. And hundreds of tragic stories were told – what the man-eater did to the families and their lives.

The locals affectionately called him "Carpet Saab." Their love for him can be felt from an incident that took place years later in 1942. Corbett was a guest at a party to entertain the World War II-disabled Indian soldiers, where a young man related to him that he had regretted that he couldn't go to see him the day the leopard was killed because he was too young to walk and his father wasn't strong to carry him that far. "And now, Sahib," he told him with pride, "I will go back to my home with great joy in my heart, for I shall be able to tell my father that with my own eyes I have seen you, and maybe, if I can get anyone to carry me to the Mela that is annually held at Rudraprayag to commemorate the death of the man-eater, I

Robert Bower

shall tell all the people I meet there that I have seen and had speech with you."

Corbett later wrote in his diary: "A cripple, on the threshold of manhood, returning from the wars with a broken body, with no thought of telling of brave deeds done, but only eager to tell his father that with his own eyes he had seen the man who years ago he had not had the opportunity of seeing, a man whose only claim to remembrance was that he had fired one accurate shot."

If you read Corbett's book, you'll know how hard-earned that single shot was. When I was in high school, I did not comprehend the subtleties of hunting and often wondered what was so great about shooting an animal with a powerful rifle? His writings have changed me, and part of the reason could be my age, or perhaps because I am in Idaho where you hear so much about hunting.

"You must fish or hunt in Idaho," Dennis told me when I first came here.

"But I am no hunter."

I liked what Carl did; he and three of his cronies got away each year with good food and wine, and spent time in the wilderness. A whole week away from work, home, and chores. Hunting was an excuse for male bonding. I even imagined I would do that one day: I would guard the tent with a book in my hand while they were out on their pretend-hunting. My romantic imagination of their hunting escapades was spoiled a few years later when Carl pulled his station wagon into my neighbor's driveway with a dead deer in the back.

It was a good size mule deer, part of the tongue sticking out on the side and a brown tag hanging on his ear. Blood on the floor. Four men formed a noisy crowd in the driveway discussing how difficult it was that year for deer hunting. I looked at the half-open, still eye of the deer and Carl's smiling face, and murmured, "I thought you go away in the mountains for tranquility."

"This deer just strolled into our camp."

And they all laughed.

The Northwest has a long tradition of hunting. Almost 200 years ago the Lewis and Clark expedition depended wholly on game for survival. Someone estimated that they needed meat the size of a buffalo to feed the party every day. Fortunately, Meriwether Lewis recruited one rugged individual named George Drewyer, a half-Indian with an English father, who was an excellent hunter and their meat-provider in the wilderness. He was a master outdoorsman. Once he killed three deer under difficult circumstances to feed a gang of unexpected Indian visitors. While he went hunting, the Indians crowded him with great curiosity. But when he killed three deer with three single shots, he earned his reputation. The Indians returned with great awe for him. Since then, Lewis concluded, if the Indians had any thought of mischief they dared not carry it out.

Drewyer had an innate knowledge of the animals and he was a superb marksman. He would go out in the morning and by evening he would bring back a couple of deer or elk to be picked up by the riverbank.

The Lewis and Clark expedition found abundant game to hunt as they moved up the Missouri River. Once Drewyer killed seven elk in one day. When they were deep in the Montana wilderness and needed animal skins to cover an iron-boat, Lewis and Drewyer killed six elk, two buffalo, two mule deer, and a bear in a single day. But hunting was not always so easy. They went hungry when they crossed the Idaho-Montana region in the winter because there was no game for hunting. And when they came out of the mountain ranges the Nez Perce and Shoshone Indians offered them salmon, fresh and plenty, but they were hungry for meat. Any meat. In the end, they ate dog meat, which they bought from the Indians. A couple of times they killed horses for food.

After the expedition, George Drewyer went back to the Indian territory again along with another well-known Lewis and Clark crew member, John Colter, for trapping and fur-trading. There is a very scenic and peaceful place, Colter's Village, south of the Yellowstone National Park and opposite the Teton Mountains. But Drewyer was not that lucky. He refused to be tyrannized by the Blackfoot Indians and gradually worked his way up the Jefferson River setting beaver traps. He was wonderfully successful at the beginning because it was a fresh territory for trappers. But one day he did not return to the camp, and his beheaded and eviscerated body and the remains of his horse were later found near his traps.

If anyone thinks hunting is easy, he has no experience. It is extremely strenuous and it requires skill. John, my friend who has become an Idaho outdoorsman, told me about his experience. When he first started hunting two years after coming to Idaho, he selected an area near Gilmore and scouted it out before the season started. He learned what "spoor" really meant. He searched for fallen leaves that were disturbed, trampled or kicked by a deer. He learned about deer patterns —when they ate, what they liked to eat, where they fed recently, and how to recognize their bedding. Only then he went out hunting. But on three consecutive weekends he returned home exhausted and empty handed. He hiked up and down the slopes, but couldn't find a deer to shoot. He wondered what was wrong, and his non-hunting wife laughed and said, "Give up John, hunting is not for us." Then, suddenly on his fourth trip, he saw a small deer sitting under a bush. It was such an easy target. He shot it quickly. Then he saw the blood trail to the bush; someone had already wounded the animal. This was his first hunt, and he proudly picked up the dead deer in his arms.

When he returned home, "Martha, Martha," he called his wife excitedly from the driveway. "I got one."

Martha came out, looked through the window of the car, and exclaimed, "John, what have you killed? It looks like a big jackrabbit, not a deer!"

Like me, Martha didn't have great admiration for these hunts.

I have no interest in hunting animals and never had. One grows up in India listening to, and reading stories that took place in hermitages or ashrams where deer roamed freely. Birds and animals provided the harmony of these ashrams at the edge of serene forests, and the word "violence" didn't exist. Most Indians grow up in an atmosphere of "ahinsa," absence of malice and aversion to killing. I was no exception to this upbringing. The Jataka animal stories that children love are 2,500 years old. The famous fifth-century Sanskrit poet Kalidas's classic novel Sakuntala uses animals as a setting to reveal the inner feelings of men and women. The docile animals serve as friends and listeners. When the sixteenth-century acclaimed singer Tansen sang, it is said that deer gathered around him to listen.

For an Indian child, animals are not just animals; they talk and provide wisdom. It is very similar to how an American child feels about his stuffed animals. The animal is his friend, and it becomes alive when there is no one around. How can one have the desire to hunt these down?

I have a hypothesis that the first seventeen years of one's life define (rather haunt) the rest of his life. How can I change suddenly just because I'm in Idaho now?

The sight of a deer reminds me of a little park in BodhGaya where Gautama Buddha achieved enlightenment, and where one can see the spotted sambar deer. They are so different from the dark brown deer we see in North America. They are beautiful yellow brown with white spots, with white bellies. What long exquisite eyes they have. In the park one can see the deer grazing in the middle of resplendent, deep-blue peacocks, some with very large, green tails spread out like fans. How lovely they are and how peaceful the surroundings. I could easily go back 2,500 years and imagine these little animals crossing the knee-deep, wide Niranjana River a little behind Gautama Buddha and making their home around the Bodhi-tree where he sat and meditated. How can one shoot such gentle animals?

"I was out scouting with my nephew last weekend," my fifty-seven-year-old secretary, Gladys, told me.

"You go hunting?" I was so surprised. She was on the heavy side and silver streaks were visible on her hair. She wore fancy glasses and I could not imagine she would go hunting. I knew she liked fishing, but hunting?

"Sure. I've done it all my life. I love to get out in the dark of predawn hours. By the time we reach our hunting area, the sun is up. It's wonderful."

She smiled. The impression of the last weekend's expedition was clearly reflected in her expression.

"Did you kill any?" I asked.

"No. We didn't find any. But I had a great time."

"Gladys, do you own a gun?"

"I don't shoot animals. I just go for fun. If my nephew kills one, I help clean it and carry it to the car."

Her round face beamed, and I could see the pleasure she had in going hunting. Gladys never married and I wondered if this was her way of remaining active and in touch with family members. This was remarkable. Often older people are left out or left at home to watch TV. How marvelous it was that she did not yield to the typical, mundane pattern of life. Is this possible only in this area where the pioneering spirit still exists?

This is unthinkable in India. Women do not hunt; an older woman's role is seen more as a mother, helper, educator, and upholder of family rules and traditions. In India both boys and girls are raised with an emphasis on non-violence and an appreciation for all life-forms. It was doubly hard for women to be hunters because they were not encouraged to develop interests in outdoor or action-oriented activities. India had a female Prime Minister, which is a long way off for the U.S., but in some ways women are less free in India. I can safely say the passion for animal-hunting is not in Indian women. Since Vedic times women have been inspired to be equal to men in all areas, particularly in the mental and spiritual faculties, but not in physical efforts. Also, society dictates taking care of women, first by their fathers, and then by husbands and sons. They need not go out hunting for food. In India, where a vegetarian diet is more prevalent, game hunting is more a hobby for rich men than a necessity.

A few years ago my friend from graduate school, Dwight, came to visit me. He was a loner but very good-hearted. He stuttered a little, and we all knew he had to study theoretical physics, because he was laconic and apparently lackadaisical. Very rarely had I seen him go out with a girl, not that he didn't want to, but perhaps he couldn't find one that fit his strict Jewish ideals. Whenever I would point out a girl to him with a typical Jewish nose, a characteristic of many at the campus, I always knew what he would say. He would find some feature of the girl that he didn't like, and invariably add, "But I won't kick her out of my bed." Dwight later moved to Israel and as far as I know he is still a bachelor.

I threw a party in his honor in my house. I invited four from my office—Don, Rex, Carl and John—who were hunters. Since it was mid-September, the discussion eventually drifted to hunting: they knew of only one person who got an elk.

"I've been practicing calls for the last two months," Don said. "Last year I hiked my boots off, but didn't see any elk. Now I know better."

"No one in the office got an elk last year," Rex commented.

Soon they were discussing John's new rifle, a Weatherby Mark 5, caliber thirty-three seventy-eight, and he described the magnificent new scope he put on it.

"How much did you have to cough up?" Carl asked.

"Four fifty for the scope and $1,200 for the rifle."

"My God," I exclaimed. "That's real money."

Dwight listened quietly. Like me, I was sure, he didn't know much about rifles. I drifted from the conversation and remembered how proudly Howard Mackenzie showed me his rifles when I visited him after their first child, Adam, was born. A Ph.D. scientist, he had recently moved to this area. He surprised me because, although I knew him in New York, I had no idea he was a hunter.

"This was one of the reasons I moved to Idaho," he told me. "My father was in the army. He taught me all about rifles and hunting."

He unlocked a metal cabinet and I saw four rifles neatly standing inside. He took one out and said, "Feel its weight and the balance."

It was a 7-mm Browning Mag, his proud possession that he used for elk hunting. He then showed me a .243 rifle, a lighter but a high velocity rifle that he used for small game. I could feel his hubris in his collections. When I was properly impressed, he explained to me why he had two shotguns (I didn't distinguish them, they were all the same to me); one was a goose gun, which was heavier. The lighter shotgun was for hunting turkey or grouse and for skeet shooting.

He expounded the details of the shotgun, but I was not listening; I was seeing a wild grouse on top of a hill. I had seen the grouse at close range when I took a few Boy Scouts on a hike up a mountain in Camp Buffalo, a few miles east of the Yellowstone Park. The grouse was ash-black and had spotted feathers. It was not frightened by our presence and hopped within ten feet from us and looked so beautiful in its natural environment. It could only fly a little distance and I felt like catching the gorgeous bird and bringing it home. The boys wanted to throw rocks, but I stopped them.

When I was of their age, while several of us were clearing a ground, a snake came out from under a bush, and our immediate instinct was to kill it. And we did–by throwing rocks at the escaping snake. I still remember the squiggle of the bloody snake before it came to final rest. We felt jovial during the act. A snake generates fear and our survival instinct had responded quickly. But the spontaneous urge to kill a bird in a peaceful surrounding in Wyoming was a different instinct, the "trophy" instinct, a desire to possess, to show off something that others didn't have.

When we came down to the camp I had the distinct feeling that the grouse looked much better alive in the woods than it could have been in any other place, dead or alive. A moment's pride to display the special catch and the story that would go with it were not worth its life.

My best friend in school played "God" with ants and selectively squashed them with his thumb. I hope as the evolution of species goes on, it will undo our instincts to kill. In the modern society where we don't need to hunt for food, could this ego be satisfied in other ways? A learned behavior for modern times?

Howard's room retook its shape, and four guns stared at me in the cabinet.

"These are all single shots," Howard told me. "I hate automatic guns."

He then proudly showed me his pistols. "I have these for self defense." The heavier .357 Magnum he carried when he went hunting, his protection against bears and bad people. It could kill a bear within ten to twenty yards. He explained to me how it came in handy on one occasion.

"Once I went fly fishing in a remote place. As I was walking away from my truck, I saw three guys pull up. Didn't look very savory to me. Either they wanted to break into my truck or make trouble for me. As they came down, they saw me with a fly rod in my left hand and the pistol on my belt. They just ran out. I didn't have to take my pistol out."

Howard gazed at me to see if I understood him, and then continued, "If one has malice in his mind, he acts differently. Hunters never act fearfully toward another hunter. Just because you carry a pistol, a hunter is not afraid of you. My pistol must have scared them because they were up to no good."

"I'm very careful with rifles," he repeated, looking straight at me, and put back the rifle after polishing a spot with his handkerchief.

"Let's go upstairs," I suggested. "Little Adam's bath must be done by now."

"No, stay. Let me show you this."

He opened a small safe at the lower part of the "closet." "Here I keep all my bullets." There were quite a few, and I wondered why did one need to keep so many bullets in the house? He explained the role of each one. These were his possessions like jewelry for women. Baby Adam could wait for us.

John turned to Dwight, "Do you like hunting?"

What I knew of Dwight, he couldn't be a hunter. Even living here for almost ten years, I hadn't gone on any hunting trips. Elk hunting, they were discussing, is especially very intense and requires skill. George Laycock called elk the "elusive, easily spooked wilderness spirits." One has to prepare for such an endeavor.

The elk (which some Indians called wapiti) is the largest animal with antlers in North America. They can be as heavy as 500 to 1,000 pounds, and measure up to five feet at the withers. And they have survived nature for a long time. (Carbon-dating results show that elk were in North America a few thousand years before man showed up.) Hunting these animals requires much preparation.

"Hunting?" Dwight stuttered, "I've never done any hunting. I don't even know how to hold a gun correctly."

"You don't know what you're missing," John remarked.

"Hunting isn't just shooting," Carl added. "It's a whole new experience."

"My gun has a new scope," Don proudly announced, "and can kill anything 800 yards away."

Carl came forward and said, "We're going to hunt in the Salmon area. Want to go?"

Dwight's curiosity was already primed. "I'm not interested in shooting, but it is enticing." He then looked at me, "What do you think?"

"It's hard work, Dwight. Not for people like you and me."

"Don't worry. He'll be with us," Don added.

"He doesn't have a hunting license," I said hoping that would end his interest. There are so many stories of accidents during hunting, especially by novice, careless and drunk hunters.

"Ah. Take him for the fun of it," Rex interjected.

By the end of the evening it was decided the four of them would take Dwight for a four-day hunting trip up in the Salmon area. I didn't want to go because I had made no preparations for such a trip and I had a deadline at the office, but I couldn't let Dwight go alone with people he hardly knew. So I also became a member of the hunting party.

Two things, I remembered, Jim Corbett learned very early in his hunting career: to get rid of his fear of the animal and never to kill without a good reason. So he primarily hunted the man-eaters. That was truly risky: the hunter can also be hunted. Fortunately, the hunting that goes on here is very different —the elk and the deer do not prey on the hunters.

The night before we left, Dwight asked for clean non-fragrant soap. "I don't want to spoil their hunting by my body odor." And indeed I heard him showering for a long time in the very early morning.

Before we left I told Dwight, "You will see a rugged and scenic Idaho, but don't be disappointed if we don't see an elk. They are smart and they stay away from the hunters."

Times had changed. About 150 years ago, one could hunt elk by chasing a small herd on horse back. The elk bumped into each other in their frantic run to escape, and a few would trip to the ground. The hunter could then butcher them with a knife. It was as simple as that. One cannot, of course, do this to a single elk—it will certainly outrun a horse.

When the Lewis and Clark team camped at Fort Clatsop on the Pacific coast, game was not available nearby, and the weather was rainy and foggy, making it more difficult to hunt. Still they killed 131 elk during the winter of 1805-1806. On one occasion George Drewyer and another hunter spent three days gradually driving a herd of elk closer to the camp so they didn't have to carry the meat a large distance. They killed eighteen elk six miles from the camp. Besides providing the needed meat, the elk skins produced blankets, leggings, and 358 pair of moccasins for the return trip up the Columbia River.

Millions of elk roamed all over this country before the Europeans came. Then the killing and hunting went in full swing. Today they live only in the mountains. The main reason for the terrible collapse of the elk population in the last century was not that elk meat tasted wonderful, but for the demand of its hide. The hide hunters, poachers, improved rifles, and the transportation system, particularly the railways, caused a demise of the elk from most parts of the country. At one time elk were killed for the teeth, especially the canine tusks – a thumb-sized ivory, which was used for jewelry. With government intervention and conservation measures, their population has increased, but nowhere near former levels. The elk population in North America is over half a million now, five times what it was around 1900. More than a third of the hunters could shoot an elk in the first half of this century, but for the last twenty-five years only fourteen or fifteen percent of the hunters succeed. Only the devoted and lucky get an elk.

An Isuzu Trooper and a Chevy Suburban left our house in the darkness of the morning with Dwight, me, and the four hunters. It took us a little over two hours to reach their destination beyond Challis and up in the Salmon River Mountains. Then we drove up the mountain on a one lane rough road only accessible by a four-wheel vehicle. The light red color of the soil fascinated Dwight. The evergreens looked greener than usual in the morning light of the sun. After climbing through the timberland for almost an hour, we parked the cars on a little space by the roadside and unloaded the gear. Don took out his binoculars and looked around. "It'll be great," he said to himself.

"Do we camp here?" Dwight asked.

"Not here," Rex smiled. "We'll go where no human has gone before."

They consulted a map and showed him a dot where they would camp.

"It's quite high up," Dwight exclaimed.

"Right," Don replied. "The rut has started. They move up for small grassy fields in the woods where they hide well."

It was almost noon by the time the camp was set up. The four hunters changed into hunting clothes and smeared their faces with black paint.

"I'm glad you didn't bring any nylon clothes," Carl told Dwight. "The animals can hear noise from far away. You stay here. We'll go scouting and be back in the evening. There's plenty of food and drink."

John said, "What about giving Dwight a firearm?"

"Not a bad idea," Carl said. "He could shoot if a bobcat shows up or something."

Carl took out a handgun from his bag, a .44 Magnum with a long barrel, and showed Dwight how to use it. He also showed him how to hang it on the belt and told him to carry it all the time. One gun was enough for both of us.

"What will you guys do today?" asked Dwight.

"We'll explore, and plot for tomorrow's action," Don replied. "An elk won't just walk into our camp."

Three days passed by quickly, or so it seemed, and each evening the four hunters returned to the camp exhausted. They had not come across an elk. Only a couple of times had they heard the bugle of a bull elk, but were not able to locate the bull. Don's calls had not been successful. "Tomorrow we'll find one," was the spirited attitude on the second evening. By the third evening it turned into, "Where the hell they are hiding?" Dwight and I silently observed how a depressing mood strolled into the group.

The first night was most jovial. Rex and Carl prepared dinner. It was thick steak and a Dutch oven dish with potatoes and onions, and strips of bacon thrown in for flavor. They also had wine, Cabernet Sauvignon. Excellent. They built a roaring campfire and spent the evening drinking and trading hunting stories.

Carl said, "My dad once bagged a deer without firing a shot."

"How is that possible?" Rex asked.

"It was in the Bitterroot Mountains and it was quite cold. One afternoon my dad had to relieve himself, and he was sitting with his pants down. He saw a good-sized deer, only fifty yards away, moving at a slow pace. He quickly picked up his rifle and aimed, but just as he was going to pull the trigger, the deer slumped, as if it was shot by him. He finished and ran to the deer. It was shot through the chest, but he hadn't fired. It must have bled internally for some time, and collapsed. He waited for someone to claim it, but no one came."

"Your dad takes his rifle everywhere?" John said.

"He always tells me, 'You never know.'"

"When I first went elk-hunting, I returned without firing a shot," Rex said.

"You didn't find any?" Dwight asked.

"I was still in high school and my uncle took me to the Skyline ridge, a few miles east of Idaho Falls, but when we got up on a hill, I saw a series of orange spots one after another all around us."

"Other hunters?" Dwight asked.

"Yes. I thought we went to a place not many knew. But it was hopeless. I thought they would end up shooting a hunter. I didn't go elk hunting for ten years."

"I'll tell you my first experience of shooting an elk," said John. "We selected a place in the Heise area, but when we went there we saw someone had already gone ahead of us. We didn't have any hope and just walked around. It was by chance we saw two young spikes below us. I shot one and my friend tried to shoot the other but it got away. We went down and started to cut it up, but I didn't know the rules well. When one kills a bull, one must carry the antler or leave on the sex organs. I kept both to avoid paying a fine and started to carry it over my head. It was a little more than a hundred pounds. Such a young head is useless, but I carried it because I thought I had to. The little antlers stuck out over my head. Then, suddenly I heard a boom, and I hit the ground. I got very scared that someone was shooting me for an elk. After a while we figured that it was a sonic boom, and I was fooled in the nervousness of my first elk hunt."

"I know a case where one lassoed an elk," Don said.

"Come on," Rex asserted, "that's impossible."

"No really. I was with him. It was November and we two were bringing down cattle in the Ruby Mountains near Elko, Nevada. Jim is a real cowboy. He was on one side and I was on the other.

"Jim came across an elk that was raking leaves on the ground and snorting. His horse stopped moving. The elk came forward, and Jim daringly threw his rope and lassoed the elk.

"Imagine that. A mess. The elk charged haphazardly, his horse screamed and wanted to run away, but Jim held onto his rope. He almost fell off the horse. He yelled for help.

"I shouted to him, 'Let go of your rope, Jim.'

"But he wouldn't. 'It's a brand new rope,' he shouted back. 'Come over and help.'

"I was on the other side of the slope with dense undergrowth and rocks between us."

"Elk are wild," John said. "You can get killed by an elk."

"So, what happened to Jim?" Dwight asked.

"I finally rescued Jim, and we had elk steak that night."

"Lassoing an elk?" Dwight mumbled to himself, "Are they crazy?"

On the last day of hunting, we saw the determination on Don's face and sincerely wished them good luck. Dwight had enjoyed these few days very much. Before coming on this trip to Idaho, he had really hoped for such a quiet and peaceful stay. Each day, after the four hunters left, the whole landscape belonged to us. Alone in the scenic wilderness of Idaho. We spread a blue plastic tarp on the ground and the few books we brought, and absorbed the scene with cups of coffee in our hands. We could gaze for hours at the cloudless blue sky, the vast green timbers, and the hills. What a scenic place it was. "This is perhaps what lured the pioneers to the West," Dwight murmured. The freedom was intoxicating.

We collected dry wood for the evening fire. Dwight strolled around while I read *The Magic Mountain*.

The sun was tilting toward the deep blue horizon over the vast wavy hills. One or two black birds flew from one tree to another. A few squirrels ran around. Red Indian paintbrush bloomed in many places, and we saw little yellow flowers we had not seen before. Were those asters?

As on the last three days, Dwight went out for a walk, keeping the tent in sight. He would have loved to see an elk in the wilderness, but he knew it was impossible; even the four hunters had not seen any. This was their last day. He strolled further away than before. In some areas the undergrowth was dense. He soon reached a gradual climbing terrain. There was stillness around and it was pleasant to be standing in the timberland. He looked out at the scenery for a long time. It was cool but refreshing.

"It's probably not that different from the top of a hill in the Adirondacks in upstate New York," he imagined.

He heard a deep-throated sound from the ridge. "It must be the sound of a bull elk," he thought. So the elk were around in this area! How beautifully these big animals hide among the timber. He gazed out at the vast green slope of ponderosa pines and Douglas fir leading to the ridge. Somewhere there was a bull with his harem and was calling to entice more cows to join him or to keep another bull away. He heard the high, shrill bugles again.

Dwight had heard Don practicing the bull and the cow calls. He cupped his hand around his mouth and tried to produce the sound of the bull. He did it several times. Since no one was around he had fun doing that. He felt free as if he were a child again. The breeze coming down from the slope carried his voice downward.

After a while he heard the noise of an animal moving through the undergrowth of the slope. He kept his eyes toward the sound, but almost teasingly cupped his hand and mimicked again the sound of the bull.

An animal emerged on the slope above him about thirty yards away. It was brushing its antlers on the lower part of the tree trunks. "It was a young bull, perhaps what Don calls a satellite or brush bull," he thought and was excited that he saw an elk. Satellite bulls are too young to enter the breeding game; they do not have the strength to fight an older bull and do not know how to court a cow. So they are frustrated animals and wander around alone. But what was it doing? Its feet scratched the ground and its antlers brushed the low branches. It moved toward Dwight. It was about twenty yards away from him now. Dwight suddenly remembered what John had told him many times: "Always remember, these are wild animals."

The elk grunted and squealed, frightening Dwight. The elk looked at him. Wasn't it too close to him? Without thinking much, he took out the gun from the belt and shot straight at the head.

Dwight got a big jolt from the shot, but vaguely saw that the elk fell to the ground.

"Oh, my gosh. Did I kill the animal?"

When the elk didn't stir for sometime, Dwight walked toward it very carefully. It was dead, lying on its side. He touched its antlers. "Wow! I have shot an elk."

Soon a pride came over him. "Those four didn't find an elk, but I've killed one. And on one shot!" A different feeling came over him; the elk didn't look beautiful anymore, just an animal. He felt the power of man over other beings, the raw power to control and dominate. "How strange!" he said to himself glancing at the distant ridge, and walked back to the camp, and told me what had happened.

When Rex, John, Carl, and Don returned to the camp one by one, exhausted and worn out, and resigned to the fact that they didn't get an elk, Dwight told them that he killed an animal, and he thought it was an elk.

"What are you talking about?" John was irritated.

"I'm not sure, but it has antlers."

"Let me see your gun," asked Rex.

One bullet was missing. "Take us to where you fired the shot," they commanded.

They looked at each other and followed Dwight where the elk was lying. It was a 4-point bull.

I have taken many of my friends and family members to the Yellowstone National Park, Jackson Hole, Craters of the Moon, and many other places, and have impressed them with many wonders of nature, but I was certain there was nothing that could surpass what Dwight and I experienced during the hunting trip and the expression we saw on four tired faces when he took them to the dead elk.

Perhaps there is an element of luck in hunting. Sometimes hunters do the right things unknowingly, which are later considered luck. If one reads Jim Corbett's books, one would find that he left very little to luck; it is all in the understanding of the animal and its world, including the animal tracks and their habits, the geography, and understanding the movement and sounds of birds and other animals in the forest, and then, it is the hunter's determination and perseverance that bring the game home. At one point, however, Corbett expressed a belief in fate or in the right time for an animal to die. If it was not its time, it couldn't be killed. No matter how hard a hunter tried. I wonder if this philosophy had anything to do with him being born, brought up, and living in India.

Why is hunting so important for many in Idaho even though it has become so hard? My friends tell me it is more than machismo. Its roots go way back in history, to the time when the Indians depended on game for their food, and then to the trappers and the hunters. When white men came to settle, they came with guns and their hunting instincts. It has remained a tradition. Truly, many hunt because they hunted with their fathers when they were young. Living the first seventeen years of their lives over again. "My grandfather hunted, my father hunted, and now I hunt." It is a father-son bonding phenomenon. But we have moved away from being a hunter and a farmer to a computer generation, where we prefer to sit behind the bluish glare of a screen and exercise our brains. Hunting is too difficult a game for this cerebral generation. Remnant hunters exist only in these areas; they are bound to wither away as a group. Only those few will survive who have taken it as an outing to be away from the humdrum of our daily lives, for male bonding, or simply as an excuse to be with nature.

Chapter Six
MOUNTAIN RIVER RANCH

I saw Michael coming down the corridor to the visitors' lounge. Sherry, walking behind him with the shiny black stripe of a leather bag hanging over her shoulder, looked positively dapper. Her curly brown hair fell neatly below her chin giving her a stylish look. "She must have gone to the 'Femina' on Lexington Avenue for this trip," I thought. "That white silk dress with chocolate polka dots probably came from Saks Fifth Avenue." I remembered how Catherine would run around for weeks getting ready for a trip. Sherry must have spent a fortune for this vacation.

"Welcome to Idaho," I said with extended arms. "How was the flight?"

Catherine hugged Sherry, as I looked at the contrast in their clothes. Catherine had jeans and an ordinary blouse, and not much makeup. The Idaho Falls airport is thirteen minutes away from our home—it isn't like going to the Kennedy Airport. Had we forgotten what it was like to receive someone at the airport? Looking at myself, I discovered I had a cowboy shirt on, which I had never worn before coming to Idaho. Michael had a beige turtleneck on with an exquisite brown tweed jacket, whose inside pocket, I was sure, had "Pierre Cardin" written on it. They glowed with enthusiasm.

"It was fine," Michael said. "But I'm surprised. I didn't know big planes landed in Idaho Falls!"

A large family was greeting a young man who just returned from a mission in South America. Two girls with shining golden hair held a banner, "Welcome back Jason." Grandparents, aunts and uncles, parents, brothers, sisters, and friends of the twenty-year-old Jason created a commotion in the small airport, almost jamming the arrival gate. Michael and Sherry skirted this group, and Sherry asked Catherine, "Is this very common here?"

"It is when someone comes back from an LDS mission." Catherine gave her a smile.

Michael looked around: a few posters on the walls—a neat and clean place, but nothing striking. The restaurant looked decent. As we turned the corner he stopped at the large exhibit on the wall—Washington's handwritten comments on the original Constitution, "We the people . . . ."

"I haven't seen this before," he murmured. "Interesting."

The single, round, metal luggage-carousel stood still for a long time before the luggage came out. There was no hurry, for the airport employees or the travelers. The spirited conversations of the passengers, and mostly of their receivers, kept the place warm and vibrating—a kind of family reunion right at the airport.

As we stepped out perfect late September weather greeted us. A silent, clear blue sky. Michael and Sherry gazed at the World War II airplane hanging over the few cars in the parking lot. Their eyes then shifted to the horizon. The mountain ranges shone in the distance, crisply reflected by the noon rays of the sun.

"What a scenery!" Sherry exclaimed. "Haven't we come to the right place for our vacation?" She pressed Michael's hand.

I showed them my favorite place at the airport, the place where the magpies live. It is a row of tall Colorado spruce trees, closely spaced on both sides of the pitch road, just outside the airport. I love the magpies—their sharp black and white stripes fascinate me.

"It has been their home for many years." I pointed out one to them. "What a magnificent shape they have!"

"You like magpies?" Michael retorted.

"Yes. Most people don't like them because they eat anything. In winter, when this place is all white, I love to see them bounding. They symbolize life in the still surrounding."

Michael looked toward the scattered few buildings.

Many say they will visit us, but very few really come this far to Idaho. So we were elated to see these two old friends, whom we had not seen since we left Long Island five years before. Our friendship goes a long way back. I met Michael in the last year of my graduate school in Stony Brook. Then, several years after graduation, when we were back again on Long Island we saw them often. Michael is a good friend. He asked me seriously before we had decided to come to Idaho, "Are you sure you want to take this job? There's nothing much out there."

We wanted them to like our new life in Idaho. After lunch and a short nap on the waterbed, another Western novelty, we took them out for a drive around town. We showed them the Civic Auditorium, the Public Library, the tallest building in Idaho Falls—the circular Westbank Hotel—the waterfalls, the Mormon Temple, and the ducks on the Snake River. We drove through the three blocks of downtown Idaho Falls. Catherine and Sherry chatted in the back-seat, and Michael silently watched the buildings. The colorful neon drawing of the lively cowgirl at the corner of Broadway and Park street glowed, on top of the entrance to the bar, as gorgeously as ever. The girl was so youthful. "It is an emblem of Idaho Falls," I told them. "I hope they never take it down."

"That's a nice figure," Michael commented, "but neon art is old. There is no market for it."

During dinner Catherine admitted that she arranged the time of their visit so that they could see the opera on Friday. The Idaho Falls Opera Theater performs only two shows a year.

The next two days we relaxed and caught up on what had happened in our lives. One day we drove to the Craters of the Moon. We showed them the Idaho National Engineering Laboratory. "They have over 9,000 employees at the lab," I told them because I was proud of the figure, almost three times the National Laboratory I worked for in Long Island.

Julie and Carl invited us for dinner. They were from Queens and were interested in meeting our friends. A small get-together of a few New Yorkers in a far away land. "They can talk with a New York accent," I chuckled.

True New Yorkers feel alien in remote societies like Idaho. It is like going to a village in India and trying to explain a flush toilet or talk about an art gallery in Brooklyn. Either you suppress your past and blend in, or you won't survive in such a foreign culture. A long time ago, when we lived in Ann Arbor, Michigan, Catherine was asked what she missed most about New York; her spontaneous answer was, "The Jews and the Italians." I was not sure if she did that for the effect, but a similar reply came from Julie when Sherry asked her the same question.

"I miss the gays."

Perhaps they miss the variety, even if it is only to look at or read about.

New Yorkers are like Brazil nuts—a hard shell outside, very hard to crack, but once they let you in, they are as soft as people anywhere else. One must, however, understand the delicate balance that exists in New York living. It is like going to the deli at an odd hour. You know you are there because other places are closed, far away, or it has something other stores don't have. And the deli man knows that, too. It is worthless to complain about the price.

It was amusing to me, who had made a 12,000-mile separation from his childhood home in a different continent, to see these New Yorkers miss Delancy street, the extra long hot dogs, the deli, the newspapers, and the crowd. They talk about the museums and the shows, but they really miss hearing the New York accent and the pleasure of complaining about everything.

"No shopping here, no good restaurants," Julie said. "It's like being in a space shuttle. You have all you need—good and healthy—but no variations."

"Gourmet restaurants here last only six months," Catherine added. "But you can have the best steaks in the world."

"What is Ed Koch up to?" Carl asked. Carl had retired from the music department of Queens College, and came here as the conductor of the Idaho Falls Symphony Orchestra. He still took delight in the machinations of New York City politics.

"He is struggling with a promotion fiasco in the police department. They designed a color blind test for selection of sergeants. A hard test, but the results have puzzled both the police and the minority groups. A very low number of blacks and Hispanics passed the test."

"How bad are the results?"

"Only two percent of the black and four percent of the Hispanic candidates passed the test, compared to eleven percent of the white officers."

"So Koch has a new headache. I wonder why the blacks did so poorly."

"They complain the tests were biased."

"The same racial issues."

I wondered if these expatriates could ever leave New York behind.

Michael admired Carl's train set which occupied a third of the living room of the two bedroom condo facing the Country Club golf course. The condo was charmingly decorated by Julie; a large painting of children in a park in Manhattan drew Michael's attention. Their living style was quite nice, but Michael could not imagine retiring here for the rest of his life. It would have been ideal to have such a place facing Central Park. "Julie, you play the cello," Michael said. "How are the musicians here?"

"There are many high-caliber musicians in this town. The Mormons encourage music for their children—both vocal and instrumental. I'm very pleased with the quality here." Julie looked outside at a man walking on the golf course. Then she murmured as if she was talking to herself, "I think I am tolerated—the New York attitude doesn't fit here. We're too pushy, often we don't know it."

Friday rolled around and Catherine told us to go early for the presentation before the show. After she left, Michael said,

"We've seen *The Mikado* several times, we don't need to hear a lecture. Just make sure we can park close by. It's already getting cold."

They put on their best clothes, Michael with a silk tie, matching shirt, dark woolen pants and his elegant brown jacket; Sherry had a dress hidden in her suitcase.

"Although you told us not to bring any fancy clothes, I'm glad I brought this one."

I loved watching them getting ready as if we were going to the Metropolitan Opera.

"Remember," I asked them, "the time we went to see Boris Godunov at the City Opera?"

"Don't remind me of that," Michael said.

Growing up in a disorderly family and with an impetuous father, Michael had developed a great liking for order and hated when things didn't go right. I suppose that was why he was good in mathematics and worked at the Courant Institute at the NYU. I always wondered if there was something that could bring out a spontaneous Michael.

I certainly impressed Michael when I parked the car on Holmes next to the Civic Auditorium. In October 1978 when we drove to Manhattan for Boris Godunov, we had planned to have a quick dinner before the show, but the Friday traffic on the Long Island Expressway ruined that. Then, there was the mad search for parking around Lincoln Center, which was impossible. We drove down to 37th Street and found a garage and had to pay in advance. I remembered Catherine asking, "Will they still be open when we come for the car?"

Several people greeted me in the Civic Auditorium and I introduced our friends. This was part of the local ritual. Being in a small town, we knew everyone who came to the opera, especially because Catherine was the make-up director.

"Only $10 for a ticket?" Sherry asked looking at *The Mikado* poster.

"Those are for reserved seats. Regular tickets are $6."

"How can they afford it?"

"You'll see. The singers are all volunteers."

We sat near the front in the middle section. The auditorium was not filled; today was the first performance. The overture started. The curtain lifted and the chorus began:

If you want to know who we are
We are gentlemen of Japan.

"The backdrop is not very Japanese," Michael whispered. "With such a large staircase in the background?"

"Small town opera clubs don't have a lot of money, you know," I said.

"I see. Japanese farmer hats and a fake cherry tree does it."

I remembered how hungry and disgusted we were when we entered the city opera for Boris Godunov. One's mood, however, changes instantly as one enters these wonderful places in Manhattan. No matter what happened before, a great solace is the Hall, and you relax. That is why New Yorkers go through all the troubles of fighting the traffic, the nuisance of parking hassles, and avoiding muggers at every step to the theater. We found we had tickets for the uppermost balcony. The crowd became thinner and thinner as we walked up four floors, and reached the top. The stage was down and far away.

"You can hear very well from here," Michael had said. "The sound system is carefully arranged."

As the first scene opened with a gorgeous setting of the Tzar's palace, the distance bothered me (we forgot to bring our opera glasses) and I soon lost interest in the scene. The voices sounded loud and unintelligible. After the first aria when the sound of clapping arose from the main floor, I felt more irritated than pleased; I felt I was not a part of the evening. It was sad, considering all the trouble we had gone through to buy the tickets months in advance and the traffic we fought to come to the show! The worst of all was that the place soon became unbearably hot—heat from the hall rose up and concentrated near the ceiling where we were. I looked at the faces around me, and finally said, "It would be more fun outside."

At the end of the first act, we walked out, and went straight to the restaurant opposite the City Opera. Catherine and I had a kind of outlandish pleasure in being able to walk out of this opera, which had been so highly advertised in the papers. We had a great time in the restaurant, and a leisurely drive home.

The sound of clapping brought me back to the Idaho Falls opera. Yum-Yum, Peep-Bo, and Pitti-Sing just finished singing:

Three little maids from school we are.
Pert as a school-girl well can be,
Filled to the brim with girlish glee,
Three little maids from school!

No big chandelier hung from the ceiling and no elegant decorations were around. The two large speakers and the red Exit letters stood out prominently on two sides of the stage.

Catherine sat with us after the first act. Since *The Mikado* was a comic opera, we got absorbed in the funny lines and laughed along with the crowd. Sherry liked Charlie Brown playing the role of Poo-Bah, and the make-up of the actors. They looked quite Japanese. But Michael compared the performance with the ones he had seen before and kept on finding little things that were not done right.

During the intermission, Michael said, "I'll buy drinks."

"Michael, it is not the Kennedy Center!"

"They don't sell drinks?"

"It's a Mormon country," Sherry whispered. "Drinking is not allowed."

The lobby was crowded. From the conversations it was clear people liked the show:

"Dianne did excellently as Yum Yum, but I wonder why Joan didn't get the role?"

"I like Steve as Ko Ko."

The enthusiasm was contagious, and Michael asked me, "You have seen many operas, what appeals to you here?"

"It is the people," I had to explain. "I can buy a wonderful cassette of *The Mikado* and listen to better music at home. But here we know the singers, the director, the musicians, the stage crew, the make-up artists. That's a whole lot different than going to a theater in New York. We are it here, Michael."

Catherine asked, "Do you want to go to the cast party?"

But Michael was not interested.

I had always wanted to visit the Mountain River Ranch; I was curious: what did they do to command such a price for a show way out in the boondocks?

"Do you want to go to the Mountain River Ranch?" I asked Michael.

"Are you kidding? What's there to see at a ranch?"

"I don't know, but I have four tickets."

"Why not?" Sherry said. "This could be a real experience. I hope it's not smelly."

The evening program was settled, but then I was worried, because they were leaving the next day. So far we had done okay, nothing spectacular, but they had agreed it'd be fun to come back again—especially for the beautiful Idaho scenery. This evening might spoil it all.

The drive east at dusk showed a different scene. The Tetons had vanished earlier in the gathering dusk, but the silhouettes of distant foothills created an impression that we were in a far away unknown, hilly land. The acres and acres of potato fields on both sides of the road added to that impression. It was lonely.

We made the left turn to Heise and went by a wall of hay, stacked high on our left, a shack on the right, and two stray horses. A few isolated trees. Nothing much around, and no lights came from any home. A quiet and dark veil was falling on the land.

Another scene came to my mind, a village far away in India. Dusk brings out a universal parallel of rural scenes. In an Indian village the evening comes with the distant sound of cow-bells, the sight of a little swinging lamp at the bottom of an ox-driven cart, a farmer returning home from a once-a-

week-market a few villages away, children in front of hurri-
cane lamps with open books in thatched huts, and hushed
female voices in courtyards. Dusk in rural areas means the
end of earnest activities of the day and a return to the comfort
of home and rest. Quite different from Manhattan, which
wakes up to new activities.

"What a country scene," Michael suddenly said. "I can feel
everything getting ready to sleep."

We soon saw faint lights ahead and knew that we reached
our destination. At the bend in the road stood a store-front
with a large space for horses and carriages. The lights were
from torches on posts in the long corridor.

"Look at the horses," Michael said. "They are for the carriages, I suppose. The place looks real."

"It's open," Sherry said, "let's go in."

The first room had farm equipment, scattered as if it were
a working room in a farm. Two saddles and several hats hanging on the wall, working boots on the floor, horse shoes, iron
rods and long hooks, metal tumblers, and many other things.
An older man strolled in the room and arranged things as if he
lived there and were looking for something. He ignored the visitors—so far as he was concerned they were not there.

In another room a girl was selling souvenirs. In the thin
light her ornamented long white boots looked very pretty, and
what a lively smile she had. "It's a real store," Catherine said.

"Cowboy shirts and boots," Sherry exclaimed.

Michael asked for bolo ties and the shapely cowgirl brought
several out for him and stood near him. Michael could not help
but look at her long black hair and sparkling eyes. What a
beautiful cowboy shirt she was wearing, one that fit her bust
so perfectly. She was certainly sexy. "I want to buy a tie,
Sherry. What do you think?"

"Are you going to wear it in New York?"

"Why not? It'll be fun to wear once in a while."

For the first time since he arrived in Idaho Falls, I felt,
Michael was at ease.

The girl took out a silver one with turquoise work and held
it against his chest. Her touch was firm and sensual. "It looks

very good on you." Her flirtatious eyes twinkled.

"Are you sure?" Michael smiled.

She was so warm and friendly. He bought the bolo tie and put it on.

Just then there was gunfire outside, and sounds of a serious quarrel. Startled, we went out. There were four men on horseback, several on the ground, and two carriages on the road. The men carried guns.

"We caught the horse thief," one man shouted .

Two of them dragged a haggard man out in front of the store.

"Where have you taken the horses?"

"I haven't stolen your horses."

"Shut up. We know you."

One man pushed him on the chest saying, "Don't you remember? Last time I let you go."

"Shall we hang him?" another man asked.

The man struggled to free himself. A shot was fired in the air scaring us further. Sherry put her hand on my shoulder. "What's going on?"

"Quiet. This is your last chance. I shall count five and if you don't tell us where you have taken our horses, I'll shoot you."

"I didn't take your horses."

"One, . . . two."

"I'm not your man. The man you are looking for is in Montana."

Then two blaring shots were fired; the man put his hands on his chest and fell on the ground. He shivered a little and became still.

A man on horseback shouted, "Let's go."

Those who were on the ground jumped on their horses, and all fled in a hurry. The man lay still on the ground.

People clapped around and the actors came back to take their bows.

"It was so real, I wasn't sure for a moment what was going on," Sherry said.

"That's what I liked most," Michael exclaimed. "The meager light and the isolation of this place make it more realistic. It was great."

A man announced, "I hope you liked this act. What you saw was not uncommon in this part of the country. The ranchers had their own laws for justice. We'll have a wagon ride now. You can board any of these carriages. There's plenty of room for all. Enjoy."

Michael got the hang of the evening. He took the lead and selected a carriage for us. It was sturdy with three rows of wooden benches, each of which could hold three comfortably. The driver and his assistant had a separate seat outside. The heavy cloth cover was flat and not round as we see in movies. Four strong horses pulled each carriage.

The yellow lights from the store front faded quickly, and we were out in the open country. It was dark and cold. As the wagon moved it creaked and the ride was bumpy. The path led us away from the pitch to a narrow, dirt road. Soon we were in a field with tall cottonwood and aspen trees and a dark hill on our right.

Voices from the carriage behind us sounded jolly, and the riders were clearly having a good time. Our carriage seemed to be filled with cerebral men and women who were more curious about what would happen next than being able to let go and enjoy. I am a city boy. Except for reading *Little House on the Prairie*, I have had no experience of hay-rides and didn't know what to do or even what to expect. We could hear happy voices from behind us and their chorus sounded cheerful:

Home, home on the range,
Where the deer and the antelope play.
Where seldom is heard a discouraging word,
And the sky is not cloudy all day.

"Look at the sky," Michael said. "I've never seen it so clear and so bright."

Above, the star-lit sky revealed itself in its magnificent glory. The Milky Way lighted our path. The star lights produced a strange reflection on the water of the Snake River— the moon was not up, but we could see the water. "Almost 200 years ago," I thought, "Lewis and Clark experienced the same open, unspoiled nature under the sky." It was wonderful.

Soon we were absorbed in our thoughts. Only the rhythmic sound of the running horses and noise of the wheels on the road could be heard. Trees passed by quickly and silently. Michael gazed outside as if no one else existed in the world. "Idaho has its own beauty," he murmured. "I'm glad we came. This is a true experience."

The wagon drove on the dirt road through farmlands. The scenes of the field and the trees changed continuously in the darkness of the night and kept us spellbound. In a while, we came closer to the carriage in front of us, and our wagon slowed down. We were nearing the destination. The distant chorus from behind became clearer again:

Buffalo gals, won't you come out tonight,
And dance by the light of the moon?

"I know that song," Michael said and hummed along. The carriages stopped in front of an old, large barn and we were led inside. Picnic tables with paper tablecloths and benches covered the wooden floor in front of a small stage without a curtain. Large beams hung above us. Walls were bare: sixty-year-old lumber staring at us.

"How is it going so far?" I asked.

"It's great," both Michael and Sherry said simultaneously.

"You know I was worried. This cowboy thing might turn you off completely."

"No, no. I'm really enjoying it," Michael said with a smile.

Guests filled up the room, including half of our table, and a lively conversation ensued. No one was formally dressed in the room. A few men had bolo ties and hats, and the ladies had decent clothes, but many were in jeans. Most were locals to celebrate a birthday or an anniversary of some sort. Soon the whole barn started to vibrate with lively conversations and laughter.

A man came on the stage and announced, "Dinner is served. Please help yourself."

It was chuckwagon food cooked in Dutch ovens: rib-eyed steaks, fried potatoes, corn on the cob, bar-b-que beans, corn bread, salad and apple pie. It was late and time to eat. That was it. There was no pretension of sophistication, everyone rushed to eat. The food was hot and tasted okay. Michael went for a second serving, saying, "We don't get this food in the East. It's pretty good."

A young-looking lady in colorful Western clothes got up on stage and announced that she'd be the emcee for the evening. I love these Western clothes, especially on slim women. She had a hoop skirt on with ruffles and lace, and a tight fitting shirt with fringe dancing on her solid breasts.

"Anyone for birthday celebrations today?" she asked. "Please raise your hands."

Several hands went up.

"Great. Happy birthday to you. Anyone for anniversaries?"

Four hands went up.

"Let's see, do we have anyone from out-of-state? Anyone from California? Wonderful."

Michael waived his hand saying, "New York," and looked at the emcee smilingly.

"Great. We have a couple from New York. Remember this is off-Broadway." She winked at Michael. "An Idaho Special. But where are your hats?"

Two men brought cowboy hats for Michael and Sherry. They put on the hats in good spirit and actually looked very nice. This little attention pleased them very much.

Two men and two girls in saloon style clothes sang and danced on the stage. *Red River Valley* didn't sound bad at all. The girls danced lifting their skirts and flirting with the men in John Wayne style clothes, hats, and guns in their holsters. The girls had so many petticoats that no one really revealed any leg. It was lively and fun.

"They are the waiters and the waitresses," Sherry commented.

Lots of applause and hoots came from the floor.

Then came three people, two men and a young, short girl, with fiddles in their hands, and they started playing *Turkey in the Straw* and many immediately joined in thumping the floor. People started singing:

> *As I was a-goin' on down the road*
> *With a tired team and a heavy load*
> *I cracked my whip and the leader sprung*
> *I says day-day to the wagon tongue*
>
> *Turkey in the straw (whistle)*
> *Turkey in the straw (whistle)*
> *Roll 'em up and twist 'em up a high tuck a-haw*
> *And hit'em up a tune called Turkey in the Straw.*

I was surprised Michael knew the song and sang along quite loudly. The rhythm filled the place.

The two men on the stage joked about the girl's height, and that she was an apprentice and learning how to play—and she went along coyly. Then she played a beautiful solo. It was so angelic that everyone stopped talking and listened to her. She thus took her revenge on her partners. All in fun and good spirit. She announced, "I just want these guys to remember that the name of our band is Sue and the fiddlers, and not the Fiddlers and Sue." Everybody laughed. They then played *Devil in the Fiddle*, and she played superbly.

When the fiddlers played very fast, Sherry looked at them intently and Michael's head and torso moved in rhythm.

An older man came to the stage. "I'll show you how a sophisticated man from California behaves in Idaho. But before that let me tell you first the three greatest cowboy lies! 'I won this buckle in the rodeo.'"

Everyone burst out laughing.

"The truck is paid for."

Another roar came from all around.

"I was just helping the sheep over the fence!"

Loud applause and laughter went around. Catherine shook her head and Sherry looked at the stage in disbelief. But Michael kept on laughing.

A man whirled a lasso on the stage. He moved it around his body with ease, while talking to the audience. "I am going to teach you how to lasso a rope. But I need some volunteers."

The waiters went around selecting men to go on the stage and took Michael and three others. "It looks so easy," Michael said. "Yeah, I want to try this."

They gave each one a rope and Michael tried, but the rope fell like a dead snake, and everyone laughed. The man showed them how to move the rope, and again it looked so easy and so smooth, but they couldn't even make a circle. To the laughter of all, they tried and tried again, and failed miserably. It was embarrassing, but Michael was having fun.

Then came four young girls with long skirts, and they took the hands of the four men, and live Western music started. Several men and women sang from one corner and the fiddlers played from the side. Lights dimmed in the barn and they started dancing. Michael was a good dancer and he caught on very quickly. Michael was so comfortable, and he blended in beautifully with the performers. He was the best dancer among the four men on the stage. "How strange," I thought, "I have not seen him so relaxed."

"Virginia Reel," the first one, a barn dance, looked very lively. It was like a square dance, but not quite. The girls went around the men with their skirts twirling, and I realized it was really a performance of the girls. Men were there to support them and they were a little stiff except for Michael. His face beamed and his body moved beautifully.

The singers then moved on to a new song without stopping, *Yellow Rose of Texas*, and the dancing changed to a Western waltz. I saw Michael leading the girl now to a wonderful rhythm. I looked with amazement at the beautiful, flowing movements of the dancers and wished I could dance like Michael. In the indistinct light of the stage, lovers were dancing in each other's arms. I could see Michael floating.

There was something magic in the tune. Suddenly, conversations stopped in the barn, and all eyes gazed on the dancers. Romance and sweetness emanated from the stage, as if the secret loves of the couples were not secret any more, and they had received approvals from everyone. The graceful movements of the Western waltz and the tune took us all to a dreamland of our own.

When the long song was over, and carriages were brought in to take us back, it was late, but I knew Michael was far away somewhere in a cowboy country.

Chapter Seven
THE MISSIONARIES

In the office we didn't discuss religion, and I mixed with a relatively young crowd, Mormons and non-Mormons all together. It didn't matter who you were; juicy stories and sex-escapades were of more importance. But one day Dennis and I were chatting, and somehow the discussion had led to local customs and practices and then to the subject of the missionaries. I told him that I didn't understand why young boys go on missions when they should be going to college. Dennis' face became serious, but I saw he didn't mind my questions. He then told me he had gone on a mission and smiled.

I could see from his face he had fond memories of the time, and I felt at ease in continuing the conversation. Dennis was medium sized and muscular. He had a large, round face with sparse eyebrows and blond hair—a common face here, usually of Scandinavian origin, and most would recognize the face as belonging to the LDS Church. I had come to know him well over the last year, and when no one was around, he was quite candid with me.

"I did my mission in Ohio," Dennis said, "and this fellow, a middle-aged man, invited us in. It was my turn to give the presentation. My partner was quiet and listening."

Dennis looked outside to the potato field, a healthy, green span stretching acre after acre to the horizon, as if he needed to recollect the old days. The long row of sprinklers spread misty water in beautiful geometric shapes. I chuckled, thinking of Dennis as one of those young LDS missionaries in shiny dark suits walking, in Miami, Ohio, from door to door.

"I was looking at him out of the corner of my eye," Dennis told me. "I was wondering why was he looking at my head so intently?"

"Did you have a funny hair cut?" I asked him naively.

"Oh no. When you go on a mission, you must have a proper haircut—clean and very short—nothing funny."

"I finally took my hat off," Dennis continued, "It was hot and I was perspiring. I asked him if he had a question. He boldly looked at my head and said, 'You don't seem to have horns. I thought LDS people grow them on their heads.'"

"You are making it up," I exclaimed.

"No. It's true. The man got up and examined my head closely. But I kept my cool."

I would have probably dug a hole and buried myself right there, I thought, or would have walked out angrily, but Dennis Young was not perturbed. He finished his talk. It is in the training they receive before they go on a mission: one must have faith and patience.

"Didn't you feel like punching him?" I asked.

"Nope. At least he had heard about our religion," Dennis concluded.

He looked outside through the office window, and I wondered about how well he remembered the man in Ohio even after thirty years.

My turn came soon. I was watching these two boys in Mormon Suits, as they call them, going from door to door and saw my neighbor, about six houses down, waving his hands vehemently and physically chasing one boy off his lawn. The boy regained his composure, straightened his jacket and went to the next house as if nothing had happened to him; his yellow-blond hair fluttered in the wind.

I examined them when they rang my bell—high school boys, not accustomed to regular shaving yet, and what guiltless faces. "We are from the Church of Jesus Christ of Latter-day Saints, sometimes referred to as Mormons. We would like to tell you about our religion."

Hm. These two nineteen-year-olds wanted to teach me about religion! I was above forty years of age and had lived on two continents in two widely different cultures. What did these two boys know about life, let alone religion? Suddenly, a rage went through my mind. I understood what happened just now six doors down. I looked at their innocent faces—babies they were, and they wanted to tell me that I should follow the LDS Church?

I looked at the shiny name tag on the jacket: Elder Prescott. "So Elder, where do you come from?"

"I'm from Texas, but my name, sir, is not Elder."

"Sorry. You have someone else's name tag?"

"No. We are called Elders when we go on a mission."

"But you are not old enough to be an elder?"

"What religion do you follow?" the other boy asked me.

"I was born in a Hindu family."

"Uh. You are a Hindu. You worship cows, right?"

"Not really."

"I know," Elder Prescott said, "you worship your God through cows and snakes."

"I didn't say I was a Hindu. But tell me what you have to say."

"We want to tell you about a visit Jesus Christ made in early America. May we come in?"

When I was in India I never heard of the Mormons, and there were very few in Pennsylvania, New York, and Michigan, where I had lived before—so far as I knew. My conscious mind didn't register them. Once in a while you heard about the Mormons in Salt Lake City, a bunch of outlandish folks following a religion bordering on Christianity, and you forgot about it immediately.

When I was coming to Idaho I was told, "You know you are going to the land of the Mormons," and I said, "So?"

After a few months in Idaho, a Mormon colleague, Dave, surprised me one day. He opened with a blunt joke about Mormons. Dave wanted to show that he was not like the other stuffy Mormons, and he didn't mind a good joke about himself.

He was friendly in nature and appeared open-minded.

Then I had to ask him, "Why are there so many more Mormon missionaries in Utah than in New York?"

"I don't know."

"Because they are still waiting for their vision."

He was encouraged by my silly jibe and wanted to keep going. "Tell me why now-a-days they use Mormons for lab experiments instead of mice?"

I looked at his smiling face as if he wasn't talking about his own people. Very few could really take well the Polish jokes about themselves, however enlightened they were. So I said, "This is silly. Tell me why the Mormon Bishop went to hell even though he reached the gate of heaven?"

"Because St. Peter was serving coffee and he didn't have time to make cocoa."

"Good. Tell me how do gold plates vanish in thin air?"

Suddenly, his face became serious, and he walked out.

While the two missionary boys were giving me their presentation, I examined the painting in the living room wall— young Shakuntala playing a lute-like instrument to a deer. It was the scene of a hermitage. Soon the grasses and the trees took shape and I found myself at the edge of a forest. A lone cottage with a dirty yellow straw roof was before me, and I could hear the rhythmic chanting of young boys. It was a rishi's ashram. I saw small spotted deer grazing and peacocks quietly sitting under the trees. It was so peaceful. The boys lived in the ashram with their guru, obeyed him, and served him with devotion. And he taught them about life, living, and death, and the spiritual wisdom which "enables one to hear the unheard, think the unthought, and know the unknown."

This is how boys gained knowledge in ancient India. And it was not meant for all; only those who were seriously inclined to devote their lives to study religion or those who would become priests would follow this mission. They had to go away from civilization to the wilderness and stayed there until they were satisfied with the depth of their knowledge. Sometimes it took many years. The serious ones would even go on to more learned rishis or on to their own search for the truth.

I thought of Shetaketu, Nachiketa, and other young boys from ancient India. Even after returning from a Rishi's hermitage, Shetaketu begged his father to teach him more about the true significance of our relation to God, and his father bade him to bring a fruit from the nyagrodha tree. When he brought the fruit his father asked him to break it.

"What do you see inside?"

"These seeds, father. They are very small."

"Break one seed."

"I broke one."

"What do you see."

"There is nothing special inside."

"That which you don't see, from that grows the big nyagrodh tree. The whole essence of the tree is inside one seed. You can't see it or feel it, but it is there. Same with us. The Brahman is within us. That is the truth, the supreme. You are a part of that, Shetaketu, you are that."

What he told Shetaketu was that God was within us, and this realization was the essence of our living. "Tattvamasi: You are that." How could this knowledge and the conviction be gained by simply memorizing a book, however holy it is?

Young Nachiketa on the other hand faced Lord Yama, the god of death, and asked him, "There is this doubt about a man when he is dead: some say he exists, others say he does not. What is the truth?"

He spent several days with Yama to satisfy his inquiry. Yama taught him that the soul is immortal and that the individual soul (whose Sanskrit name is Atman) is identical with the universal Supreme Being (Brahman). Just as we cannot see our own eyebrows, we cannot perceive the supreme life force within ourselves. That is the greatest knowledge we must master.

To me most important are the quest—and respect—for knowledge. One must question everything and accept answers only when one is convinced of its truth. Self-searching and self-experience are the basis of my life. I looked at the two Mormon missionaries in clean shirts, suits, and shiny shoes. They had no experience of their own, and they dared go on telling others what the true faith should be.

Next day I told Dennis how my neighbor chased away two missionaries. "They must have had a lot of these experiences," I stated.

"And many more," Dennis confided.

"Really."

"Well, let me tell you about my friend Elder Judd's experience. When he was in New Haven, he was invited to come to the apartment of this man. Judd was pleased that the man did not give him any hassle, and simply said, 'Come tomorrow.'

"The next day when Judd and his partner settled in a small room, the man's study, he sat on a sofa away from the boys, and said, 'Go on.'

"Elder Judd opened his notes and started talking—looking at the man's eyes. The man slowly moved his eyes up toward the ceiling, and Judd naturally followed his eyes as he was talking. Then he noticed. The whole ceiling was covered with *Playboy centerfolds*—from one end to the other. Judd was from Richmond, Utah, and had not seen a *Playboy* magazine before.

"He quickly looked down and started his presentation again. But his concentration was spoiled, and the man slowly raised his head again toward the ceiling. Judd could not help but look at the beautiful pictures of almost naked young girls, their breasts hanging down from the ceiling. The LDS church had taught him that looking at a naked girl is a sin—very unholy. He stuttered. Then the man looked at his pants and between his legs.

"'Don't you like girls?' the man asked him.

"'Yes, but we are taught to respect them.'

"'Ah! Let me tell you what happened to me when I was young like you . . . '

"Elder Judd went to his supervisor the next day and said, 'This guy invited us and he was very nice, but I had this peculiar experience.'

"Before he could say anymore, the supervisor asked, 'Was it in the apartment on Dover Street?'

"'Yes. How did you know that?'

"'Was it on the top floor? A small room with pictures on the ceiling?'

"'Yes.' Judd was flabbergasted.

"'That guy has been doing this to Mormon missionaries for some time. He invites the boys and watches their reaction to the pictures and then tells them dirty stories.'

"'You could have warned us. It was very embarrassing.'

'You see, then, I'd have to explain all this to you, and I couldn't do that!'"

I understand why the LDS Church sends out young boys to preach the religion. They hope that by seeing these well-dressed, young, healthy, clean-shaven boys and pretty girls people will be inspired to become like them. And they do succeed that way, particularly in deprived neighborhoods and undeveloped countries. From my Indian heritage and perspective, one gains wisdom when one is old, and only then does one have something to tell others. These boys can only repeat what they were told. In the East, truth is accepted on the basis of personal experience. That is why people become monks, leaving home and the luxury of life, and go to the "forest" in search of the truth.

But the Mormons are devoted to their religion in an unquestioning way. Right from birth they are taught a reverential faith for the LDS Church and its sacredness. Their temple is not just a building where one worships—the way most people look at their churches. The Mormon Temple is sacred, like the temples of the Hindus, and true members live their lives centered around it. As an example, life is not complete for a Mormon who cannot get married in a temple. And one must live a wholesome life to get married in the Temple. This is determined by the ward bishop, the lay priest, who watches over them. So there both boys and girls behave properly—no bad thoughts allowed. However, knowing the current TV generation I wonder how they can stay so pure, and it is a wonder how even a single boy gets married in a temple.

I think in the LDS society boys are swept away by the aura of the church and the family pressure of getting behind their relatives and neighbors. A little competition and upmanship do wonders for them.

"I can also go to the lions willingly. Is that it?" I asked Dennis.

"That's not it," Dennis told me.

"Why do you, then, waste the most formative period of your life?"

"To us, life is not all work or making a decent living. We must nurture the soul and the life after. It's an honor to go on a mission. And it's not easy. One must qualify by living according to the prescribed lifestyle of the church and must show his devotion—true faith. One must be willing to give two years of his life for the mission. How many can do this?"

"I see. A test of your faith in the church."

"It's a training. It makes a boy into a man. The LDS people are not so stupid as to think that these young boys will convert many, although that's the intent."

"You mean they all come back as mature individuals?"

"Some do. On the mission, they are guided every moment of their life—what to do, when to do it, even what to think. Some like that very much and are trained to follow the disciplined approach to their later life, but some fall apart when they return because there is no one to tell them what to do anymore."

I visualized the innocent faces of the two boys who came to my house. One day they would be proud that they came all the way to Idaho Falls and gave their two years, going from door to door; and in that process they matured by bantering with the Catholics, Presbyterians, Evangelists, and even a few Hindus. What a way to grow up.

Chapter Eight
Be Crazy About

"**I** stayed up last night because Max was sick," Lorna told me with a sad face. She put her elbows down on the desk and held her head. Her blue eyes didn't have their usual shine. The bluish glare of the computer monitor stared at us from the side, and the cluttered pile of papers on her desk told me nothing would be done today.

"I'm worried," she looked up with the pensive look of an apprehensive mother. "Max is behaving very strangely. I haven't seen this before. Not even with Angela when she was sick, my first daughter."

I looked out the window. The potato field behind her office was all hard and brown. Acres and acres of the field seemed to extend to the distant mountain, cut only by the log-posts for the electric lines. The rows of the last planting were still visible by the lines of slightly raised soil. The land looked barren.

"What's the problem?" I asked her.

"Max didn't eat anything last night. Before I went to bed I felt he had a temperature. He wouldn't look at me. He stared at the wall. That got me worried because he was fine during the day. I offered him a drink, but he wouldn't take any. He acted worse and worse as the night went on."

"Did he eat anything unusual?"

"He's on a strict diet, you know. Unless he has picked up something from the garden."

"So many things to worry about. You look very tired. Why don't you go home and take care of him?"

"I have to make an appointment. He is sick but the symptoms aren't clear yet. Jenny's looking after him this morning. I'll see."

Lorna's wheat blonde hair was not neatly combed today, and dark shadows arched beneath her eyes. She looked at the pile of mail on her desk, but her mind was not at work. How could it be? Max was only six months old. I remembered how excited she was when she brought new-born Max's pictures to the office.

It was early April. She barged into my office, bubbling with joy. "We have a new colt. Max was born Friday." She lay down a packet of photos in front of me.

A reddish-brown baby horse standing next to the mother with thin legs that hardly supported its weight. A streak of white color on his head.

"I named him Max because of his shoulders," she told me. "Look, how strong they are. He's a purebred. The father was a champion at the Utah race."

She went around the office explaining the details of the pictures.

Many in the office had horses. At first it was a shock, then a curiosity, but by now I had gotten used to animated conversations about horses, the pains and the pleasures of owning one. My first surprise was when Tom walked into a meeting, haggard and tired. He said he struggled the whole night, trying to save his horse, but it died. Big Tom was in charge of a group that investigated what happens during a nuclear reactor accident. He worked with sophisticated mathematical programs, called codes. I couldn't imagine the laboratory researchers to be so affected by horses. The meeting stopped, and everyone was more interested in knowing the details of what happened to the horse than the details of the hydrodynamics code. But I kept quiet, this was Idaho.

Dennis once told me, "Horses love the man who feeds them. That's why you can buy a horse and he'll be yours in a few days. Other pets aren't like that." Willis said, "You have to be

Robert Bower

careful with horses. They do things instinctively. They don't think. The other day, Wagner's horse, an Appaloosa, moved his head up suddenly, and hit his wife. She had a big bruise and is afraid to ride any horse now."

There is an unspoken mystery of owning a horse. I have heard different reasons. Mostly, I heard, "We enjoy riding the trails you can't hike to." But I saw them going only a few days during the year at best! "Do they do all this work for keeping a horse just for a few days of riding in the woods?" I had asked myself. Some said they loved the graceful shape of the animal, especially when they ran: "I can watch for hours when my horse runs around the fence. What powerful muscles! How smoothly it moves through the air." Some would say, "It's for my daughter," and would not explain any further. Some would give me a blank stare and say no more, implying, "How could you be so stupid to ask this?" Women were more enthusiastic than men and often expressed a mystic relation with the horse. I had thought that the ability to master a large, strong animal and being able to lead him to any place she wanted to provides a thrill a woman does not find anywhere else.

There is certainly a unique relationship between a horse and its owner, the intensity of which I didn't understand.

Only a few months back, there was a small crowd in Lorna's office gazing at her pictures and recollecting stories of their own newborns. Pictures of Max circulated from one hand to another: Max sitting in the shade; a picture of his mother looking at him; Max drinking milk; Max next to the fence; Jenny, Lorna's daughter, caressing Max. The packet also had several pictures of Lorna's backyard with bales of hay stacked up on one side. The mountains in the photograph, delineated in crystal-white snows, looked so near to her house in Blackfoot.

"The mother first rejected Max," Lorna had told me earlier. "She went away after the baby was born. But she came back. The bond developed after he started to drink her milk." She was describing the details of each picture to me, and I realized Max was not just a newborn horse; it was her new baby. Lorna was in her early forties and had three teenage daughters whom she was raising alone for the last ten years because her husband was killed in an accident at work. She had told me how terrible it was when her husband died. She belonged to the LDS church, got married right after high school, and was very happy to be his companion in every way; her husband was her leader, and he decided everything for her and the family, and she simply followed. She didn't know or have any interest in knowing anything else. "We did whatever he wanted to do. Our social life was around his friends."

I looked at her wide eyes and said, "You were very happy. Weren't you?"

"Yes. My husband was also very playful. We had water fights even after our children were born." Her face beamed with happy memories.

Then her world had suddenly crumbled. The news just came, and she was lost. Her youngest daughter was only two years old. It took her years to stand on her own feet. Eventually, she learned to do everything by herself. She told me she wondered sometimes if she was a new person now or if she had earlier simply suppressed the capabilities she had.

My acquaintance with horses was only with the worn-out, regular carriage-horses in Calcutta (not the healthy ones you see in Central Park, New York) when I was very young and, then, with the mounted police for traffic control. What else would one see in a big city? But soon the carriages were replaced by automobiles and the horses vanished from the normal scenes.

My first memory of horses is from when we first came to Calcutta to live, and it was of fear. In the darkness of the night, we came out of the colossal Howrah Train Station, on the other side of the Ganges River in Calcutta, and in the dim light I saw the line of carriages in the middle strip of the road. The horses had blinds on their eyes, and it made them look creepy. They were eating straw and moving their heads and feet occasionally. My six-year-old instinct told me they could hurt me if I were near them. I remember grabbing my mother's hand. What made it worse was the surrounding. Crowds were all around us, all walking frantically. Coolies walked fast with huge loads on their heads, and overwhelming noise came from all directions. Most of all, the horses appeared chancy. I felt I could be separated from my family any moment, and then I would be lost forever. We waited while my father and uncle settled a price with the carriage driver. It sounded like they were quarreling, and the old Muslim driver with a long white beard wearing a lungi was frightening. The thick tails of the horses swiped at the flies. Then we entered the dark carriage, all eight of us sitting on top of each other. The physical closeness of the family and the rhythmic noise of the wheels soon put me to sleep. After coming to Idaho, I learned to see that horses are not to be scared of, but loved, a strange notion for a man who grew up in a city with ten million people. A horse can be a pet!

While I looked at the crowd in Lorna's office talking about their horses, another scene from Calcutta came to my mind. My father was standing in front of the small room in the first floor and asking, "Who brought the puppy that made such a mess in the room?" In a little boy's voice I admitted that I found the puppy in the neighborhood and wanted her as a pet. "Well, then, go and clean her poopies." In India we never had to do such menial work (there are sweepers and cleaners for such dirty jobs), but I had to clean up the mess because the puppy was mine. My father would otherwise throw her out. That was how I got my pet, and everyday she followed me a distance to the school.

How proud I was when the grown dog, Kaalu, produced a litter of six puppies in the balcony of our three-room flat on the third floor of our house. I watched the little shiny ones come out, and how Kaalu licked them clean, one at a time. Their skin was like glistening velvet.

I remembered the animal smell of the babies. I secretly took one to bed, and it peed at night. My mother found it out and that did it. "A dog in the bedroom? Inauspicious animal. Out, out. They must be out of the house today."

I don't remember now what happened to the puppies. Probably they were thrown out of the house and left to survive as street dogs. There were many like that in the neighborhood. They lived on the little food they could find in the garbage bins.

My vision came back to the office. I heard Lorna saying, "In winter my horse loves it when I bring a tub of warm water to melt the ice under her hooves. She stands still and looks at me tenderly. I can feel the bond."

"I have the same experience," our safety engineer, Lynn, said, "when I feed grains to my horses. They eat from my hands so gently."

"Horses are like dogs," Jack shouted as he passed by, "only dumber. And much more expensive to keep."

"Jackass," someone commented under his breath, "he hates animals."

They ignored Jack's comment, but I thought there was some truth to the expense part. Even a saddle costs somewhere between $700 and $1,000. The feed and regular maintenance with shots would easily come to $200 a month. A trailer costs $3,000 to $4,000, and you need a three-quarter-ton truck to pull the trailer. That is $25,000 and more. And the gas-mileage goes to hell when you pull two horses. A horse was certainly not for me.

Lorna did not come to work for two days. On Thursday, when she came in, she was smiling: "He is doing better." She went straight to her desk. Later, Lorna told me what had happened during the last few days. "Running fever, diarrhea. So bad, we couldn't keep him hydrated. He had colic. We loaded him up and took him to the vet. But the moment we entered the vet's office he felt better."

"Finicky horse, eh?"

"This happened three times. Every time we took him to the vet he was perky and fine. The vet wasn't sure whether we were crazy or not. Max's eyes and gums looked good. He had only a low fever. The vet gave him a shot to keep him calm. We brought him to Idaho Falls. You want to go see him?"

"Sure. But why is he here?"

"For observation. The vet for large animals has a better facility here. They'll record his symptoms every hour."

"Like human patients?"

"Of course. Would you expect less for your pet?"

I was taken aback by her bold assertion. It was new for me. Pets in Calcutta didn't receive the care and the attention they receive here; emotional bonds were sacrificed quickly in the face of reality.

We only have a cat and a fish tank in our house in Idaho Falls. We hadn't encountered any big problem as Lorna had now and I didn't know what I'd do under such a situation.

I suddenly remembered the day in Calcutta my seven-year-old baby brother put on long socks and shoes, which he hated to do. "What are you up to?" I asked.

"Didn't you see, there were two horses on the road? I'm going to see them."

"Why the long socks?"

"Tetanus. Horse dung has tetanus germs. The germs can jump two feet up in the air."

He went out to see the animals up close.

During lunch time, I went with Lorna to see Max. He was kept in an indoor stall. A thin small horse—obviously weak and standing quietly. He barely moved his head. A tube came down from the ceiling joist to his neck and injected fluid from a plastic bag to keep him hydrated, as they do in regular hospitals. Outside light through the large doors kept the stall bright and cheerful. Fresh straw and a water tub were there. Lorna went inside and caressed him. Max liked that and moved his head a little. "He's doing better," she said. "The vet hasn't figured out what's wrong with him. The blood test didn't show anything. He's on a general antibiotic. But it seems to be working."

She brought the hose from the outside and started to clean the stall. A large horse was in another stall, and no one else came while we were there. The place looked like a private clinic with several clean rooms. This must cost her some money, I thought.

Lorna adjusted the tube around Max's neck, and checked the fluid level. She wanted to stay longer, but I reminded her about the office.

On our way back, I wondered if I had not seen such caring for horses or other pets in India because I grew up in the city. But all life form is highly regarded in India. Perhaps affluency brings a new dimension to this equation. I asked her how she could spend so much time for the horses.

"I know what you are thinking," she said. "I'm not crazy. I can't just let the colt die!" She stopped for a few seconds, and then continued, looking at me once, "The horses become a part of your life. When you have a horse and you are its only rider, a special relationship develops between the two of you. It can't be explained. One understands the other without any spoken word.

"You develop a oneness with the horse. You can ride the horse without reins. The horse knows by your touch and your body movement where you want to go. You can also feel if the horse wants to go a certain direction, and you let her. The horse's eyes and body movement follow the owner instinctively. A sixth sense they have."

"A relation with a pet that can only be experienced," I mumbled.

"Horses are not as warm and friendly as dogs, but they give their charisma, the only species that allows you to take part with them. It's almost like molding clay when you are on top of them. They enjoy that as much as you do. You actually become one with your horse.

"I heard camels and elephants may surpass horses in intelligence, but they don't respond as quickly as horses. The human touch and the relation do magic for both."

On Monday morning, Lorna went straight to her desk and sat down. She didn't look happy. I had to come over and enquire.

"We took Max home over the weekend because he was doing so well. But on Saturday, he lay down and put his feet up. His colic was back. We took him to the vet. They did a lot of tests. Took samples of stool and blood and did the GI track, everything was good. But we knew he wasn't healing. The vet said he didn't know what was wrong with him. If it continues he said he would recommend we take him to Pullman. The university has the largest animal hospital in this area. Big Equine Center. They can do tests that can't be done here."

"Pullman's about 500 miles away," I exclaimed. I couldn't imagine how she could even think of driving that far with a horse.

"If I have to, I'll do it," she said.

I thought of the last days of Kaalu. One afternoon, when I came home from school, Kaalu didn't greet me on the road. She usually met me a block from our house and followed me home. My mother said she was on the veranda making a mess. Kaalu was lying down and the floor was red. Her throat and behind were wet with blood and she looked worn out. Her tail didn't wag, even when she saw me. "She must have gotten into a fight with the dogs in the street," my sister reported. I patted Kaalu's head. Her tail moved a little.

Dogs were always fighting for food. It was a part of their life. Even if a few like Kaalu got left over food from the house, they wanted more, but the dogs had their territories defined. If one sneaked into another territory for food or whatever, the dogs in that area would attack viciously and chase him away.

I didn't know what happened to Kaalu, but clearly they did a job on her, the wounds were deep. She wasn't strong enough to defend herself against many. It was a truly dog-eat-dog world out there. My mother asked me to remove Kaalu from there and clean up the place so it wouldn't smell.

I took Kaalu down to the little backyard of our house, a ten-foot-wide strip, where we occasionally planted a few flower plants. She lay on the dirt. I brought water in an earthen pot but couldn't think of anything else I could do. A trickle of blood kept on oozing out from the wounds. The concept of taking her to a vet didn't occur to me. No one did that where I grew up and I was sure everyone would laugh if I mentioned it. Nature makes them and cures them. If one doesn't survive, there are many more around. This was their fate. I hung around her and when it became dark I went inside.

Before going to school I took some food from my plate and kept it near her, but Kaalu didn't show any interest. As I walked away, I saw several crows on the fence eyeing on the food and I felt the scorching sun. It would be a hot day.

Lorna said, "It'd only be a ten-hour drive. I can do it. I'll take Jenny with me."

The fax machine beeped. I looked at the pile of work on her desk, and something made me say, "You can buy a new colt for about $500." But I didn't finish my words when I saw her blue eyes and realized I shouldn't say what I was thinking. "I guess you have to do the best you can. I was only thinking of the financial debt you are getting into."

"I'm in trouble anyway. Max's father came from the Hagerman Ranch in Twin Falls—a thoroughbred. He was a well-known race horse in Utah. The stud service is expensive. We had to leave Max's mother there for a week. That and all the blood tests for the record had already cost us $2,000."

"My Gosh! How much can he bring?"

"It depends. We have to train him, which costs a good sum of money. And then he must win some races. It's a long shot." She looked away from me. "I know it's all a loss."

I came back to my desk and thought of how Kaalu died. The last block I had run home from school to see her. She was lying with her eyes closed. She looked all dried up in the sun. The water bowl had fallen on the ground, water had drained out. The food plate was clean. I was sure she didn't eat anything, and I knew she couldn't get up to go to the drain for a drink. The wounds looked black from dried blood. Her whole body was lean and stiff. I patted her and held her head up. A breath came out and her head dropped. I knew that was it, but I could not cry or even scream. I stood there and looked at the dead body for a while and then walked away.

When I dropped the books on my bed and lay down, my mother knew Kaalu had died. She didn't say anything to me. It was not a big deal to anyone. I heard her telling my sister, "Make sure the sweeper takes the body out to the garbage bin."

A month passed by. Lorna kept us informed of the horse's progress, but Max was never well. One day he was good, the next day he wasn't. It was mostly bad news and I thought he was going to die. Then, Lorna didn't come to work for three days. I started to worry about her and wondered if Max's sickness was reminding her of her husband's death when she could do nothing. Was she fighting an old battle that she would have fought, but couldn't?

Thursday, Lorna came back effervescent, the original Lorna we were used to. "I took him to Pullman, and they found what was wrong with him," she told us with a big smile.

We gathered around her to hear the details.

"Max was colicky on Friday and lay down on the ground and moved his legs in pain. I couldn't stand it any more and hauled him to Pullman.

"Jenny and I reached the animal hospital at midnight, but the place was open and busy. A vet came out and opened the big door and we pulled in. It was such a big place you won't believe. They had all the equipment to hoist a horse if necessary. They checked his vitals and put him in a nice stall and told us to come back early in the morning. I'll tell you the place was better than any medical facility I've seen.

"We went back at 8:30 and two teaching veterinarians examined Max from head to toe, and ran a scope with camera to the stomach. They couldn't find anything especially wrong. 'Perhaps an ulcer in the intestine,' one of them commented. They put him on a special diet.

"Next morning Max colicked, and they got a first-hand knowledge of his problem. Max laid on his back with his feet up. They gave him a pain-killer. They walked him around and he finally settled down. They again suspected some kind of ulcer, and said if they couldn't find what's wrong, they would have to open him up. 'That's the only way to know for sure.'

"So, Sunday they operated on him. You should have seen Max, so many tubes coming out from his body. They found an ulcer which had burnt through the intestine and then sealed it. Two quarter-inch openings and adhesions. Food backed up. When that happened any movement caused pain. So they spliced the intestine.

"Max was walking on Tuesday, and so we drove back. The road was bad. It was snowing, but we didn't mind." She looked up to me. "I was so happy Max will live."

"Wonderful," I said, "How is Max doing at home?"

"No. No. He's still in Pullman. We'll go back in a week and get him." She started to sort out the mail with new vigor.

Chapter Nine
An Excursion on the River

I will go to the bank by the wood and become undis-
guised and naked,
   I am mad for it to be in contact with me.
                           - Song of Myself, Walt Whitman

Once, about 100 years ago, people lined up along the Ganges River near Calcutta to see an ochre-robed sadhu. He had spent decades in the Himalayas meditating and had acquired so much power that he could walk on water. A man rushed to RamaKrishna, a humble priest at the famous Kali-temple who was considered a saint by many, and told him about the holy man.

"Sir, please come and see for yourself. He is going to cross the river on foot."

"You said he acquired this power by meditating in the Himalayas?" he asked.

"Yes, sir. You should see his long matted hair."

But RamaKrishna was not interested. On further coaxing he smiled, saying, "I can cross the river by paying an anna to a boatman, why should I spend all my life learning only to walk over water?"

I think of this story whenever I drive by the Snake River and especially in winter when it is frozen white. In India it is hard to imagine that a river can become solid. I didn't meditate in the Himalayas, but I could walk on the Snake River in winter. If I were to prove my point, I know exactly the place for this feat. It would be the bank opposite Keefer's Island, where a small cabin still stands and represents early settlers in this area.

The winter scene on the Snake River is something out of this world. In the morning it becomes surrealistic near the Keefer Island—a mist hovers above the snow-white, unevenly-frozen, solid river; vapors rise from several fissures in the ice; and the silhouette of the cabin can be seen in the background of the unbroken white. Silence is the overlord of the still surrounding. Two or three months later the view becomes focused —white ice chunks drift by the island and the bluish color of the river makes them very special, like amateur paper boats let go in the streams by children after a heavy rain. The curvy river-bank becomes distinct, and commercial buildings on the other side become visible. The river is coming to life for a new season.

The Snake River is an attribute of Idaho Falls, as the Ganges is for Calcutta. But how different the two rivers are! Not only in their color, width, and flow, but in every way they are different except for the high reverence each enjoys in the two regions. I have lived on the banks of both of these two rivers and I have come to love them in different ways. I could easily go back 200 years to the time when only American Indians roamed the Snake River Plain on horseback and similarly to the time 2,600 years ago when the Ganges ran through wilderness, and Gautama Buddha walked along its shores.

The Snake River is the first object one notices from the plane before landing in Idaho Falls. Indeed, the river looks like a snake from above—a long, slim, black body slithering through the sagebrush. What a tiny little river! What a contrast to the mighty Ganges River in Calcutta with its almost-half-mile wide muddy, brown water, where big ships bring goods from all over the world and old-fashioned wooden, battered boats drift in water with discolored sails held by bamboo poles. Barrel-shaped roofs over a small space in the middle of these boats provide shelter to the boatman and his goods.

Buoys bob up and down with the waves of the Ganges, but no motor boat disturbs the surroundings.

The mountains looked misty green from my living room window, and the sky deep, summer blue. The sun's warm, golden rays flooded the earth over the lush green potato fields. A series of large cottonwood trees stood dignified at the corner, one side lighted by the sun. I was engrossed in my vision of the Ganges River when a Suburban pulled into the driveway. My reminiscences were broken with the sound of the door bell. Tim, a local doctor, and his wife, Cindy, were at the door. I was waiting for them. We were going to float the Snake River today. Two weeks back, they had come over to our house.

"Want to float the Snake River?" Tim had asked. He was bubbling with enthusiasm.

"Is it dangerous?" I asked spontaneously in my habitual insecurity.

"We won't float white water," he had added, "just the gentle part of the river. It's scenic. It'll be fun."

I could never resist the allure of the river. The Ganges had instilled this in me—an intense fascination with flowing water. I agreed to the trip immediately. Although we had been here for two years, this would be our first trip on the Snake River.

Tim practices family medicine in Idaho Falls. He is not a big macho man. His round, thin metal-rimmed glasses, pushed to the base of his nose, reveal a pair of bright intelligent eyes, medium-size and brown. He has faint eyebrows. Light brown hair neatly combed to one side with no sign of a receding hairline. Almost a square face with very little cheek bone showing, no one would quickly know his age—almost forty.

We have seen him often with weary eyes from delivering babies in the middle of the night. The fascinating part of him is that in spite of a busy schedule, he is always interested in reading the classics, finding consolation in past human glories and lamentations in deeds not done, paths not taken, even in our own lives. To him living in Idaho Falls is not about people or old buildings or history or civilization. It is about man's rendezvous with nature. Any opportunity he has, he is out hiking in the mountains.

Tim grew up in Colorado and came to Idaho Falls at the same time we did. He is not a typical Idaho man, but he reminds me of an archetypal picture of Idaho: a solitary man casting a line on a remote stream, men with backpacks on a mountain trail, or a small family camping in the wilderness, amid the serene beauty of nature, as if nothing else exists in the world.

With the rubber float on top of Tim's heavy-duty Suburban we headed out east on Route 26. It was a perfect day: no cloud in the sky, the pitch road shining in the morning light with fields fresh green, and distant mountains crisp. A few miles out of town and four children busily talking in the back, I wondered, in the cool breeze of the open window: what else could be better in life?

We floated from a boat ramp in Swan Valley below the Palisades Reservoir. A playful young couple in bright yellow-orange clothes launched a canoe from the same ramp. A date on the river.

The gap in the green scenery, the ramp, vanished from our sight very quickly. Branches of small willow trees stooped on water from the bank. A few ducks swam in between the branches. We drifted to the middle, and a new scenery emerged: a serene mass of water flowing gently with two rows of dwarf, green bushes lining the two banks. There were few tall trees, and no mountain loomed around.

As the initial excitement of launching the raft died down, we quietly floated the river. The current carried the raft along. Its clear, black water has always fascinated me. I have seen so many different streams in its water from many spots on its bank. The curves of the river and its boulder-filled bottom make these currents. As I watched the surrounding, I suddenly felt there was something very unusual. The background noise we were so used to was not there—as if someone had raised a wand and made a new world, where silence was

Jarmila Pech

prime. Only the sound of the flowing water and our own voices could be heard. No other sound, but nature's own! And what
a beautiful sound the water made. I tuned my ears and heard
the streams talking to each other—kuul, kuul, kuul, kuul,
kuul, kuul. "Go, my friend, go." Why hadn't I heard this before?

We gazed silently at the scenery. I remembered from the
long past when I had taken a boat-ride on the Ganges River.
An excursion arranged by my college, the huge steamship was
filled with students. The noise of the engines and our com-
bined, boisterous voices had drowned all other sounds. We
were young, and interaction with new and old friends was predominant for us, not the beauty of the river. The river was only
an excuse. The sound of the river was lost in the hustle and
bustle of city life. We did not notice the beautiful, small clusters of banana plants on the bank, or banyan trees drooping in
the water, or centuries old ruined palaces, or the long steps of
the ghats where people were bathing and worshiping the
sacred river, or the meager smoke rising from unmarked cremation sites with mourners standing and vacantly looking at
the river. Only the tall, shiny chimneys from factories that

occasionally appeared drew our attention because they were signs of progress.

"Do you want a drink?" Cindy asked, and I shifted my view from the high bank of the Snake River. The river had cut through lava rocks here and it was fifty feet straight up; pines, cottonwood, and willow trees on top and dogwood and other bushes on the ground made it look like a jungle. Some bare roots clung to the side of the eroding bank. How dark green was the riparian vegetation. The crystal blue sky shone brightly above us, making the trip a wondrous experience through the wilderness. I felt I could float forever on this river.

The Snake River originates in the southern border of the Yellowstone National Park, with many little streams joining together. It flows south toward Idaho Falls, turning west in Pocatello toward Twin Falls, and eventually going north all the way to Lewiston, thus covering almost the entire state of Idaho in a semi-circle. The Ganges River is 500 miles longer than the Snake River, and it is much wider. After it descends from the glaciers in the Himalayas, the Ganges flows south and south-east through the plains of north India. The fertile land it helped create abounds in green scenery, but it is not wilderness anymore. The Ganges rolls through populated plains, whereas the Snake River's ice-melt water flows through gorges, plains, and wilderness. The cold temperature of Idaho and its enormous mountain wilderness have prevented that exponential conglomeration of humans along the Snake River.

In Thomas Jefferson's time, early explorers thought of the existence of a river that could open a passage to the Pacific. Whoever found this river would control and conquer the West, so Jefferson commissioned the Lewis and Clark expedition. They found no such mythical river but they were the first whites to see the Snake River, in 1805 in northern Idaho via the Clearwater. Later in 1811, Wilson Hunt's expedition came beside the Hoback River in western Wyoming and found the Snake River and thought that its athletic waters, sweeping through the valley, would take them to the Pacific Ocean. Their optimism to discover the water passage was foiled by the Snake's many rapids. They wrote, "Its terrific appearance beggars all description—Hecate's cauldron was never half so agitated when vomiting even the most diabolical spells." The mountainous wilderness of the Northwest does not allow a smooth passage to the West Coast. The Snake River comes close to being the mythical river people hoped for; it is the only river that drains the western slopes of the northern Rocky mountains into the Columbia. But it was impossible to conquer.

Such daring expeditions by courageous people are forgotten now. Once I was in Washington, D.C., and searched through the Smithsonian corridors to find the items that Lewis and Clark sent back 200 years ago. I couldn't find it anywhere and finally asked the guard, "Where is the Lewis and Clark exhibit?"

"Lewis and Clark?" he asked me. "The concert for tonight?"

I looked at his faultless face and realized that Lewis and Clark is of no importance in the East. It probably never was to the extent it is in the Northwest. I eventually found two small table top displays that contained a few pieces from their expedition. The beauty and the exuberance of the Snake River country is unknown outside this region.

Soon my mind slid back to that other river trip; how I had gazed with wonder when we reached Diamond Harbor where the Ganges River opens up to meet the ocean. The river is so wide at this place that I felt small and frail. Neither the river nor the ocean can claim this body of water, and I heard a call from the ocean—an excitement mixed with fear and adventure. My mood changed from college boy glee to mythic musing. I perceived the presence of a nearby, underground place where 60,000 sons of King Sagar were burnt to ashes by fire from Kapila Muni's angry eyes.

Their father, King Sagar, wanted to perform the Horse Sacrifice ceremony which would proclaim him as the king-ofkings on earth. Before the actual ceremony a horse was color-fully decorated and allowed to roam free. If the horse wan-dered across the border into an adjoining kingdom, the people of that kingdom would have to pay homage to the horse and to the king it represented. If a king did not allow the horse to enter his kingdom, then a war would ensue. When there was no king left who challenged King Sagar's supremacy, a great Yajna would be performed and the horse sacrificed.

The ceremonial horse was protected by King Sagar's 60,000 sons who were fierce soldiers. However, Indra, the king of heaven, was worried that King Sagar could become too power-ful and might even challenge him one day. Indra was clever and conceived a plan to thwart Sagar. When the horse strayed near the ocean, he stole it with his powerful magic and took it to the underworld, where the mighty sage Kapila Muni was meditating. Indra let the horse browse near the Muni.

The princes searched everywhere for the horse which had suddenly vanished and eventually they came to this area. There, they saw the beautiful stallion. In their joy of discover-ing the horse and excitement, the princes rushed to capture the horse, ignoring the Muni.

Kapila Muni's meditation was broken by the clamoring noises and buffeting he received as the 60,000 rushed passed him. They did not show him the simple courtesy of respect. In his anger, burning fire came out of his eyes and as he looked at these ignorant mortals, they were all burnt into ashes.

The horse was later recovered by King Sagar's grandson, and King Sagar completed the Yajna, but the souls of the burnt ones couldn't go to heaven. Once uttered, Kapila Muni's curse could not be lifted. He only said that if Goddess Ganga could be brought to their ashes, the touch of her sacred water would release them.

Two generations later King Bhagirath led the colossal effort to bring Goddess Ganga, the Ganges River, down from heaven, and her sacred water finally freed his ancestors. The souls of Sagar's sons were purified by the touch of her water and went to heaven. From that time on, the Hindus have performed the last rites for the deceased with the sacred water of the Ganges

River. They cremate the dead on her bank, throwing the ashes from the funeral pyre in the river so the soul, like King Sagar's sons, would go to heaven.

So hallowed is the Ganges River.

Rivers are also sacred to the American Indians, the first inhabitants of the Snake River, but in a different way. Each part of the earth is sacred to them. Rivers are more so because they quench their thirst and carry their canoes. One hundred and fifty years ago, Chief Seattle said, "You must give the rivers the kindness you would give any brother." Not having a mirror, the Indians also identified themselves with the river because it was there they could see themselves. After a Sweat Lodge ceremony they would walk down to the river to clean themselves. The Shoshones and the Bannocks spent winters on the Snake River banks because it was warmer there compared to the hills, and many springs provided fresh water and the trees protected them from bad weather.

Legend says that the waters of a river decided the fate of the American Indians, and it could as well be the Snake River. The grandfather created a woman and a child from clay to complete the world and baked them for four days. When they were perfect he walked with them to the river, where he gave them the power of speech.

The woman immediately asked, "What is this state we are in, breathing, eating, and moving?"

"This is life," he answered.

"This is nice. Shall we always be like this?"

The grandfather hadn't thought of that. He pondered for a while and then said, "Let us decide it together. I shall throw a buffalo chip in the river. If it floats you live like this forever. If it sinks, people will die and come back to life after four days."

The woman did not like the buffalo chip. She didn't have any experience of the world. She picked up a rock and said, "I shall throw it in the water. If it floats we live forever; there will be no death. If it sinks, we will die."

And she dropped the rock in the river.

We floated along the Snake River. Time seemed to have no meaning, no importance. Only the sun changed its position and we knew it was midday. The flowing water of the river, the deep green banks, and the sky above made up the trinity of this float trip. The sky was shiny, crystal blue at the beginning, but now it became white blue. We couldn't gaze at the sky for long, but its presence was God-like. The sky was especially spectacular when the banks were high and the sun's orange lights streaked through the trees.

Catherine and Cindy talked about getting sunburn, and they put suntan lotion on themselves and on the children.

Tim maneuvered the boat to a small island in the middle of the river. The boys jumped out and pulled the rope to the sandy beach. A little island to ourselves. The children ran into the woody center of the island to explore. "Be careful of the poison ivy," Catherine shouted at them.

Black birds flew from one tree to another. Very few humans came to visit their island—a cause for excitement. Tall cottonwood trees with many branches covered the island. Tiny, pink wild roses lined the edge of the miniature forest.

"Let's open a bottle," Tim suggested and sat down on the wet sand.

"Monday through Friday I work like a dog," he said. "I need to get away as often as I can."

"When we were on Long Island," I said, "we often went to the Fire Island. That was to get away for the excitement of the waves. This is just the opposite. Get away for the solitude."

Catherine, and Cindy opened the cooler and took out food and drink. I looked at the pink cloth on the ground. Little fish swam in the design among reeds sticking out of the water. On one side lay smoked salmon, Norwegian crackers, Gouda cheese, and a bottle of semi-dry white wine. A shiny orange-brown roast-chicken and pasta salad came out of a plastic bag. Cindy put melon, strawberries and grapes on the cloth, saying, "This should be enough."

"I can see," I told Tim, "why people get away from the town."

"Most people don't realize this," Tim said, "but our work is often very boring—I see patients for colds and headaches. I'd love to work on interesting cases, but they rarely show up. But patients affect us deeply, especially when we see a terminal case." He gazed at the white and blue rubber float dragged halfway onto the beach.

He'd told me this before, but I didn't realize why getting away from the office was so therapeutic for him. There are different reasons for different people to be in the outdoors. Instead of relying on drugs as many do, Idahoans have an opportunity to be in the wilderness—the mountains, the valleys, and the streams. And nature provides a welcome substitute for the analyst's couch.

A river touches the inner soul of an individual. This is especially so for the introverts and the book lovers. Tim was no exception. The life of a medical doctor in this country is very intense, to say the least. Outsiders look at most doctors as competent, respectable individuals, who are a little money-hungry; but from their side it's a different story: constantly hassled by hospital administration and government regulations; always on their toes so that no mistake is made; long hours of work; continually tired and worried of being sued by someone; and no great glory waiting for most of them. So, if they make some money and have the biggest house in the neighborhood, they feel they deserve it. But they have no time to enjoy them, they only glow in the warmth of their possessions. However, Tim was not a run-of-the-mill doctor; he opted to be a general practitioner because that had the most variety of medical work. He didn't have the biggest house or an expensive foreign car. His money was spent on books and lecture notes, and Idaho provided him a natural simplicity of living. When he was out on the river, he didn't have to think about his patients, and he was unreachable by phone; he could open up and feel free.

Living in Idaho is truly different. Here, I thought, it is essential to find one's place and one's role in life—not to the extent that one understands who he is, but at least to come to grips with what his role is. One does not have to become a loner to appreciate the beauty of being alone.

The children came back from their exploration of the little island, Tim's son holding a dead bird, and his daughter saying, "I saw it first." Nikhil and Rajeev, holding long sticks, followed them behind, thrusting and parrying their "swords."

"We saw rabbit holes," Rajeev proclaimed.

On the float again, we let ourselves be carried by the gentle, curving flow of the river. The river came out of the gorge. The broad, brown hills with light green sagebrush at the bottom and clusters of darker trees on the bank portrayed a beautiful still picture. I wished it to remain that way for eternity.

A bald eagle swooped down and I saw with amazement its distinct bright, white head. "They really live here," I told myself. How gracefully it floated in the air, brown wings spread out like a big plane and its white head and white tail shining in the afternoon sun.

The hills were barren, but the view took me back to a time 100 years back. Behind the leaves of the trees and the fields, I saw a young Shoshone Indian girl's round face with a long braid on her back. She wore a red and blue dress and was talking to a few tall, white men. I could see many tipis around her with smoke coming out from a few. The girl was wavering her hand like the motion of a swimming fish. How lively she was: "See, how the salmon moves. We live on salmons. We are the salmon people." But the mountain men didn't understand what she was saying. The white men came along the river and the river was mostly in their mind. So they misinterpreted her sign as those for snakes and called them the Snake Indians and their river the Snake River. The river was not named because it meandered like a snake or snakes lived on its banks.

The Snake River has always drawn attention in the Northwest since the time of Lewis and Clark. The river was first known as the Lewis River, but the Shoshone name survived in the end, although the exact date when it came to be known as the Snake River is not known. Many events and

Indian skirmishes have taken place on its bank. That is why the Snake River always reminds me of the Indians. I visualized how the Indians lived nearby and imagined them riding on its bank. Perhaps their canoes floated the same spot we were traveling. Their early interactions with the white settlers were disconcerting. Although sad and sometimes brutal, the Indians' forced accommodation of the white people often led to cross-cultural, humorous situations.

One hundred and thirty years ago, the superintendent of Indian Affairs, Captain Porter, was sick with tuberculosis and spent most of his time in bed. He was bald and wore a wig, but since he was sick and dying, he often kept it on the bedpost. Many Indians visited him for business. A leader of the Bannock Indians, Bannock Jim, came to see him unexpectedly. Captain Porter stayed in bed. Bannock Jim sat in a chair, but looked around in the room and finally gazed at the wig on the bedpost. He couldn't take his eyes off it.

"What's that?" he asked.

"Oh, that's a scalp!" replied Captain Porter without thinking much about it.

They talked about the business Bannock Jim came for, but all the time Jim couldn't take his mind off the wig.

"Where did you get the scalp from?" he finally asked.

Unconsciously, Captain Porter took his velvet skullcap off and rubbed his clean bald head and sighed, "The Sioux, he did it."

When Bannock Jim saw his smooth bald head and looked at the wig, he jumped out of the door and hurriedly rode away. A scalped man and still alive! It was too much for the Bannock Indian.

We passed by a flat land; all was still green, but more like a marshland with poplar trees. They were spaced out, tall columns that did not branch out sideways. There were white colors on the trees as if someone had spread powdered salt over them. Two trumpeter swans swam near the shore. A calm, surreal picture. A dream from the long past of my youth came back to me, where I walked on a narrow path between two endless lakes strewn with pink and white lotus flowers in a sea of dark green, round lotus leaves. For a long time I had walked on the path, but I had no destination. The joy, like now, was simply being there.

The river widened on the left going round a bend and the water looked like it was not moving at all between the small green island in the middle and the left shore. The sky was above and below, and the reflections of the trees stood still. This is the place, I was sure, beautiful nymphs came out on a moonlit night to play in the Snake River. And a place where Shoshoni women came to see their round faces in the water.

This is also a place where the beautiful Daphne could come and play with her maiden companions. However, the sad story of Leukippos, who fell in love with Daphne, came to me.

Young Leukippos was the son of Oinomaos, the lord of Pisa. He loved Daphne the first day he saw her but he knew that he could not attain Daphne; Daphne had run away from all men who approached her. As his love for Daphne grew, the handsome Leukippos thought of a way to reach her. He grew long hair, and made beautiful braids. He then put on the dress of a princess, and went to Daphne.

"I am the daughter of Oinomaos," he told her, "I would like to go hunting with you."

Daphne found him appealing and he was innocent like a virgin girl. She also liked his devotion to her. Soon they became great friends. And why not? He was a brilliant huntress and came from a grand family, much better than her other companions.

But Apollo became jealous of Leukippos's success in love.

When they came to the River Ladon, the place was so serene and secluded, Daphne and her companions wanted to swim naked in the water. They quickly took off their clothes and jumped in the water, but not Leukippos. He stood on the shore transfixed by the chaste beauty of Daphne and knowing that he was in trouble.

Daphne missed him in the water and signaled her companions to the lonely Leukippos standing behind a tree. They rushed to him and in their playfulness ripped the clothes off his body; then they stood back. What a muscular male figure it was!

They got their hunting spears and did not hear his cry of love for Daphne. They stabbed him to death on the bank of the serene river.

We quietly drifted on the river. No roads or signs of civilization could be seen from the water, but we knew they were there only a few hundred feet away, just as this trip was a hide-away from our daily lives.

"Look there," Tim pointed to the shore. A mule deer with its head up from eating looked at us with as much curiosity as we looked at it, and went back to eating. An animal in its own setting.

It is fortunate that a large part of the Snake River country is protected by the government and a few floaters on the river can get a glimpse of the natural life of the wilderness. Those who drive through the state go by the developed farmlands and cannot experience what truly the Snake River country is. Don Moser has described it beautifully in a few lines: "The geography of the Snake River country is confused and confusing. Rivers loop and meander and turn back upon themselves. Mountain ranges lie in a maze that baffles the eye and sets a man's internal compass spinning. A wonderfully mixed-up country, and wonderfully diverse." From our rubber float we were seeing only a quarter of this diversity.

The Ganges River is sacred, but I don't know of any story of a sacred origin for the Snake River. My Navajo friend tells me all rivers are sacred, not just the Ganges. I like that; the Snake River is as sacred as the Ganges. What would happen to South Idaho without its water? No agriculture, no cattle, just dust. The Ganges River is very sacred to the Indians because she is the free-spirited Goddess Ganga, Ma Ganga, who originated from Vishnu's toes, and to whom all Hindus go for blessings and for salvation from this life.

Stories abound on the Ganges River. Not only a bath in her water is holy: if the bone of a dead man touches the waters of Ganga, that person will be assured of a place in heaven. And Mother Ganga accepts all with open arms, even the worst sinner, because there is good in every individual. When a Hindu dies, the most wonderful thing that can be done for him is not a great obituary column in the local paper or a funeral service with dignitaries and friends saying wonderful things about him, but taking the remains of his body to the Ganges River.

Cremation on the Ganga's bank is so well ingrained in the Hindu religion that, when someone dies, the death announcement says the Goddess Ganga has received him—the word used is Ganga-Prapti (Ganga-received). No such religious reverence applies to the Snake River.

There is a folk story from the Indian state of Andhra Pradesh about a family who was so poor that they did not have enough food to eat. One day, the daughter-in-law, in her despair, asked her mother-in-law when she would like to "receive Ganga." The wise mother-in-law had lived in poverty all her life. She told her, "Daughter, I want to see my grandson before I go to Ganga."

As time passed, the daughter-in-law produced a son. Now there were more mouths to feed, and sometimes she did not have any food to eat at night. After a while, the daughter-in-law asked her again, "Mother, now that you have seen your grandson, and he is healthy and strong, is it time for you to go to Ganga?"

"Oh my daughter, I am so happy with your son, how can I go to Ganga without seeing him married and happily living?"

Eventually, the grandson grew up and was married as the custom demanded. However, the condition of the family did not change at all; it only worsened with too many people to feed and too little food they could buy. Desperate and unable to stand hunger, she asked her mother-in-law, now quite old, "Mother, you have seen your grandson married, couldn't you go to Ganga now?"

"Oh my daughter, I am too old, and I am feeble. I cannot go to Ganga alone. Now that you are also a mother-in-law your-

Robert Bower

self, let us go together to Ganga."

That was the last time the daughter-in-law asked her mother-in-law to go to Ganga.

The dark waters of the Snake continued to move us—slowly and imperceptively—through the silent, incoherent, tall cottonwood trees. The riparian shrubs sprawled close to the water as if to be united with the river. And a sharp, blue sky peered from behind. But in place of the jubilant disposition of the boat trip on the Ganges, a different mood strolled in. This trip had reminded me of the Ganges, of my past. I wondered if the Snake River is an external entity, while the Ganges is internal? The Snake River is serene, it's beautiful, it has the youthful rhythm of a young maiden, and one can sit by it for hours and not be bored, but it does not let one go deep into one's own soul as the Ganges does. A few free hours on the Ganges will connect you to the scenery beyond her banks, to the depth of your own life, to your ancestors, to the thousands-year-old stories, to the continuum of the human race before you; you cannot help but go to a spiritual world.

Tim's words brought me back from my ruminations: "In Colorado I did a lot of white water rafting. Big rapids. It was exhilarating. The thrill of conquering nature." He stopped and looked away toward the end of the river. "But now I like the gentle floats. A sign of old age, I suppose." Apparently, we were both thinking of the past. Two middle-aged men silently lamenting the good old days in two different places.

We saw other floaters in the distance and knew we were nearing a little village, Heise, and this scenic ride would soon end. How time flies on the river. We achieved a lot but didn't do a thing today; and I cannot explain this to anyone who hasn't experienced it.

The land was flat, grassy and green with cottonwood trees here and there; and the pink rays of the late afternoon sun spread their wings on the clear blue sky above. A lonely man cast a long line from the shore. I silently gazed at the flowing river and felt that I was only a visitor for a very short time while it has been flowing like this for centuries. And it will keep on flowing when I am gone. Suddenly I wanted to connect myself more deeply with the Snake River. A Bengali song from the long past came to me and kept on ringing in my mind:

Oh River, this only question I ask:
Tell me where your country is!
Do you continue flowing without an end?

Oh River, this only question I ask:
You have no ties to tie you down,
Is it because you have no home?

Oh River, this only question I ask:
On this bank you destroy, while over there you build.
What do you do for the one whose both banks are laid bare?

Oh River, this only question I ask:
Mistakenly, you consider me an outsider,
Have you no free time to spare?
Couldn't you tell me a little of your happiness and your sorrows?

Chapter Ten
POLLYWOG POND

I was sitting next to Amanda on Delta flight 1767 to Salt Lake City, the regular morning flight out of Idaho Falls. There is only one other jet flight at midday, but that takes people to the East Coast late at night. So we often took this flight.

Many were sleepy at this hour and had their eyes closed, but Amanda was awake. She opened a thick book, but looked around to see whom she knew. Then she asked me, "So where are you going?"

"The holy land, where else?"

"I'm going in the opposite direction. To Richland."

"Richland? What's going on there?"

"The usual quality assurance audit, but I'll go to Spokane for the weekend. My parents have a ranch. I go there with my children every summer, but I'll visit them since the government is paying for the trip, anyway."

I never knew she grew up on a ranch. "Cowgirl upbringing, now an engineer?" I wondered, and looked at her intently, although she never gave me that impression. Amanda was in her mid-thirties, pleasant looking with an oval face, a small forehead, small brown eyes, and thin lips. Dark walnut-brown, long, curly hair fell over her shoulder.

"You miss the ranch life?" I asked.

"I didn't grow up on the ranch," she told me. "I spent my childhood summers there. My brothers and I had always looked forward to it; as soon as school was over we badgered our parents until they took us there." She closed her book. "You know what I loved most? Catching the little frogs." She smiled, happily reminiscing. "There was a pond in the ranch and it flooded when it rained in July. We ran around in the water and scooped up the little ones. It was so much fun. We called it the pollywog's pond."

Children here love to catch little toads and frogs. They are a novelty. We didn't care for them in India. They were everywhere in rainy season. All the fields became little ponds where they grew and lived. If we turned over a rock or a brick, we would find a toad under it, sometimes a very big one. They were ugly and scary. Someone told me, "They can spit at you, and if it touches the skin, it will grow into a mold and it will never heal." I now think it was the same boy who told me, "If a mad dog bites you, little baby dogs will grow in your tummy. Then the doctors will have to use a long needle, a foot long, to inject medicine in your tummy." Can you imagine how frightening that was!

In the evening the frogs croaked in unison, and their sound came from all directions—a rhythmic, deep-throated, baritone symphony that never changed and never ended. We went to bed with that noise.

I remembered I once saw a snake with a frog in its mouth in the open drain by the road, which was flooded in the rain. The snake couldn't swallow the frog, it was too big, and the frog struggled, but couldn't get out of the snake's mouth. It was a pathetic case, and I didn't know what to do—kill the snake for his greediness or kill both of them. I helplessly watched for sometime and then walked away. Insects, geckos, and frogs were all around us; they were simply a part of life, not a novelty.

"So, do you still catch little frogs?" I asked Amanda.

"I help my children catch them." She gave me a pleasant smile.

The plane was moving up through the clouds. I gazed out through the window and soon saw a small pool at the Sealander's Park. Several children were running around and playing in the pool. My view focused and I saw my own children there. It was a few years ago, my wife, Catherine, and I were invited to the INEL summer picnic at the Sealander's Park, and we went with our children. I didn't work for the company that managed the federal laboratory, so I stayed with the children and walked around the park. On one side was a lava field, extending far out—a sea of irregular, rough, reddish-brown lava rocks, 12,000 years old. Here and there a pine tree grew in that barren land. I held up my older son to see the view, and then he clamored to go there. I was afraid of the rattlesnakes resting in the nooks and cracks of warm rocks, and I didn't want to venture out. I steered the children toward the other, greener side of the park, where there was a small footbridge above a tiny stream. Large willow trees lined the path, and since it rained recently, it was wet. Children were running around, screaming in pleasure. They were chasing dragonflies, and some had little frogs in their cupped hands and in plastic cups. We soon reached a ten-foot-wide pond where many children were catching tadpoles in little cups.

Rajeev and Nikhil ran into the pool before I could stop them: "Daddy, Daddy. Help us catch tadpoles. We'll take them home."

"Tadpoles?" I shivered at the image. I didn't know how to catch the slippery little thing and hated the idea of a frog in the house. I said, "You don't want them," but my children said, "It'll be fun, Daddy."

Rajeev pulled my hand and I reluctantly went to the pond. I put my hand in the pool but couldn't catch any. A man was standing near me. He said, "That's not how you catch a tadpole or a baby frog. Here, take this cup and scoop it out."

I saw with horror that Rajeev had already caught one in his cup. He asked Nikhil to hold it and went for more. I simply watched what fun the two boys were having at the little pond.

They triumphantly brought several tadpoles home and their mother put them in a nice jar to admire them. They fed them almost everything they ate, and I don't remember how or why but the tadpoles died.

Next week when it rained, my two children clamored to go to the park where they could catch little frogs. "Daddy, all the boys are catching them," Rajeev told me. "Josh brought one to the class yesterday. He kept it in his pocket." My wife said, "Why don't you take them? Spend some time with your children."

I had some office work to do and the Sealander's Park was far away, so I found good excuses. They went away with sad faces, but I was still not interested in tiny animals. As a matter of fact, I never took them to catch tadpoles. Catching frogs was not my forte.

Looking at Amanda, I wondered if I had blundered the opportunity to spend quality time with my children, and now they would grow up as psychological misfits in this country. It is truly hard for many of us, who grew up in a different culture, to understand and appreciate the way of life here. So we encounter idiosyncratic problems in raising children. One can teach children only what one knows and what one had been exposed to. As an adult we can choose to participate in the activities we like, but when it comes to children, they have to go along with what other children are doing, and we cannot shed our responsibilities to provide them the opportunity to join in the fun. But some things cannot just easily be done.

After our discussion, Amanda finally closed her eyes and I remembered the Pinewood Derby. I went to the Indian Guides with Rajeev because that was what the dads did. "Aren't you a dad?" Catherine told me, "So you go with him."

In the garage of a neighbor's house Rajeev and I met with six other little boys and their dads. The leader, Larry, had so many tools in his garage it looked like a shop. He showed us how to make decorative leather patches and headbands. Each boy had to select a name for himself and make a badge resembling something from his adopted name. The idea came from the American Indians. Father and son work together on the project; that was the essence of the Indian Guides organization—a kind of male bonding for father and son. Then he said, "Next week you all bring something to show."

I asked myself, "Do I have to make something like what he did?" I never held a tool in my life. In India you didn't play with real tools. You didn't even own any. No way was I capable of making any of these. But I saw Rajeev eagerly looking at the many decorative things hanging from the man's neck. Another man had a necklace with many different colored beads and bear-claws. I heard Larry say, "You can buy a leather belt from the store on Yellowstone Avenue and make designs on it. Use a drill press to punch holes."

"Drill press? What was that?"

Then we went inside, and when we sat down in a round circle in the den, Larry said with glee, "It's Pinewood Derby time again."

I heard a chorus from three dads, "Yeah!" And I wondered if it was a horse race that we'd go to.

"We have three weeks," Larry said. He was also the Cub Scout leader. "Last year one didn't use a high quality lubricant and failed miserably. Remember to use fine carbon powder. You can buy it from any hardware store."

"Where do they use the lubricant on the horse?" I wondered. "For a good bowel movement the night before?"

Larry was emphasizing, "Remember, it is to be made by the kids. You are there to help them. That's how it works."

I looked at Rajeev and it seemed to me he knew what Larry was talking about. We bought a packet and came home.

In the bright light of our dining room I opened the package and saw a smooth, rectangular pine block, two metal rods and four small, black wheels, and felt relieved that the rods fit nicely in the grooves and when I put the wheels it moved like a car. So it was not that hard. We could do it.

Next week at the meeting, Larry had a little red Mustang, which you could hold in your palm, on the coffee table. Its metal coating was shining under the light and it looked like a miniature model bought at the factory. Sheepishly he said, "My son and I did it last year."

It looked like a varnished, metal car to me.

"It deserved the first prize it won," Chuck, another dad, said. He admired the details of the car.

"I think I'll make a Model T this year," Larry told him.

I didn't know what came upon me and I asked him, "Did you make it from the pine block that came in the package?" and all the dads' faces turned toward me.

"You'll be surprised," Larry told me, "If you sand it well and put several coatings of good paint, it will look like that."

I thought the pine block was so smooth. Why did he have to sand it again? But at least I got an idea for Rajeev; I must buy some colorful paints for him. The dads discussed several techniques for adding weights (to the maximum amount allowed) so it would run fast. One man said he glued pennies at the bottom; one dad said he had screwed a few washers at the back and those looked nice as taillights for the car.

The seven boys sat quietly and watched their dads discuss what needed to be done for their cars. They wanted to go to the basement to play with the toys Larry's son had, but the fathers didn't let them. I saw a pale-looking boy, Andy, gazing at the paintings on the wall. He was more interested in the Indian riding through the country. I felt his father was so engrossed in the discussions that he was oblivious to his son's presence.

I thought of my own father. He never did any fun activity with me, nor with any other brothers and sisters. That was not the style. India is the old country: the father is a formidable figure, he is the head of the household, to be listened to, to be obeyed, and certainly not have fun with. He decides what is good for the children and the family. Father was distant; the only interaction with him was studying, particularly math, English, and Sanskrit. Later, I realized how gentle he was, but at a tender young age, when fathers are playing companions here, teaching their young ones sports and scouting, in India they stayed away like a great sage. Like the set path of a flowing stream, I followed what our older brothers did, and played with our own age-group children, the same games they had played for generations.

In my grandfather's time there was a day the boys were naughty in the village—it was not an approved event, but daring boys participated anyway. The day was called the nausta-chandra night, the spoiled moon night, when the Moon was full and the watermelons were just ripe. It was a night the boys sneaked out of their rooms and had fun with the farmer's vegetables and fruits. They ate some, but they mostly destroyed a lot by their play. The farmers also played tricks on them and chased them away. Complaints poured in the next day, but soon those were forgotten. My granduncle, who later became a well-known folksinger, was caught in such a nausta-chandra raid; he didn't see the farmer quietly lying on the ground among the vines. He was not let go that night and brought in the temple courtyard of the village for punishment. The village elders decided he would have to build a trap or a bell of some kind so the farmers could be alerted if someone tried to steal the fruit. That was the only time I knew of in the family when a father got involved with a son to build something. My great-grandfather ended up helping my grandfather's brother build a scary ghost-like figure to keep the boys away from the fields. And that worked because boys were afraid of skeletons standing in the field. Who knew—it could be real.

Finally, Larry declared that he had arranged for the ramp to be at the school next week so we could try out how our cars would perform and what adjustments were needed. He would also have an accurate weighing machine there and would help us to add weights to the models.

When we came home, I asked Catherine how we could cut the edges of the block to shape it more like a car. She said I must use a jigsaw and told me that it wasn't expensive. I was proud of her that she knew what tool to use.

At work Willis confirmed that, yes, I needed to buy a jigsaw. He said I must also buy sandpaper if I didn't have a belt-sander. I bought a jigsaw, sandpaper, fine carbon powder lubricant, and silver, black, and white paints. I went home bubbling with energy that I knew how to help Rajeev do the project.

I didn't care about his homework that evening. As soon as dinner was over, I cleared the table and took out the jigsaw. "Boy, the blade felt so loose, how does one use it to cut a tiny block of wood?" Rajeev said he would hold the pinewood and I could cut along the lines he had already drawn on it.

Catherine was passing by the two enthusiasts and said, "Don't cut your fingers!"

I thought she was right. Rajeev could not hold the block strongly and the blade could slip and cut his fingers. I got an idea to hold the block at the edge of the table with one hand and use the saw with my other hand. However, that made only a scratch on the block because I couldn't hold it firmly. The saw vibrated monstrously and it was impossible to get a grip on the wood. I got up on the table and put my left foot on the wood, but the moment I was going to bend down to use the saw, I hit my head on a blade of the fan. Ouch!

"Are you hurt, Daddy?" Rajeev asked, and I didn't answer.

I pressed the block hard with my foot and tried to cut the corner. It made so much noise that Catherine came over.

"Are you crazy? You are going to get hurt working like that." She took Rajeev away from me. "You need clamps," she said.

That was a great idea. "Why didn't I think of it before?"

Willis advised me that I should have a vise. "Don't you have a work bench?"

"I have two garden benches," I told him.

He looked at me for a second or two, and then said, "Well, try the clamps. If it works, fine. You need to have some clamps anyway."

I brought home two bright orange clamps, and as soon as dinner was over the father and the son went at it again. However, the clamps could not be held by the dining table – somehow, either the angle was wrong, the table too thick, or the corner too slippery. And Rajeev was not strong enough to hold the clamped block of wood while I used the saw. We struggled and sweated. I got the chisel and a hammer to carve out parts of the block. Wood chips spread over the floor and the table.

Catherine peeked through the door and was very pleased. She had a funny smile on her face and said, "Male bonding, eh?"

Actually the father-son bonding was at its lowest point at the moment. I wished I was not involved with this stupid thing at all, and I had the feeling Rajeev would rather get away from the room if he could. He only said, "I have to get something for Show and Tell tomorrow." The whole purpose of the Indian Guides was proving to be an impossible task.

I shaved along the outline of the block as best as I could. I had to use a hacksaw, chisel, hammer, and the jigsaw. The model became pointed in the front, and the back remained somewhat rectangular and fat. But it looked like a car, and Rajeev said, "It's good, Daddy." So I gave up further shaving the wood.

"Now, if you sand it well, and paint, it will look like a great car," I told him.

Rajeev painted the carved-wood silver—both on top and the sides; he then painted white windows on the sides, white headlights, and black fenders in the front and back. When we put the wheels on, it indeed looked like a racing car. I was not involved with the painting and had left it completely up to him. I was happy that he did a very nice job. We ran the car on the floor and it went smoothly. His brother joined him in running it back and forth. It was a pleasure to see the success of the project. Rajeev took the car to bed with him.

At the practice run on the ramp, however, as the car developed a little speed, one wheel came off, and it hit the sidewall; the car slid upside down to the bottom. I gazed in disbelief. It was the worst failure I could have imagined. I picked up the pieces and was wondering why the car came apart, when Larry came over and said, "This happened to me on my first car. Don't worry. Just make sure the wheels are held tightly. Use a little glue and put carbon powder on the axle before you run it." He then took the car and weighed it. It was very light; I had cut out too much.

I was disheartened that I couldn't even do this project meant for the kids. Larry told me that we should glue nuts at the bottom of the car. He gave me seven nuts. The tournament was only three days away.

Rajeev was silent on our way home.

"Let's go to the Baskin-Robbins," I told him because that was his favorite treat, but he wanted to go home.

The final day arrived and we went to the gymnasium of the Junior High School. We had fixed the car as told, and Rajeev had painted it again, and it looked great to me. We entered our name and gave the car to one of the busily working Pinewood Derby officials and sat down on the bottom, flat step of the gallery.

This was our first experience with the event. There were so many cars on the table, and many of those looked truly marvelous, like miniature models of real cars. The dads hovered in groups and discussed finer details of building these cars. The weight must be in the front, but in a balanced way so that it does not topple, and the shape was very important for aerodynamics reasons. The most important of all were the wheels. I gathered that some of them had turned the wheels on a lathe machine to make them perfectly smooth. Any little friction would take away its speed. I was overwhelmed with the knowledge they had and felt very inadequate. I wondered if it was really a project for the dads, and the boys were only an excuse.

The competition started and the dads became silent. One by one the cars were brought, the name of the boy who made it was announced, and his car was run on the ramp. One official recorded the time each car took for the course. The dads watched intently.

The wheel of one car came out, just as it happened to our car during the trial run. The father's face became grim, and I could share his embarrassment. He took the broken pieces from his son and walked out of the room. I started to pray that it wouldn't happen to Rajeev's car. When Rajeev's turn came and the car was placed on top of the ramp, I held my breath and Rajeev's hand. We both watched as it nicely came down in one piece. Its timing was not great, but I was elated that it completed the run without breaking down. One official of the tournament looked at the car with much curiosity and placed it on a separate table.

Now that ours was done, I relaxed and watched the race. Some of the boys were playing outside on the corridor, and a few stood at the back of the gallery. They had no concern for the races. When Andy's car from our troop came down the slope, it performed marvelously, the fastest car so far, and his dad raised his hands up in the air shouting, "Yes."

I saw that Andy was not on the floor; he was on top of the gallery looking out toward another boy. His dad and Larry shook hands with pride.

The whole competition took almost two hours because each car ran for three times to record the best timing. Finally, the time for announcing the winners came, and I told Rajeev that I would like to stay to see the rest of the program although we knew that we didn't win any. "Sure, Daddy," and he stayed with me.

First, the fastest running cars were announced. These were the grand prizes, coveted by the adults. The first prize went to a boy from another troop, whose father, I understood, was a machinist at the federal laboratory. They received a long ovation from everyone. The second prize went to a boy from Rexburg, and Andy won the third prize. He came down from the gallery, took the prize and gave it to his dad. His dad kissed the car and hugged him, "Didn't we do great this year?"

"Yes, Dad." He walked away to play with his buddies.

When the honorable mentions were announced, one boy, whom I did not know, started to cry loudly. His car didn't win any prize. His dad consoled him, "We'll do better next time, son." But it was no good. The boy punched his dad on his back and kept on crying, "You promised, Dad. You did."

Then the winners in several other categories were announced: the best looking car, the best design, etc. Suddenly I heard Rajeev's name. How could that be? Ours was one of the slower cars and did not stand out as anything special. Rajeev went to the stage with a look of surprise on his face. He received a prize for the most innovative painting done by a boy. His car was not the best-looking car, but it was clear that it was designed by him. The official stated that Rajeev's car was the only one that looked like the boy had more to do with the design and painting than his dad. Everyone applauded as he collected an impressive trophy. He was beaming as he came back with his prize. "Thank you, Daddy," he said and gave me a hug.

I knew I wasn't able to do as fine a job for Rajeev as the other dads had done for their boys. But Rajeev didn't know this, and he was elated that his dad helped him win the trophy. For a moment, I felt my hapless feeling go away and I was truly happy.

The plane had crossed Idaho sometime back and was flying above the Great Salt Lake. The sky was clear blue in Utah. As always, I stared at the mountain sticking out in the middle of the placid lake; it glowed in the morning light.

When I turned, I saw Amanda looking at me in a questioning way. She asked me, "Are you afraid of small animals when you go camping?"

"Camping?"

"You know, going away from home with tents and sleeping bags?"

I simply smiled. I was shy and hesitant to tell her the truth.

Chapter Eleven
THE POETS' CLUB

But those who ate this honeyed plant, the Lotus,
Never cared to report, nor to return:
They longed to stay forever, browsing on
That native bloom, forgetful of their homeland.
                    —*The Odyssey*, translated by
                                R. Fitzgerald

We had this "Poets' Club" in the early '80s that was remarkable for showing me a different side of my colleagues. No poetry was read. It was a "Happy Hour" association that met at the Little Tree Inn. Its sole purpose was not to discuss literature but to enrich our after-work lives, especially for those who were single. The half-price drinks and free hors d'oeuvres made the atmosphere congenial.

Bill Scoresby invited me to the Poets' Club. "Are you doing anything after work?" he asked me the second Friday after my arrival in Idaho Falls.

"Nothing particular. My family's not here."

"Want to come to the Poets'?"

"Poets?"

"Some of us meet on Fridays after work. Just come." He left with a ludicrous smile on his face, heightening my interest.

Bill was a charming, likable fellow. He was officially higher ranking than me. I had met him at the office only for a short time when I came for an interview. But I immediately felt his warmth.

My first surprise in Idaho came from him, although now I am not sure what was the portent—Idaho or Bill himself? He had taken me around to show the town. After we had roamed the eastside for sometime, I told him about my moving problems. I didn't want to drive from Long Island to Idaho with two young children, one not even a year old. I would come a month in advance of my family, but I had to have a car in Idaho Falls when I came. I thought I would buy a small, second-hand car, but how could I do this from New York?

"No problem," Bill said in a laid back fashion.

"No?" I asked.

"Tell me what kind of a car you're looking for, I'll see what's available."

I had no idea what was on his mind. I tried to guess it by looking at his face. Bill was forty years old, tall, slim, and quite handsome with dreamy eyes. His short, dark brown, curled hair was combed sideways with a distinct parting line. He had a clean shaven face with a short, thick moustache. Stylish, metal-framed glasses adorned his face. I saw he was serious. From my East Coast experience I could only think of the hassles of buying an old car and how one could be cheated if one wasn't careful. I could not imagine what he could do for me but I told him what I was looking for.

A week later I received a call in New York from Bill. He had found a Honda station wagon with low mileage—just the kind of a car I was looking for—and for only $4,000. Small cars were hard to find in those days, and Bill said he got it checked by a mechanic. The problem was the owner was leaving Idaho the next day for Washington. Did I want to buy the car? If you lived in New York, you could not buy an old car on the phone because you would be afraid the seller was lying about the car. But I sensed sincerity in Bill.

"How can I send you the money so fast?"

"Pay me when you get here."

He hung up.

How could he do this for someone, a colleague-to-be, who had not arrived at the office yet? He didn't know me at all. Was Idaho that different? No one would do this in New York or any-

where else in the world. Put up one's own money or take a tem-
porary loan so the new employee would have a car when he
arrived?

Bill showed up at the airport with my new Honda. He had
even had it tuned.

"I was in Seattle last week," Bill mentioned to me casually.

"On business?" I asked.

"No. I visited my son. He lives with his mother. In fact, I
stayed in their new house. She married again."

"No problem staying in ex-wife's house?"

"No. I'm friendly with her and her husband." He gave me a
smile. "My wife is Chris. You'll meet her soon."

In the dim light of the spacious bar I met the members of
the Poets' Club, mostly from our office but some from EG&G.
Betty was a lawyer, who had a fourteen-year-old daughter in
Texas. There was Shannon, a pretty Mormon divorcee, who
worked in contracts and was relatively quiet and very pleasant. Two young ladies, Susan and Karen, came from the public relations office. Bill, Armando, Ken and Paul were regular
members. Paul was married and a quiet type, but Armando
was clearly the social director. Come to think about it, they
were all outsiders to Idaho except for Shannon and Susan. A
few, like Jack and Dave, came occasionally but they didn't
drink alcohol.

Conversation topics included a wide variety of subjects,
even why one would work for the government. Betty said that
her father retired from the government, and even in his time,
the government workers had argued over the same subject.
Many of her father's colleagues received offers from private
companies with higher salaries and left. But in the long run
they had lots of troubles and her father was glad he hadn't quit
his government job. So Betty was going to stay with the government. Her concern was her daughter, how to take care of
her from Idaho.

My father had retired from the British government in
India. In the subdued light of the large restaurant, I remem-

bered him in the small room on the third floor of our house in Calcutta, neatly writing the expenses of the day in a notebook. The light in the room was always dim, almost like now. Darkness of the night surrounded the house. Only the fast rhythm of sitar music from a distant radio and faint voices of neighbors floated up. He sat at the edge of the bed with the ink bottle on the table and a pen in his hand. He dipped the pen in the dark-blue bottle and added the expenses on a separate piece of paper before recording them in the book, one page for each month. At the end of the month he summed up the expenses, and would say, "This month was a little tight. Next month will have to be better." This went on every month. I didn't understand how it could go on, but whenever I asked for money to go to the city for studying, he gave me the bus fare. Perhaps government workers, all over the world, learn to live within their means.

Then the vision of an older man came to me, a local man who always wore clean, white, starched dhuti and shirt. Standing on the stairs of our house he was calling for my father, "Majumdar-babu, are you home?"

My father was always home. I took him to my father in his room which was the drawing room and his bedroom.

"Come. Come." My father would receive him warmly and offer him a chair and signal me to ask mother to make tea.

They would talk about the weather and the local events for a short time, and then sheepishly he would say, "End of the month. I'm in a tight situation again. Could you loan me ten rupees? I shall pay you back as soon as I get paid."

My mother in the kitchen would protest in a low voice, "He always comes to borrow money, and I have to leave everything and make tea for him?" She made tea and I took it over to him.

He would say, "No. No. Why this trouble?" and take the cup. "Aren't you having tea, Majumdar-babu?"

"I just had tea." And he would go to the next room to get the money.

He would leave the house with ten rupees, not much money really, $2 in those days, the price for a pair of sandals. When he left he would fold his hands in the customary greetings fashion and say, "Namaskar. I shall return this soon."

My father would simply fold his hands and nod his head. He disliked the incident, but he always lent him the money, and the man also returned the loan.

I saw Bill nodding to a person at the next table, and the Poets' Club retook its shape. The tables were filling up, and the noise level had gone up. So this was the place for Friday evenings, I told myself. Several from our group went to the buffet.

"Is your daughter in Texas with her father?" I asked Betty.

"No. She's with my sister. I'm divorced."

I looked at her with sympathy and curiosity. She was in her late thirties, but looked older. She took a sip of her drink and said, "I was married when I was eighteen. It was for love. Then I caught him with a woman in our own house. See what life is?" She laughed.

I was shocked at her openness. "Sorry to hear that."

"I was such a good housewife," she said. "I didn't know what goes on in a man's head." She stopped for a few seconds. "I've come a long way, man. I struggled. I went to college and finished my law degree, and now I'm raising the girl by myself."

She took another sip. Was this the place to let her hair down? I wondered. At the end of the week, this club was perhaps the place to relax and let go of the office, and get ready for the weekend. Hardened by experience, I thought, Betty must be a good lawyer.

"The other day," Betty was telling me, "I met this guy in Jackson Hole, and he wanted to be sociable. He thought I'd spend the weekend there." She stopped and leveled her gaze at me. "I can see through men."

Bill went to another table to visit someone. Others brought back a lot of hors d'oeuvres to share. Paul said, "Don't let Betty spoil your interest in women," and gave her a smile.

"Who wants to go for dinner with us?" Armando shouted from the end of the table. "Then we'll go to my house."

"Have you met Robin?" Bill asked me a few weeks later.

"The new girl in the Legal Department?"

"Yes. She's single. Why don't you invite her for the Poets' tonight?"

I had met Robin before in the small, one-room cafeteria and been struck by her simple beauty. When you were young, you didn't need to try hard. In the case of Robin her wide eyes on a larger than usual face and a set of beautiful teeth would catch anyone's eyes. She was tall and slim but not thin. Her olive face glowed as if tanned recently from a trip to the Caribbean Islands. She had finished her internship in San Francisco and accepted this job. She had a pleasant personality and was well educated. Something about her told me that she came from a well-to-do family. When I asked her why she had come to Idaho, she told me it was her first job.

Robin came to the Poets' Club and sat down next to me. Bill occupied a chair in front of her. She was quite at ease in our company. Bill bought drinks for us and managed to have the conversation going among the three of us. Robin told us about the Oakland office. There she mixed with the young crowd and went out on Fridays to check out the bars in the Bay area. I observed Robin glancing at Bill in a curious way.

"You'll find Idaho much simpler and nicer than San Francisco," Bill told her.

"What's there to do here?" She flatly stared at him.

"Wait for two months and I can take you skiing. Then you can judge for yourself."

"It's a deal," she smiled.

Bill and I went to a nuclear reactor safety meeting in Albuquerque, and he took me to a dance club after dinner. It was a huge bar with several rooms for dancing, all crowded. Many beautiful women were there with Spanish features, olive skin and long, black hair. Bill danced with a couple of girls and then sat down.

"Great place isn't it?" he said with a grin.

"Yeah, if you want to meet someone," I said.

"I don't want to take a girl to my room, but I love this place. Not like Idaho Falls! So many people out here and having a good time. You meet new faces, new challenges. You know I get bored so easily."

"Do you go to the Stardust in Idaho Falls?"

"Oh, that's a meat market. No fun there, the same divorced women looking for men. Idaho Falls has started to bore me. Everything is routine."

"But you have so much going in Idaho Falls, ski clubs, travel groups, so many things. All the people I know envy you."

"Nah. They don't know me. Their problem is they're stuck in a set pattern. They love it, but I don't know how they do it. My parents stuck together, but I'm not sure how happy they were. They're all like my parents."

Another night a new girl, Ronda, came to the Poets' Club. She worked in public relations for EG&G. My wife, Catherine, who couldn't come often because of our children, was also there. Ronda was slim, very tall, and single. As soon as she had a drink, she became gregarious and talked incessantly, entertaining the whole group. I didn't know what came over her, she spilled out the gossips of the town, especially who was sleeping with whom, who went on travel with the general manager who had no need to go, and who got promoted at everyone's surprise. She rolled her eyes, pitched her voice high or low depending on the situation; all her anecdotes were humorous with a possibility of being true. Catherine barely concealed her surprise, "In this nice, little town?" when Ronda laughed loudly saying, "Hey, men are men everywhere, even in Idaho." She then moved on to genealogy. She was doing some research on her family who came to Utah with Brigham Young. She told us that she found plenty of skeletons in her grandmother's closet.

"Really?" Paul smirked, "In a good Mormon family? I thought they never write anything not nice."

"I'm going to write a novel about it one of these days." Ronda said.

"I wondered how the co-wives treated each other," Catherine asked.

"We can't even handle one wife," Paul commented.

"My grandfather had three wives," Ronda continued. "What I found is that he married the youngest wife when he was fifty and she was only fifteen, and she ran away."

"She couldn't stand him or her heart was set for someone else?" I asked naively.

"You have to wait for my novel," Ronda said smilingly.

"She was probably running away from the other wives," Paul interjected.

"The interesting part is that the other two wives helped her get away," Ronda told Paul. "There is a good story here with intrigues among the wives and their frustrations."

"Life was much harder then," Dave made a grand statement. "There was so much work to be done, no one had free time to waste, both men and women. And I'm sure men provided for and took care of the wives very well. I bet there was more harmony then than what we see among husbands and wives now-a-days."

Bill was quiet during these discussions and looked at the two couples dancing on the floor. In a little while he got up and walked away. In the jolly atmosphere of our table, I wondered if Bill was a lonely man and felt detached from the mundane, silly, little humors and events of our lives.

Bill's wife, Chris, came to the Poets' Club one evening. She was young, short, muscular, and had a very pretty, attractive face. I thought she couldn't be more than twenty-four. They were so good together. Chris worked for Delta Airlines; she was often away and couldn't come to the Poets' regularly, but when she came, she was friendly, open, and effervescent.

Bill had good taste in women, I thought.

Soon the snow came although Thanksgiving was still ten days away. The mountains were white for some time, and the extent of the white stuff on the ground told me it was here to stay. A few weeks earlier at the Poets' Club someone had told me, "You must love the winter if you are going to live here." Then he added, "I can't wait for the snow to come in."

Bill came to me saying he and Robin were going skiing. "You want to come?"

"I have skied only once in my life, I'm not good at it."

"I'm a very good skier, I'll teach you."

They picked me up on Saturday when it was still dark, and we drove to Grand Targhee. The ski lines were short, and the place vibrated with bubbling enthusiasm. Many came to start the season. Robin said she wanted to try out the Bunny hill first. That was for me, too.

I was alone on the chair and absentmindedly swung my feet. In the early light of the sun I admired the sea of pine trees on the opposite hill and the big Douglas fir below the lift, sparkling with crystal white, fresh snow. The Tetons stood near in the sky proudly displaying their three peaks. The silent white all around me was simply magnificent, so different from my tropical upbringing. It was the white of a bride's dress, the sign of purity, of virginity. The contrast with an Indian bride's dress became more vivid to me.

An Indian bride's dress, a sari, is always colorful, most often red. Marriages are still arranged in India. The shy, innocent bride dressed in the bright sari sits in a small room in her own house, surrounded by onlookers. She has very little control over her marriage. Unfamiliar mantras are uttered in the wee hours of the night and she is married to the boy she doesn't know. But then a strange thing happens—they fall in love and spend the rest of their lives caring for each other and for their children. How it happens is a mystery to the Western world where marriages are based on personal choice alone without regard to family, often after living with each other for some time.

I thought of what Mamata, my class friend's wife, told me in New York. She did not have an arranged marriage. She came from a Brahmin family, but my friend wasn't a Brahmin, so her family wouldn't agree to the marriage. They eloped. It was a long time ago, and I was in America then. They had a hard time because of a boycott by her family, but they survived. They settled in New York with their two children, who were much older than ours. What I remembered now was not their marriage, but a scene she related to me. When she was very young, she had lived in a joint family with her uncles. Children didn't have separate rooms to sleep in. She and her younger brother slept in the same room with her uncle and aunt. The adults had the bed, but she and her brother slept on the floor. It was a common practice.

We had had several drinks, and Mamata must have been in a reminiscing mood.

She said, "You know some things we hated when we were young, sometimes they turn out to be so wonderful. I was thinking of my uncle. I used to be so mad at him. My little brother would fall asleep very early, and I was supposed to be asleep too, but I used to be awake when my uncle came to bed. He would smoke a cigarette, then my aunt would come after finishing her work in the kitchen. She would turn off the light and tuck in the mosquito-net. They talked a little, very little, of household chores. Then I'd hear a little noise from their bed, shuffling of clothes, and some movement. In a short time, I knew what would happen because it happened every night. I used to get so mad at my uncle. He would get on top of her. I could sometimes hear her moaning. I stayed frozen in my bed on the floor. I didn't understand why my uncle tormented her every night. They didn't know I was awake. I was angry, and I felt sorry for my aunt. She was so sweet to me. I wished I could stop that for her, but then in the morning I'd forget about it completely." Mamata gazed at the large Batik painting in our living room for a short time, and then turned toward me. "After thirty years, and seeing what struggles we go through everyday, I now envy the relationship they had."

Thinking of the days in Calcutta, I was distracted and got nervous when it was suddenly time to get off the chair and I fell down. Bill was ahead of me and helped me get up. Robin teased me, "You'll be a perfect ski companion for me."

"Oh. Go ahead. I'll come down slowly."

I watched the two going down the hill, Robin following Bill. She had bought a new pink and black ski outfit for this season, which looked gorgeous on her. Seeing the other skiers who whooshed by, I knew Bill was purposely making slow, broad turns for her. Still under the chairs at the steeper slope I saw Robin fall down; one of her skis detached and stayed a few feet away. She lay there with a hand stretched for Bill to pick her up. I saw them laughing and enjoying the event as if they were two young lovers.

Bill taught me how to shift my weight to the right foot when I turned right and shift my weight to the left foot when I turned left. Robin stayed with us while I practiced. Once in a while Bill would look at Robin and make silly comments. "Robin is an expert skier. She falls perfectly."

She was only mildly abashed. "Last time I fell because you came too close to me. Remember?"

Skiing was not in my blood, I couldn't let go of my fear. It was more fun to watch Bill and Robin ski. In the beautiful surrounding of the ski hill, I wondered if Robin was acting more intimately with Bill than a colleague normally would. Bill was enjoying her company, but I was not sure if he was doing anything unusual for her. He was behaving as the natural Bill I knew.

I wondered what had happened to Chris and remembered the beautiful enlarged photograph I had seen in their house, both looking very young, a picture taken during their honeymoon. They appeared so happy together.

The severe winter in Idaho finally passed, the snow melted, and the hint of spring was everywhere. My wife and I were going to the Waremart after dinner and decided to drop by Bill's house. I called before starting, and he said, "Sure, come over. Maybe we could do something together this evening."

Robin was in his house. They had just finished dinner and were washing the dishes. Bill was jovial and teased her in a rather intimate fashion. Robin ignored his silly, sensuous remark and kept smiling.

There was love in her eyes. She had fallen for Bill, I surmised.

Robin was showing my wife a silver bracelet she bought recently, and the two were having a serious conversation about shopping, when Bill said, "You're like my mother, a spender."

They ignored him, but I was curious. I asked Bill, "Did your father argue with your mother about spending money?"

"Nah. They didn't argue. She spent whatever she felt like. Sometimes she went on a spending spree and bought stuff she never used or even looked at again."

"Your father didn't say anything to her?"

"No. My father was afraid to. There was something between the two that I didn't understand. My father went away occasionally, and my mother would be silent for a day or two and then go on shopping."

"So each business trip cost your father a lot of money."

"I didn't get to know my father well. He died when I was in high school. I didn't really know what he did that bothered my mother."

My eyes shifted to the kitchen and the cabinets. Everything was very neatly kept, even the dish towel hung nicely folded from the hook. Just like his office, neat and tidy.

One morning a month after I had seen Robin in Bill's house, as I turned from Holmes onto 3rd Street, I heard a crash. I looked back and saw a small, sporty, green car smashed in the front and Chris getting out of the driver's seat. I went to her quickly and held her hands. She was shaken. I stayed with her while the police came. Bill was away on travel. We went to the small cafeteria in our office. She called her mother.

After she had spoken with her mother, she was calm. She gazed at the dull, one-story Credit Union building across the way and said resignedly, "Bill is wonderful. I love him. But we are separating. You know that?"

I was shocked. They were married only for about two years.

"What did you say?"

"Yes. It's true. We like each other, but we've decided we shouldn't be married. I'm still young, and he's not ready for a lifelong commitment. He'll eventually be unhappy. So we decided to be friends. My parents also agree."

I watched her face, her eyes, her expression. There was no anger, just a slight sadness that could be overcome easily. Why did Bill do this? And how he could divorce such a beautiful, vibrant girl. I didn't understand the situation at all. Did the intensely cold Idaho winter do strange things to young married couples? Or was it Bill who got cold feet whenever he saw a steady, fixed situation? Bill and Chris, such a cheerful couple together, they made all other couples jealous.

I thought of the simple life of Mamata's uncle and aunt. In spite of all that was going for Bill, and his affluence, could he ever be as content as them? Was Bill merely reacting to his parents' poor relationship?

The Poets' Club continued its Friday-evening assemblies. In the partially lighted room, the gang always appeared cheerful with drinks and hors d'oeuvres in front of them, and an expression of relief from the last few days of the worries of meeting deadlines. Robin had somehow dropped out of this club. Betty didn't come for a couple of weeks and I inquired. Several looked up and Paul said with a big smile, "She's in love."

"Betty?" I exclaimed.

"It's true. She met a physicist from the Westinghouse Company, and he sent her a dozen roses at the office. That did it."

"How could it happen to Betty?"

"That's what life is," Paul said and took a long sip of Canadian Club from his glass.

"Did you know Shannon is in San Diego?" Armando said. "She met a guy from the Navy. I think I'll look for a job in a warmer place. The cold is getting to me."

Bill got up and went to visit friends at other tables. He didn't participate in gossip of others' affairs.

Months passed by. Robin went to Washington, D.C., for some sort of attorneys' training. I also had a meeting there and we decided to meet and spend an evening together. We went to the Kennedy Center for Performing Arts and saw a Greek tragedy. Then we roamed aimlessly in the federal buildings' area. She drove and talked. Eventually we ended up in her hotel-cum-temporary-apartment. She went to the refrigerator and opened a bottle of red wine. She was in a talkative mood. There was something we both wanted to talk about but were shying away from. Finally, I asked, "I haven't seen Bill for sometime. Where is he?" I was afraid because I didn't know where they stood with each other, but after a drink it didn't matter.

Robin looked at me for a few seconds and said, "I'm so miserable."

The glass stopped in front of my lips and I stared at her. She then said, "Did you know Bill was married three times?"

"I thought only twice."

"No. He wanted to go to Denver to ski and said, "We could stay with my ex-wife."

"That's scary."

"He said it very casually, but I was amazed." She again looked at me with her big eyes. "It's then I snapped out."

I must have been drunk and said, "Why don't you marry him and train him right?"

"Bill can't be married to anyone, really." There was a melancholy tone in her voice.

A reorganization took place in the office, and I was sent to the laboratory fifty miles away which was known as the "site." I became busy with my new work, and the daily two-hour commute took a toll of my free time. I saw my friends at the Poets' Club when I went there but slowly lost touch with Bill and others who stayed in town. Soon after this Bill retired from the federal government and went away. He had planned it this way. He had joined the Navy when he was young and the Navy paid for his college education. Those years were counted toward his retirement, so he could retire at age forty-two. Bill simply vanished from the scene, and I lost touch with him. I heard he was working somewhere in New York state. Robin went back to the Oakland office. I went to the Poets' Club occasionally, but somehow it was not much fun any more.

Several years passed by and Idaho Falls grew on us. Our children were in high school now. The office expanded, and I was promoted to a Branch Chief's position. I had to travel a lot as part of this job. I was in Albany at the State Building for a meeting. During lunch our group sat at one corner in the large cafeteria. The tall glass walls showed a beautiful early winter, the ground sprinkled with light snow surrounded by dark leafless trees. There was no sign of any wind and the still scene scintillated in orange rays of the sun. I thought of the skiing trips to Targhee.

At a far corner in the cafeteria I saw a man who looked familiar. He was eating alone and gazing outside. Wavy, white-streaked-brown hair covered his head, and I recognized him by his elegant metal glasses. I quickly went over.

"Bill?"

"Ah, Debu. What're you doing here?"

I immediately felt the same warmth from him as I had felt in Idaho Falls almost fifteen years before.

"Tell me. How are you doing? A long time isn't it?"

"I'm okay." He smiled, but it didn't have the gregarious enthusiasm of the past. Perhaps he was tired, perhaps age does that to us.

"How's the social life? Any Poets' Club here?"

"Is that still alive in Idaho Falls?"

"That died long ago. Betty and Armando moved to Texas. Paul, Dave, and Jack retired. Many new faces at the office. The old camaraderie is not there any more. Tell me about you."

"Nothing to tell, really. I live alone. If you're free let's meet in the evening."

I said that would be great and left him.

Bill had a two-bedroom apartment in a high-rise. He quickly straightened the living room, arranging the pillows on the sofa and some papers and magazines on the coffee table. He took away the old cup to the kitchen. His style of decoration had changed. No pictures of the Targhee skiing area, the Tetons, and farm horses, but a large print of Whistler's "The Princess from the Land of Porcelain" hung as the centerpiece of the room. It was the picture of a slim, beautiful, Italian woman in a Japanese kimono. In that living room I felt her face emanated sadness.

"This is different from your Idaho house," I told him.

"Yeah. I don't have the same urge for neatness anymore. Very few come to this place, anyway."

"No ladies?"

"No." He smiled. "How about if I cook something simple to eat?"

"That'd be great. I'm more interested in catching up with you."

He opened a bottle of Chardonnay. "This'll be our Poets' night."

It was a long evening, but he never mentioned Robin, and I didn't bring her up.

On my way out at the door I asked, "You miss Idaho much?"

He stared at me for a while, as if the memories were crowding him all at once, but then he only said, "You can't hang onto the past."

Chapter Twelve
A PLACE TO HANG YOUR HATS

The hemlock hedge was tall, like that of our house in Long Island, and I touched the healthy plant that sparkled in the afternoon sun. Their soft green branches made a cozy border in the large backyard of the ranch style house. The flowerbed was dense with mums, irises, lilies, and several other flowers that accentuated the setting. A contoured rose garden curved around the lawn. How beautiful a garden they had built, though the summer here lasts barely for two months. While I admired the garden, the sound of the vibrant party floated out of the living room. It was the summer get-together of the Idaho Falls Opera Theater. All volunteers—many expatriates from different parts of the country—made this club. I was there because of my wife, Catherine, who loved operas and helped them with stage makeup.

"Don't you admire this garden?" Mrs. Nelson spoke to me from behind. I hadn't realized she was there, strolling alone like me. About fifty and slim, she looked very graceful.

"Oh, it's beautiful," I said. "They must spend hours in the garden."

Her husband sang in the opera club, and she helped with the fund-raising. They were from Illinois. She inspected the campanula.

"I guess you don't have these flowers where you were born."

"I come from Calcutta," I told her. "Very tropical. All different flowers there."

"Very fragrant, right?"

"Yes. I love the tropical, sweet aroma."

"Do you miss Calcutta?"

I looked at her. No one usually asks a man this question. Hers was a congenial voice, and I said, "Yes, I do, but I don't think about it."

She came closer. She was wearing a long, dark blue, cotton skirt and a white blouse with embroidered small, pink and blue flowers on the sleeves. Unpretentious, she had very little makeup on.

"When you think of your home in this country, where would it be?" she asked me.

I was startled and my body moved in a jerk toward her. The depth of her inquiry cut at the heart of many like me. Perhaps it was hers, too. She gazed at me with interest, and I saw a melancholy face. I was certain she hadn't asked this to make a conversation.

"Well, it would be New York," I told her. "I spent ten years there."

"I have begun to think of Idaho Falls as my home," she said. "My parents are dead, and there's no connection any more to Peoria, where I grew up. That place is so different now."

"In one way or other, we are all foreigners," I thought. But, before I could say anything, a call came from the kitchen window, "Mrs. Nelson, we need your help."

"I'll talk with you later," she smiled and went inside. I had thought she was one of the settled folks here but I wondered if she still felt the need for belonging to a place she could call her home.

The few couples in the garden started to move inside. Dinner was being served, but I lingered in the backyard, thinking of an incident that had happened last month at the Safeway on 17th Street. I had been at the fish counter.

"Mama, Mama, look at the man," I heard the young voice of a boy talking to his mother and pointing at me. "Is he black, Mommy?"

My eyebrows came together for a second. The boy's shiny, golden blond hair glistened in the intense, white light of the supermarket.

"No. He is a foreigner. Now be quiet." The mother tried to pull him away, but he continued looking at me with wide eyes.

"Why is a foreigner here, Mommy?"

"I don't know. You ask too many questions."

When I passed by the boy, I smiled and said, "Hi."

"Where are you from?" He asked me.

"I'm from India."

"Oh. How long will you stay here?"

He was not smiling, and the clear blue eyes stared at me. The innocence of children can't be beat. He knew well I didn't belong here. The only question was how long would I be visiting this place, his country.

I have been in the U.S. for twenty-five years, a citizen of the country, but where was truly my home?

"I don't know," I told him.

Happy voices from the living room led me inside. Catherine stood at the door. "Where were you?" She took me to the eating place.

The three-leaf long dining table was covered with dishes from one end to the other. The light from the chandelier shone brightly, and the intricate, lacy tablecloth enhanced the beautiful serving dishes and their colorful contents. Hamburgers and hot dogs were on one side with the necessary condiments, but the rest of the table was a gourmet delight. I saw sushi, yellow biriyani pilaf, dumplings, several sausages, salmon mousse, and a variety of salads. Catherine's tanduri chicken was also there. In this land of opportunity food was so plentiful; it was an art, I thought, to learn to eat less.

In my time in India, we had great food only at weddings. The vision of a thin, old Brahmin came to me. He was walking on a dirt road with his teenage son. A faded cotton dhuti, which he moved occasionally to cover his chest and shoulder, was wrapped around his whole, sun-dried body. Little puffs of dust flew up from his worn sandals. The obedient boy was silently listening. "You'll see lots of different food, some dishes you haven't seen in your life, chops and cutlets, good fish—rui and ilish maach—and goat meat. Don't eat much of the ordinary food, like vegetable-curry. Eat the meat, the fish, and the sweets. You know we can't afford these in our house. That's why I'm taking you with me."

In the middle of the dinner, the boy picked up the brown earthen pot of water from the floor and drank it empty. The father, sitting next to him on the floor, looked at him with angry eyes. "I brought him here to eat good food, and he's filling his stomach with water," he grumbled to himself. "How stupid."

The father was truly disappointed. On the way home, as they were crossing a large rice field, the father kept on harping: "I took you to the feast so you'd get to eat good food, fish and meat. But what were you eating? Filling up your stomach with water."

The son walked quietly for a long time. Then he couldn't take it anymore, and said, "Baba, I drank water so I could eat more."

The father was now angry beyond question and burst out, "How is that possible?"

"The water settled the food at the bottom of my stomach so I could eat more."

The father looked at the son for a few seconds and, then, finally slapped him. "Then, why didn't you also tell me?"

My sister had got me on a dieting track the first day I arrived in Boston in 1964. I had to wait for a long time at the Montreal Airport to catch a plane to Boston and had wandered around the airport aimlessly. I had only $24 with me and was afraid to spend it, my emergency money, so I didn't eat anything in Montreal. When I entered my sister's house, I smelled Indian food. "They'd feed me a great dinner," I thought, but my sister offered me tea and a piece of plain cake, and told me, "You must be tired. Jet lag. Go to sleep now. We'll open everything tomorrow." They meant the stuff I brought from India.

My brother-in-law winked and said, "Want a glass of wine? It'll help you sleeping."

Wine? Only bad people or the really rich drank wine in India. "Has he changed here so much?" I wondered.

Robert Bower

The bed was soft with springs at the bottom. What a country, I thought, no hard bed, no bed bugs either, and the lights were so bright everywhere. I questioned why the lights were dim in India and drifted into a deep sleep.

In the morning I was still tired and had tea and toast, but the butter did not have the taste I was used to. The bread was also not crisply toasted—not as hard as we did it in Calcutta. Then my sister served me cold milk from the refrigerator and Rice Crispies. "How awful," I thought.

"Don't you heat up the milk?" I asked.

"No," she said. "Too much trouble. You'll get used to it."

For lunch they served me a sandwich, an apple, and a Coke. No one asked me if I needed more food. I could have eaten several sandwiches, and what I really missed was a plate of rice. I remembered the everyday-lunch in Calcutta—a mound of steaming rice on a shiny metal plate with a little salt and a wedge of lemon on one corner. A bowl of dahl (lentil soup) would accompany this, shaak (fried spinach), sometimes slices of deep-fried potato or egg plant, and fish curry. Occasionally there would also be another vegetable curry. And my mother would be there giving me more rice from a big haree (vessel).

In Boston, I was hungry in two hours after lunch, but no one mentioned food. No afternoon snack. "Do they practice staying hungry?" I wondered.

Instead of serving me more food, my sister asked me, "Do you want to go shopping?"

"On empty an stomach?" I asked myself. "One may fall down from the bus." I said to her, "No. I have jet lag." Actually I had food-lag, but couldn't tell them. It was America, I should follow what they did.

Next day when I mentioned food in the afternoon, my brother-in-law told me to try an avocado. "It's so good."

I looked at the green fruit. It had a rough skin and did not look appetizing. "How can one eat a green, unripe fruit? Are they crazy?"

I was hungry again, so I decided to risk the avocado. I tried to peel it like a mango, but the skin was too thick and hard. I cut a slice and saw the light green flesh inside. I put it in my mouth. Ugh! It was not sweet. It was not soft like a ripe mango either. What was it? A vegetable? I looked at the smiling face of my brother-in-law who said, "Isn't that a wonderful taste? Like a soft nut with a gentle flavor?"

I simply wondered what had come over them and decided that as soon as I had my place, I'd have rice, dahl, and fish curry every day for the rest of my life.

Catherine's voice brought me back from my ruminations: "Debu, see the stuffed grape leaves. Suzie made those. She's new in Idaho Falls."

Mr. Alexander was ahead of me. "I have to select my food carefully," he told me. "Too much cholesterol in these foods. But they're so good. I'll take small portions."

I saw his plate was full, piled high.

Catherine and I took our plates to the living room and occupied two chairs. Several others were there, eating: the Willards, Tallmans, Knechts, Fernums, and Roberts.

Bob looked up and said, "We should do one where there's lots of food. A gourmet cook poisoning her own lover by mistake. What you think?"

"*Mikado* is just right for here," Mike asserted. "Exotic, but not too foreign."

I looked around the room. Everyone was white. And all were well-to-do people, all professionals, including most of the wives. In this tiny town far from the two coasts, where the real opera singers were, they had kept the spirit alive. One had sung with the Pittsburgh Opera but she came here because of her husband. Singing was a hobby for these people.

"Blacks sing so well," I whispered to Catherine, "too bad we don't have many in Idaho Falls."

"We have one in the opera club. Ladona. She sings well. Daisy and her husband join in the chorus sometimes. But you know what I learned? I found it difficult to make them up," she replied. "How do you put a black person in *Mikado*?"

"They do it at the Met."

"Here people want traditional operas. Those weren't written for the blacks except for Aida and Othello. But those will be difficult to do here. It's hard to make their skin light. I've got to put yellow color first to cover their skin before I can use normal color. Otherwise it'll have an ashy appearance. Last time we had Ladona in the chorus of Merry Widow; during the show they put a blue light on her, and she looked green. It was horrible. It will be expensive to rearrange the lights just for her. We can't do what they do at the Met."

"I guess it's difficult for them here."

Everyone has a handicap of one kind or another, I have mine and they have theirs. There are so few blacks in Idaho Falls, I wondered if they felt they lived in a foreign country. My black friend, Dr. Donna Johnston, the anesthesiologist, told me she was often asked in supermarkets and department stores how she liked this country. People were always surprised she didn't have an accent. How could she? Her family history went back 200 years in America, while the families of those who asked her these questions came only in the early 1900s.

"Weren't you insulted?" I asked her.

"No. It was their ignorance, not mine." She smiled warmly at me.

"Foreigner" is really a concept, I thought, of how you feel and how you are viewed. These two are somewhat connected, but the connection can be severed. The more self-esteem one has, like Donna, the easier it is to overcome how you look or are viewed by others. I was certain Donna would fit in any part of the world. She was truly a global citizen.

I thought of the program we had had at the University Place. It was Black History Day and our office had invited several people to speak for a celebration of diversity. The Mayor of Idaho Falls was one of them, but he didn't come and had sent a councilman in his place. The speakers sat on the stage, and I could see the councilman was bored and shifted his legs often. When his turn came, he jumped up and gave his speech. He said that it was good to have us in Idaho Falls. "Enjoy our town while you are here." In other words, "Don't forget you are a visitor here, not a part of the community." During the question-and-answer dialogue he was not there. I had seen him sneaking away by the back door as soon as his speech was finished. He did his part, as required; why hang around any longer?

The few foreigners that were here came because of the large nuclear laboratory. They had a culture of their own, as if a separate micro-world of a few existed in Idaho Falls. They had their own get-togethers, picnics, and tours. They came from different countries and the only thing they had in common was their foreignness. They were professionals, all short-timers; and they knew it. Their foreign accents were a novelty for the locals.

One day I was downtown and went to the bank there. I usually bank in the small branch near my office where everybody knows me. It was lunchtime and the line was long.

"I want to take $100 from my account," I told the teller and gave her my account number.

She looked at me—a young girl in her early twenties with beautiful blue eyes.

"Your Social Security number?"

I told her.

"Do you have any identification with you?"

No one asked me this at the branch office, but I showed her my driver's license. She examined it carefully. She gave me the cash. I then asked her if she asked these questions to all.

"Yes. Our bank requires this."

"I'm glad you are protecting our money," I said in a serious tone, "but you didn't do that for the people ahead of me." Sometimes I get annoyed. "Next time if you do this to one, do it to all."

She stared at me silently, and I left. This was nothing new for me and I didn't blame her. When you are foreign-looking and settle in a place, you learn to accept certain local responses. I should blame the situation. But why did I have to face this often while the others around me didn't have to?

However, I knew it was a normal reaction to a foreign-looking person in any place, not just here. Outward appearances define us. I thought Stephen Spielberg and several other film directors were courageously breaking this barrier. They purposely made Yoda very short and ugly with big ears. E.T. looked hideous. Only children could see through their outer appearances and perceive their true identity. Just because they looked different they weren't unintelligent, unethical, and uncivilized. I admired Spielberg's vision. But changes are slow to come.

I'll always be considered a foreigner in this country. I look different, I speak with an accent, and I have finally realized I also think differently. The first seventeen years of one's upbringing can't be thrown away easily! My son told my wife recently, "Mommy, I don't know why people say Daddy has an accent. I don't hear it."

Perhaps the trick is to get close enough, then the differences are not seen anymore. One can see the "inner you," not the "external you."

Sometimes I see a similarity between us and physically handicapped people—they are soul-mates in a world that the ordinary, the normal wouldn't understand. We know how people react to our presence. Perhaps a more poignant comparison is with a fat, young woman. She can do everything normally, but she must behave in a certain way to be accepted in the society. She must be a little nicer, more humorous, and sympathetic to others. If she is sloppy, argumentative, and dresses badly, the response of other people is more negative. She is like a foreigner in her own country.

What really is a foreigner? No one is born a foreigner and no one feels a foreigner inside. The first twenty-three years of my life, I was just like everyone around me, but circumstances led me to live in a different country. I know foreignness has nothing to do with where one is born. It is, as my friend Donna says, how at ease one feels in a place. Although the hankerings to go back to one's childhood, to those familiar sights, sounds, and events, will always be there when one lives in a different place, I submit that it's not the land which makes one feel foreign. It's not a place but something within oneself, an inborn thing.

Mrs. Willard announced that the video of the last opera was being shown in the family room. It was *The Pirates of Penzance*. We trooped downstairs. The room was already crowded. All the singers, costume designers, stage crew, make-up artists, and helpers were there to appreciate their work being shown on the television screen. Someone had turned up the sound to full blast. I stood near the door.

Soon it became a little rowdy because many wanted to comment on the costumes, the stage, the lighting, the performances, and especially on the comic acts. But I was a detached observer, an outsider.

When the show was over, I said, "I wish I could be on stage, too."

"Why not?" Joan told me. "Come for the next rehearsal. We will get you in."

"I don't sing in foreign languages, you know," I winked at her. "If you do an opera that needs an Indian character, let me know."

"Don't you have operas in India?"

"Indian life is an opera itself."

"You silly man, we'll have to find a role for you."

I met Suzie Ansari upstairs admiring a print of Monet's Water Lilies.

"How do you find Idaho Falls?" I asked her.

"I like the people, but it's not like Beirut. I lived there for many years. I'm still adjusting to America. When we went to Lebanon in the '60s, we had to do the same thing. We learned the Muslim culture. We got so used to living with two religions. I miss it now."

"When I first came here," I told her, "I made so many mistakes because I didn't know the culture. It's funny now."

"That's so true."

"I remember when, at the beginning, someone told me, 'See you later,' I stared at him and said, 'When?'"

"Sometimes the cultural differences end up in sadness."

"Even in Beirut?"

"Yes. I remember a young friend, Muriel. She worked at the embassy. She was single and met this guy, Kamal, who taught physics at the university. They became friends and then lovers. She thought it was a fling while she was in Beirut. But Kamal told her, 'Our love is eternal.'

"That put her in a different situation. She was a docile girl and thought it was fine. She was happy to be with him and decided to build up their relationship. She suggested he help her to improve her Arabic. They tried for a while but he was impatient, and it didn't work out.

"Then she told him she wanted to write dialogues in Arabic and he could help with her writing. She taught English writing classes to Lebanese students in the evening and wanted to be a writer someday. The first piece she wrote was a little anecdote.

"It was about walking down the Masjid Road and seeing a beautiful jewelry store and going inside. She was looking at a necklace. After a while she noticed that an Italian fellow was also interested in the piece. He started a conversation with her.

"He said, 'Do you like it?'

"Muriel said, 'Sure. Who wouldn't?' and she gave him a smile.

"'Then I should buy it for you. You are so pretty'.

"They both had a good laugh. Neither of them bought anything and they walked out. As they came out in the street, he invited her for coffee.

"She was surprised, but agreed to go with him to the outdoor cafe. He was quite a handsome and gregarious man. 'Shall we meet again?' he asked her.

"She said, 'Why not?' and gave him her address

"Muriel gave the little piece she had written to Kamal for correction, but he charged out of his study as soon as he read it, asking, 'When did you meet this guy?'

"Muriel replied that she didn't meet any Italian in a jewelry store. She made it up. But he said, 'No. You cannot make this up. You must have gone out with this man. Tell me the truth.'

"She told him, she didn't go out with a man, really. She was incredulous at Kamal's reaction.

"'You can't fool me,' he told her, and stalked back into his study.

"That was the end of their relationship."

"I can understand him, the jealous man," I told Suzie.

"I thought you would." She said with a faint smile on her face.

Sometimes cultural differences and upbringings play such a hilarious role, although they are not hilarious when we're face to face with them. I thought of my first flight to the U.S. and remembered the nervousness of a twenty-three-year-old man from Calcutta, who knew nothing of Western customs. In fact, I had rarely spoken English until then, and I felt like a little tribal boy venturing out from his village to the most advanced country in the world. I stayed overnight in Frankfurt, West Germany. I don't remember how I managed the airport customs, the people, the traffic, and how I reached my hotel. It was a miracle. In the darkness of the night and the new city, I'm sure it was like a dream, and I simply followed whatever I was told to do. The hotel was a big one at the center of the town. I had never slept in a big hotel before, at least not in one where I didn't speak the language, but I quickly fell asleep.

When I got up in the morning, I looked at the commode and wondered how to use the white porcelain thing. There was no hole on the floor with space for two feet. How did you do it? And where was the mug of water?

Then I saw a newspaper in the room—it was in German. I spread it on the floor around the potty and pondered the best course of action. The safest was to lift the wooden thing and put my two feet on top of the porcelain commode, and even if I made a mess it would be contained. It was difficult, but my years of yoga exercise came handy and my light weight (102 pounds) allowed me to climb on top of the commode and somehow I completed the job. Then in my horror, at the sight of what I saw, I put a lot of those rough tissue papers in it, and rushed to the shower. The water was very cold, much colder than water in Calcutta. I wondered if the Germans liked a cold shower after they go potty.

Then I went down to the lobby and someone pointed out the dining room to me—a big room with elegant tables and chairs, white beautiful tablecloths and cutlery. I looked at the waiter and asked for chicken because I was afraid they might serve me beef. Being a good Hindu, one thing I certainly didn't want was beef. So when the food came I was delighted—I could see it was not beef. There was no gravy on the chicken; it was not like curry, but it was okay. I wiped my hand with the cloth napkin and went after it. I ate a little of the meat but was very interested in tasting the marrow in the bones because in a mutton curry the marrow was always cooked well and tasted very good. I chewed the bones, but it didn't taste that good. I then wondered where to put the splintered bones—on the table or on the plate?

Chicken was not common food in my time in Calcutta. In the past, the Muslims raised chickens, and so the Hindus wouldn't eat them. Not only that, the devout ones like my grandmother wouldn't even allow chickens near their houses. I remembered the first chicken I tasted in India. We had to go out of town on a picnic for this. We started very early in the morning and took a train to a remote village outside Calcutta.

There we bought two live chickens and some vegetables from the open market and went to my uncle's empty house.

We usually ate goat or lamb and we didn't know how to cook chicken. Our friend, Shibu, put some spices and a lot of water to boil the meat. But more water came out of the meat; and soon it looked like a vat of yellow water with a few pieces of white meat floating. It became a broth, perfect for a sick patient.

I left most of the meat on my plate in the hotel in Frankfurt and a pile of chewed chicken bones at one corner on the plate. I prayed that I wasn't supposed to put them on the floor for the sweeper to clear later.

Don came to me and said, "You know, Debu, I like opera because I grew up with it. I wonder how you find it."

"I come for the comic parts only." I teased him, and we both laughed.

"No. Really. We were a host family to foreign students in Kansas. We took one student to an opera, I think it was *La Traviata*, but he didn't enjoy it. He didn't understand the story, and he said it was too noisy, the soprano was too shrill, too high pitched for him, and the plot was silly."

"Hey, I like him. He said the right things." I squeezed Don's arm in mock humor. "It takes a long time to appreciate operas. Even for many who grow up here, doesn't it?"

A long time back an Indian friend of mine, Prakash, had told me about his host family, the Peters. They wrote to him before he came over to the States. Mr. Peters was a stockbroker in Philadelphia and they lived in Swathmore. They met him at the Greyhound bus station in Philadelphia, took him to the university, and got him settled. It was certainly a great help to him. Then they brought him to their home. They showed him the college there, the town, the golf course, which Mr. Peters loved, and the Longwood Gardens.

On Thanksgiving Day they took him to their home again. Prakash delighted in the ritual with the turkey, the corn bread, the yams, and the pumpkin pie. On Friday they went to the local theater to see *Annie, Get Your Gun*. During the per-

formance, Mrs. Peters whispered to him often to make sure
that he understood the story and enjoyed the play. At the
intermission, he stood with Mr. Peters, a tall and taciturn
man, in the lobby and watched the people interacting with
each other. He was the only foreigner there, but few looked at
him with any serious curiosity. He heard Mrs. Peters' voice a
little distance away:

"Oh, really, he's from Nepal? We have one from Calcutta
this year."

"A Bengali, yes? We had one several years ago." A dignified
man wearing a suit and a hat was talking with her. "Very
docile people. Mention Tagore and they will melt away."

"Didn't you have a foreign student from Ethiopia last year?"
she asked.

"Yes, yes. We taught him how to use knives and forks. It
was a funny experience."

"Oh, you've always managed to find the most exotic students. By the way, how are the Evanses? I heard Mrs. Evans
was sick recently."

"They are fine. Bring your student to our house sometime.
Perhaps they could meet each other."

Mrs. Peters came back. She was very satisfied and said,
"Don't you love this hall, Prakash?"

Prakash told me he didn't visit them anymore. They were
very nice people but he didn't want to be a part of the host family program. He then murmured something about pet dogs, but
I didn't understand. I loved my host family and am still in
touch with them, but sometimes I wonder what motivated
them to go to all the trouble to take care of and entertain the
foreign students. Prakash said casually, "The more exotic the
country, the more the prestige."

I was shocked. "What?" I asked.

He just looked the other way, and I thought how he made
himself more foreign than he had to.

Everyone feels foreign sometimes; it may not be due to the
language, physical appearance, or the accent, but to estranged
circumstances, to situations where one feels unaccepted, to

contact with old friends who have grown in different ways, to deaths of beloved ones. Sometimes, I feel that way too.

My consolation is that a new class is emerging in the world —an educated class—which has gone beyond regional boundaries, and finds more commonality among themselves than among their closer neighbors. They are well read and have common visions and aspirations. This is global citizenship. They may never leave their home countries, but they would feel more at ease with each other than with their own countrymen. I wish I belonged to this global village, to the new generations of boundary-less, knowledge-hungry men and women growing up in all parts of the world.

I was absorbed in my self-analysis when Gayle came near me with a wineglass in her hand. I knew her through professional connections. She worked for a small company that did technical work for the government. I knew she was single and her children were grown and out of the house.

"I didn't know you were involved with the Opera Club." I expressed my pleasant surprise to her.

"I help them when I can. Good to see you here."

"You must know everyone in Idaho Falls. Don't you?"

"Remember, I've been here since 1975?"

"A female engineer in Idaho Falls in the '70s. That must have been a singular experience." There was inquisitiveness in my tone.

"You tell me! Sometimes I felt I didn't belong to my own group."

"That bad?"

"Working as a female engineer was an experience at the beginning. Most of the time I was left out of the office chitchat. Sometimes many forgot I was a female and created awkward moments. Oh it is funny when I think of these now."

She smiled and I knew she had gone through a lot in this town. I find that women are more understanding, more sympathetic to others. They can easily put themselves in someone else's shoes. They can become global citizens easily. I once went to a speech therapist in New York for her advice. She said, "Your accent? Why do you want to change it? We understand you fine. It's charming. It adds to your personality." But in the business world—still a man's world—it is often not an asset. Prejudices have no role in that world but, still, any deviation from the normal is less welcome. I wondered if most women are in the same boat with foreigners in the business world, where the message to a foreigner is not sympathy, not a helping hand, but a stern warning: "Learn, man, learn as quickly as you can because you are alone in this world."

I understood very well what Gayle communicated to me without saying it. She left me, and I kept on looking outside at the twilight. The garden looked dark except for the recessed lights at the edge of the lawn and the lights on the deck. In the distance, the hills had disappeared but the lights from the houses made their presence known.

People started to leave the party. Mrs. Nelson was in the kitchen arranging dishes when I entered. "It was a wonderful party," I told her. "Great food and a good group of people. They treated me well even though I'm not a musician."

"I'm not a musician either, but I have inched into this group." She laughed. "You are doing better than me. They like your open inquisitiveness. Musicians have big egos, but they don't mind you."

"Really? I thought they just tolerated me."

"No, no. It's much better than that. You bring an element of foreignness that is charming." She had a naughty smile on her face. "It would be boring without people like you."

Now I had to laugh loudly. "Mrs. Nelson, I'm glad you told me this truth. I can sleep well tonight."

She looked up and said, "You have found your home."

Chapter Thirteen
OH, CALCUTTA

"Mr. Elmer is not here, but I can take your insurance payment," the partner of my agent at State Farm told me. "Come to my desk."

I sat down on one of the two chairs, and he went to print my insurance statement. I watched his slim, tall figure, working with the little machine. About seventy years old, he was quite adept at what he was doing. His desk was clean with only a few papers, a pen set, a stapler, and a hand calculating machine. No fancy paintings hung on the walls, just a calendar and a picture of an Indian on horseback; the office was not posh by any standard. Mr. Anderson came back with the papers and, as he sat down, asked me casually, "Where are you from?"

"Calcutta, India."

"That's what I thought," he said looking straight at me. "I spent a year there during the War."

"Really?" I have met many like him over the years. Such a revelation is always a little surprise, but I have enjoyed listening to what they remembered of their stay in India.

"We lived in Barrackpore and drove to the fort in the Calcutta maidan. It was very hot. I made many trips to the Burmese and Chinese borders."

I presumed he went on bombing missions. Very few remember the word maidan for the large open space—a huge, sprawling park—between the Ganges River and the exclusive hotels and business section of Calcutta. "The Chourungee Road and the Park Street," he told me, "were the main hubs we hung around." An impressive fit for an old man from this tiny town of Idaho Falls to still remember the names of such a distant place. Who really cared for Calcutta, the Black Hole? Most who went there during the war forgot their rough experience as soon as they came back; they did what they had to do and that was it; their memories become vague like a half-remembered dream, but not for Mr. Anderson. He told me the details of the town, the trams, the movie halls, the market, and people walking everywhere. He didn't get to know the people but he liked what he saw.

"Did you enjoy the spicy curry?" I asked.

"We mostly ate ration, and we had our water in large bags that we used. Once a week I went to eat at the Grand Hotel. Food was very good there." Then he gazed at me for a few seconds, almost absent-mindedly, and said, "It was okay for me as an adventure, but I can't live there. It's so different. I wonder how the few Indians I see here do. They have a decent living, economically secured, you know what I mean, but totally cut off from their social framework."

Startled, I looked at his penetrating eyes.

Just a few days back my classmate in high school, Professor Pal, had written me a letter and wanted a short article from me about living in America for the coming class-reunion. I had left Calcutta so long ago that I was not sure what to tell them about our life here, and especially when they had no clear idea of Idaho, where I now live. Disparate places in the States lose their identity from such a distance. When we lived in Michigan, I received a letter from a friend in India who was coming to New York with an immigrant visa, asking if I could pick him up at Kennedy Airport. The notion of space and time vanishes when one thinks of the States from India. In their mind the U.S.A. is one homogeneous country. What could I write about living in Idaho Falls? And especially how the people from India fit in this society?

The two cities are on opposite sides of the globe, the only obvious similarity being that a river runs through each city. The river, the mother of civilization, molds character, but how differently the two cities have evolved. The Snake River nurtures a fishing, hunting outdoor life, a love for nature and a spirit of freedom, and the Ganges nurtures a calm, spiritual life. One lies in the mountains at 4,700 feet above sea level and the other at an elevation of thirty feet. One is essentially landlocked, and the other connected by sea to the world. Idaho Falls didn't exist when 300-year-old Calcutta was at the center of international trade. One is still a small town in the Old West, and the other is trying to catch up with the modern West. Globalization is imminent with satellites, television, and internet, but will they ever catch up with each other?

Two distinct cultures, histories, and living styles exist in the two locations. Could I truly reflect on the fur traders, miners, and the American Indians who made what Idaho is today, or describe adequately the aspirations of the people who live here now? Similarly, could I truly answer Mr. Anderson's query? How does a first generation Eastern Indian feel about living in Idaho?

"It's a dilemma, I'm sure," I told Mr. Anderson. "A complex, emotional issue. It doesn't have one answer. It was difficult even for the very-willing Europeans, who were farmers, tradesmen, and unskilled laborers. The East Indian case is more complicated because of the very different society they come from, and also because most of them initially came to the States for higher education, not intending to stay. Coming to Idaho is new for East Indians. I'll come back another time and chat with you." I paid him a check and left for home.

But he had plucked a chord in my psyche. I held the foreign aerogram from my friend and gazed at the distant peak of Taylor Mountain. The mountain range beyond the foothills shone beautifully in the afternoon sun. The air was cool and the Canada geese were flying south. Trees hadn't changed color yet; they usually don't display much color in Southern Idaho. The spectacular reds and oranges of autumn are rarely seen here. The sudden appearance of cold weather doesn't allow enough time for the trees to change color. The leaves just wither away.

Where I grew up in India, trees were always green. They didn't lose leaves as they do in cold countries. Only in spring did light moss-green leaves appear on dark green trees, announcing the birth of a new season. Then a fragrance of mango flowers spread in the air. This was the time my mother would fry the newly-emerged, yellow-green neem leaves in oil and feed those to us as an antidote against diseases. She served them with sweet, deep-fried, small pieces of eggplants, but the neem leaves were still extremely bitter. We ate them as the first course because we had to.

My older sister said, "After this, everything tastes wonderful."

Truly it did.

But my mother had died while I was in the States, and I don't think of neem leaves any more.

No snow on Taylor Mountain yet.

I walked up the green, spiral metal stairs to the roof of our three-story house in Calcutta. No mountains, but one can see flat roofs of discolored plaster-houses of various sizes, shapes, and colors everywhere. Water tanks on the roofs stand out as eyesores, and clothes-lines display a variety of colorful cotton saris. If you squint your eyes toward the southeast, you can see the top of the famous cantilevered Howrah Bridge. About a third of a mile long, this bridge symbolizes Calcutta of my high school years—with trams, cars, old red double-decker buses, lorries, hand-pulled carts loaded with goods, rickshaws, and masses of people crowding the only path over the Ganges River from the city to the main railway station in Howrah. The bridge reveals a panoramic view of the two industrialized cities—Calcutta and Howrah—on two sides of the wide river. A few dark, aged boats move slowly through the sluggish current, and there are always a few people bathing on the ghats. On the bridge's footpath sit a few beggars—men with no arms and old women with babies clinging to shriveled breasts—hoping for a paisa from the passers-by. The City of Joy was filmed near this bridge—an ideal location because, as long as I can remember, the perfect movie set was already there, waiting.

No commercial boats carrying goods move on the Snake River as they do in the Ganges; no traffic jams in Idaho Falls either. If one drives for ten minutes in one direction, he will be out of this town. In summer the large potato fields lay beautifully green next to its lonely roads; and in winter they are silent, white seas. The not-so-distant hills provide a picturesque background, and nearby lava rocks remind everyone of the geologic origin of this area. Calcutta is a contrast, being on the flat delta of the Ganges.

Ten million dwell in the city where I grew up. How can I describe to Professor Pal living in an Idaho town with only 50,000 people? And with 30,000 cars. (In India cars are the private preserve of the wealthy and taxi drivers who don't own their cars.) And how is it to live with people who have so much but are engrossed simply to maintain their living standard? My memory of India is from the days of my youth when my parents took care of my needs, but here I am on my own, a significantly different experience. Am I fit to honestly answer Mr. Anderson?

More than 300 years ago, Calcutta was established by Job Charnock as a defensible settlement on the Ganges River for the East India Company. Ninety-six miles upstream from the Bay of Bengal, it was an ideal trading post. Although the name can be traced to a 500-year-old Bengali poem, the city came into existence as business grew around three little villages that were there in the marshlands and jungles of the river. The name "Calcutta" originated from the British pronunciation or mispronunciation of one of the villages, Kalikot.

The story goes that Job Charnock, the controversial administrator of the East India Company, saw a flaming pyre on the Ganges River and standing next to it a young, long-haired Bengali woman, the widow, who was to be thrown into the flames. He fired a shot in the air and rushed to rescue her. The young woman looked at him helplessly as the others fled. A dazed, slim Bengali woman at the moment of her journey to heaven to be with her husband, whom she most likely did not know well. Job Charnock took her home and lived the rest of his life with her in her native land. Charnock resided in India for almost forty years and died there.

To many the emblem of Idaho Falls is the Mormon temple, built in the '40s. From a distance it is a white geometric ziggurat tower stepping gradually to a spire holding a golden angel, Moroni. To some, it is the artificial falls that was created on the Snake River for the city's hydroelectric generator. To me, the Snake River is the identifying mark of Idaho Falls, as the Ganges River is for Calcutta, although many may think of the Victoria Memorial as the symbol of Calcutta. Humans must have dwelled along the Snake River since they lived in Idaho, but 200 years ago no white man ever stepped foot on Idaho, and only a few Indians were there. The first Idaho census of 1870 recorded only 6,168 Indians. The number was, of course, low because they certainly did not line up to be counted by the white man. But the Indians hadn't heard of Darwin. The American West was Darwin-at-work for the humans. And the Indians couldn't survive the competition from the technologically advanced race.

I can imagine the Indian guide on horseback leading Colonel Craig, a pioneer who married a squaw and for whom Craig's Mountain is named, near Camas Prairie, and his joy as he saw light breaking beyond the dark mountain. "Idah'ho," the Indian exclaimed as he pointed to the break of dawn on the mountain. That is how the name of the state originated. No one knows which tribe he belonged to and whether the Indian meant "Look there," "Light," "Sunrise Mountain," or simply the Indian name of the place. Although "Emerging light" or "The sun coming down the mountain" would have a deeper and a more romantic connotation for Idaho, the common meaning of Idaho is known as the "Gem of the Mountains." It was the gold and gems that brought white men to Idaho.

Contrary to this romantic story of the name of Idaho, 100-year-old Idaho Falls was named in 1891 by a petition because land promoters from Chicago thought it would promote the town better than its original name, Eagle Rock. It also rhymed well with other Idaho towns: Post Falls, Twin Falls, and

American Falls.

Idaho Falls was a hunting ground for the Indians, but they weren't forcibly displaced to establish the town. A ferry and a private toll bridge on the Snake River helped to make it a name in the 1860s. Idaho Falls was initially a little crossroad for miners going north to the gold mines of Idaho and Montana and travelers to the West. Then it became a little town for the farmers. Later sugar-beet-growers and tourists to Yellowstone and Grand Teton national parks helped it grow. Finally, in 1949 the need for a remote nuclear testing station put Idaho Falls on the list of significant places in the U.S.A.

A shining yellow school bus went by with young faces gazing out the windows. Their innocent faces reminded me of my very young days in Calcutta. We walked a lot, actually to everywhere—markets, schools, games. Here children go to school by bus, even though it is only a ten- or fifteen-minute walk. In Calcutta, I enjoyed walking to school—I looked at all the stores, observed the people on the street, and joined with other boys along the path. It was more fun than sitting in a bus and gazing out at houses in silent neighborhoods. We didn't have school-buses; that would have been a luxury in my time. Once I stopped to watch a man climb a tall coconut tree with only a short rope around his ankle like a rubber band. He went up fast, just like a monkey, and he had no fear. He cut the coconuts which fell to the ground. I was absorbed by how effortlessly the bare-bodied man did the job and almost got late for my class.

Later when I changed to another high school, I had to walk first for almost fifteen minutes to the bus stop for the public bus. That was also a different experience because the buses were so crowded they would often not even stop. If it was less crowded, meaning there was a little space near the entrance, it only slowed down, and you had to run along side and quickly grab the metal handle with one hand and at the same time find a spot on the step of the bus for one foot. This was a skill we quickly acquired.

Getting off a bus was equally difficult, but the drivers were kinder to women. They stopped a little longer for them. Once the bus was so crowded that we were crammed like sardines in a tin can, and a man shouted loudly when his stop came, "Ladies, ladies to get down. Please stop the bus."

The bus stopped and people made space for him. He got out and immediately walked forward without waiting for the lady he had been shouting for.

When no lady appeared, the annoyed conductor asked the man, "Where is the lady?"

The man looked back at the bus, "The lady? She is, of course, in my heart," and he increased his speed.

I had to take a second bus to reach my new school. This was easier because I could get on at the terminus, but getting off that bus was a different story. I did this routinely for many years, all through my high school senior year and college days. The journey from home took almost an hour, but we never complained. Occasionally, my older sister went at the same time and bought my bus ticket. That gave me a little money to buy a small snack on my way home. Here such a journey would be considered a great hassle and a waste of time. Here high school students must have cars in their senior year, otherwise they are outcasts. What a difference!

However, that avoids the pickpocketers. I was given a beautiful peach-colored Parker pen by a local group when I graduated from high school, and my mother told me to use it only in the house. In fact, she kept it in a trunk under her bed, where all her valuable stuff was stored. After sometime, I questioned the gift lying in a trunk and took it out secretly. I displayed the pen proudly on my front shirt pocket. But as I came down the stairs of a double-decker bus, I clearly and helplessly felt a hand lifting the pen from my pocket. In the midst of the congested bus, the rush traffic outside, and the few moments the bus stopped in front of my college, I could do nothing but get off. I lost my pen on the first day I took it out and I couldn't tell this to anyone. I had to save for many months to buy the pen and put it back in the trunk.

There are no pickpocketers in Idaho. In Calcutta, we thought pickpocketers existed all over the world. In fact, a prominent story in Calcutta was that once the best German pickpocketer and the French pickpocketress were traveling on a luxurious boat to New York, and they met and fell in love.

The German said, "You are the best in France, and I'm the best in Germany. If we get married, and have a son, won't he be the best pickpocketer in the world?

She simply smiled in agreement.

They were so enamored with the idea of having the best pickpocketer in the world that they got married by the captain during the voyage.

They settled in New York and in due time, a son was born. But, alas, the baby was born with a defective hand; his right fist was closed. The doctors were puzzled and didn't know what to do. Their medical knowledge failed them, and they finally said, "We can use surgery when he becomes a little older."

"How sad, we have a boy with closed fist in our family of pickpocketers," he murmured.

"Our dream is gone," she said.

The baby came home from the hospital with melancholy parents. Except for his closed fingers, the baby was adorable, and the parents soon fell in love with the boy.

After a few months, they decided to go to a ball, their usual place of business. This was a very special event, and she took out her most valuable jewelry. She went to give the baby a kiss. The baby's eyes sparkled as she bent over, and she felt a pull on her neck. The baby's hand was firmly holding her beautiful, shiny locket, and a ring fell off his hand.

"That was the ring the delivery-room nurse lost," she exclaimed.

In India as the sun sets and birds settle noisily in nearby trees, children come home from playing. This was the rule and it had happened this way through generations. We washed our hands, faces, and feet, and sat down with our books. No long telephone calls in the evening and no TV shows; they were not there. The only sound that could be heard is the sound of children reading and that of their mother's cooking on coal-fired stoves.

Sometimes I dozed off in front of the book and my father would say, "Why don't you eat your dinner and go to bed?"

"No, no. I'm not sleeping," I would say and start reading more loudly. But my voice would soon be lower and lower, and I dozed off again. Then my mother would call us for dinner.

Older high school students got up very early in the morning to study because that's when the mind is most alert. It is the Brahma-muhurta, the time when one can perceive the Brahman, the soul of the universe. If I was late, my mother would wake me up saying, "The light is on in Ranju's house, he is already studying. Don't you want to get up?"

But when we met with friends, we all proclaimed, "I'm not studying much, are you?"

Education has always been important in India. The tradition comes from the Vedic times when students went away to hermitages to learn from the sages. Knowledge is power in the West because you can influence someone or some issues, but somehow education and acquiring knowledge were always important in India for their own sake.

Thousands of years ago when the sage, Yagyavalka, wanted to retire from family life and wanted to spend the rest of his life as a monk, he divided his belongings for his two wives so they would live well. But his wife, Maitreyi, asked him, "Lord, what shall I do with the wealth if it does not lead me to the ultimate knowledge of life? Give me that instead." The zeal for knowledge, not just a good living, has always been an essence of Indian upbringing.

So many memories came to my mind as I held the letter from Calcutta. I thought of food, such an important item in India, is not so important here. This is the land of plenty. The quandary here is how to restrain from eating too much. Only a week after her stay in this country, a housewife from India went around saying, "What a country! Simply open a can and eat. What a country!" In a few months we watched her pass through the doors sideways.

Food in Idaho is primarily no different from anywhere else in the U.S., except potatoes are cheap and plenty (free for the picking if one has the interest), great beef (which Hindus haven't tasted in India), free trout from the streams, and fresh salmon.

In the U.S. one can eat anything one wants anytime of the year. That wasn't true in my time in India. I went to market everyday in Calcutta for vegetables and fish. Meat—goat or lamb—was very special, perhaps bought once a month, and only about two or three ounces per person. My mother never knew what to cook until I came back from the market. We ate different food in different seasons. No cauliflower, cabbage, tomatoes, or peas in the summer. In a hot country and with no refrigerator in the house, all food was cooked and consumed within a few hours, so lunch and dinner were cooked separately, keeping mothers busy in the kitchen.

Once I pressed a fish in the market and said, "Soft. Old fish, eh?"

The dark, shriveled fisher-woman looked at me for a second. Wearing an old dirty-white sari with faded blue borders, worn out for being thrashed on cement for everyday cleaning of the fish-stains, she sat on the floor with one foot on the wooden base of the big sharp fish-cutting machete. "Let me see your hand." She pressed my muscle saying, "Soft, eh. How would it feel lying here for a few hours at this temperature?"

A feisty lady. But I guess you quickly became one in India.

A few months later I was collecting money for Saraswati Puja—a religious ceremony for the Goddess of learning—and I wasn't doing well. People worship the Goddess in their home and weren't very interested in donating money to young boys to perform separate pujas in the neighborhood. It was considered only fun projects for the boys.

I saw the fisher-woman walking with her load on her head selling left over fish. In half jest I asked, "How about contributing a little money for the puja?"

She put her load down: "What puja?"

"Saraswati puja."

"Do you study hard?"

"Oh sure."

She gave me a 25-paisa coin from a little knot in her sari. It was so unexpected. What does a poor fisher-woman care about learning? I started to give her a receipt, but she picked up her load saying, "What shall I do with that?"

And she walked away.

Clean, lighted supermarkets here. We see the faces but do we really get to know anyone who works there? Do human relations grow here purely based on needs?

Truly, Idaho is so convenient to live in. My first surprise in Idaho Falls was when I found I could park my car in the downtown next to the Bon Marche or any other store I needed to go in. The second surprise was when a salesperson spent time with me on the phone looking up an item, its price, and some other information I needed. This just doesn't happen everywhere else in this country! Telephones suddenly get disconnected in big cities.

Shopping in Calcutta, on the other hand, is a phenomenon, a pleasure and a pain at the same time. I remember a shopping trip in Calcutta when my wife, Catherine, bought a gold necklace. These jewelries are intricate works of art and not available in the States. As soon as I announced that we would go shopping, there was a commotion in the house about who was going to go with us. No one goes shopping alone in Calcutta. And at this stage, no one thinks of the traffic and the turmoil of the journey to the center of the city. Shopping is not a chore, it's an outing. Soon came a long discussion of the sister-in-laws as to who was going to wear what saris. Then someone invariably said, "Let's have tea." By then two hours had passed and they hadn't even discussed where to start shopping. There are three separate areas one could go for twenty-two-karat gold jewelry. After deciding that we would go to Bou-Bazaar, the bride's market, it was time to get dressed. That certainly kept them busy for another hour.

After rickshaw, train, and bus rides, we reached the bride's market. Jewelry stores lined both sides of the street for several blocks. These stores contained beautifully crafted, shining jewelry inside locked glass cases, dazzling in their elegance. A man can easily buy anything from these stores with equal pride, but not so the ladies. They went over the necklaces with sharp eyes—they were either too thin, too heavy, too ornamented, too plain, too gaudy, or some didn't have the right pattern. So, as expected, they walked out of the first store undecided. After a group discussion on the footpath, they marched to the next door. This was very normal. My sisters went to several stores, and, finally, the major concern boiled down to which style would look best on Catherine's beautiful pink skin. The group couldn't agree on one and no one asked or listened to what Catherine desired.

After visiting several stores I said, "Let's go to a restaurant and we can discuss the matter over," and all agreed. Actually, this was a normal part of the shopping spree, especially for an expensive item like jewelry, which always tops the list of importance in Calcutta.

On the way to the restaurant Catherine asked me, "How does one buy anything with so many deciding?"

I smiled because that is how things are done in a Bengali family. There is a consensus building process. One doesn't buy something just because she likes it. It must be liked by others , too. Then they will go from one store to another for the best price, even if it means saving only a few dollars.

Catherine wanted a simple but unique necklace from Calcutta. I pointed out a store with two guards with rifles standing on the gate. "Chanda Jewelers. That's the store to buy jewelry."

"Are you a fool?" my sisters told me. "They are thieves. You'll pay double for the same jewelry."

I guided them to the store. "Just see what's there."

The store was a cut above the ordinary and fitted better with the Western style. Catherine took the lead while others hesitated. She showed me one, "What do you think?"

"Oh, this will go very well in New York."

My plan was to end the shopping, but my older sister said, "It's beautiful, but aren't you paying too much?"

Catherine looked at me with a queer, helpless stare in her eyes: Do we have to go on searching for the ideally priced, unique jewelry?

It was dark when we returned home. We had spent a whole day buying one necklace!

Shopping in Idaho Falls is so convenient that it lulls many from big cities to settle here. It does not have the fancy stores of the big cities, not even a Nordstrom, but it's adequate for a decent living. Before coming to Idaho Falls, I asked what kind of stores the town had.

Mr. Gonzales, the personnel director assured me, "This is a big town. We have everything. We've Sears and Roebuck."

That is it. Sears and Roebuck. That is America.

I always remember the five star Grand Hotel in Calcutta when I pass by the dilapidated sign of "Grand Hotel and Bar" on top of the building in Idaho Falls at Broadway and Yellowstone Avenue. In the early 1900s it was the elegant Eleanore Hotel occupying almost a block on each side of the two streets, but most of the building was destroyed in a fire. In 1940 a little part of this building became the Grand Hotel. It was once the abode of high class prostitutes in Idaho Falls. In the '60s the bar was the town's attraction and was visited frequently by sheep herders and out-of-towners from as far away as St. Anthony and Ashton, over fifty miles further north. On paydays the sheep herders came in from the grazing grounds in the mountains, and the hotel manager helped them spend their earnings. With a little coaxing, they often bought a round for all present. Eager women in the bar soon led them to rooms upstairs. There is no trace of its glorious days now—a very ordinary three-story building straight up on Broadway, all closed up.

What a contrast to the Grand Hotel in Calcutta, which makes you forget you're in Calcutta. The heat and dust and the crowds outside suddenly vanish. It becomes Aladdin's world, instead of the India we know. The best art work from paintings to shawls to jewelry cover the walls and large brass pots with plants surround the place. White-robed Indian attendants with red belts and Maharaja-style hats salute and wait for your command. You step on the thick, red, ornamented carpet and wonder, how did the atmosphere suddenly change? Several restaurants serve Russian, French, European, or Indian cuisine, and tall palm trees line a blue swimming pool in the inside courtyard. It is no wonder that Mr. Anderson still remembers his weekly night-outs in this hotel. For a young soldier it must have been paradise in the middle of a deadly, tropical desert.

Outside the Grand Hotel you see the great Calcutta Maidan —the open ground which stretches to the Ganges River two miles away—where the soccer and cricket games are played, lovers come for strolls, and political rallies are held under the 160-foot-tall Octherlony Monument. One of the best museums in Asia, the Indian Museum, is on its left. The white marble Victoria Memorial, a museum of mixed European and Mughol architecture, further left of the Grand Hotel, contains the history of the British Raj. Behind it is the New Market, not really new, but where you can find anything you want—literally anything. You can easily walk to the Park street, the place for the Westerners, and for restaurants and night clubs in Calcutta. Idaho Falls falls asleep at nine, but not the center of Calcutta, this place. The outside may be sleeping, but inside another Calcutta wakes up.

However, the real Calcutta can only be found in the coffeehouses and perhaps at the canteens of the universities. There the Calcutta intellectuals spend most of their time with hot tea and coffee cups on wooden tables and where tall ceiling fans, darkened by oil and dust, circulate the warm air. They constantly discuss politics, literature, music, film, and all other form of art that flourish in Calcutta. It is the Calcutta of Rabindranath Tagore, whose name the West vaguely remembers now-a-days. In Idaho Falls there are no "coffee houses" or university canteens. Similarly there are no cowboy bars and no country music in Calcutta.

I cannot say for sure where the real Idaho Falls is. However, I feel it is in the pioneer spirit of the people. They came here on individual drives to make a better living, and that individuality is still the essence here. Only it has transformed to a love for living with nature. The pickup trucks in each driveway and the guns many possess still symbolize that drive—to be free and able to go to any rugged place they want to.

The East Indians are docile people. And no one I know of thinks of carrying a gun or buying a pickup truck to be away from the maddening crowd. Job opportunities with the Idaho National Engineering Laboratory and the State University have brought them here. They are not of the type Idahoans are supposed to be. Food, shelter, and physical protection, the basic needs in Maslow's hierarchy, are well taken care of for the immigrant Indians as Mr. Anderson had pointed out; but deep down in their hearts they are ill-at-ease with the all-materialistic, living-for-the-present Western society, as it was not imbibed in their traditional upbringing. Unable to integrate themselves with the activities of the society, most Indians, nay most Asians, live a separate life. They hanker for social acceptance. But the sympathy they look for doesn't exist because everyone is a pioneer here.

Once, after a few drinks in a party, I asked my East Coast friend, Jerry, what he missed most in Idaho Falls. Perhaps there was a melancholy tone in my voice, an expression of regret, a regret for leaving Calcutta, the place of my youth, for ever.

His eyebrows came together for a moment as if I had asked a very wrong question. He glanced at the wall for a few seconds and then said quite seriously, "Most people I know are too busy living a good life. They aren't interested in anything else."

"You mean people here are not academically interested?" I perked up. "Show no curiosity beyond this region?"

"I think they are afraid to. It's not that they lack the intellect, but there is something that stops them. So many blank faces I see. Anything different simply passes by without any concern. If I start a conversation of any substance, I get empty stares. I miss the diversity, you know the kind that exists in a college town."

Jerry was serious, but I said light-heartedly, "I thought it's that way by design. No confrontations allowed. A questioning mind? Big trouble here."

"I don't mean to create problems, so we become like New York City. What I mean is I want to know and discuss the greatest minds of the world. But I don't find any interest from anyone. Can you imagine mentioning Nietzsche or Kant?"

"Perhaps a happy living is contradictory to an expanding horizon," I said. "You know what happened to Gautama Buddha. He was kept within the palace, protected from the outside world. He was happy until he stepped out and saw the real world. He then had no other choice but to get out."

"The outside world exists," Jerry asserted, perhaps a little annoyed, "we cannot deny it even if many would like to in Idaho."

I thought of the writers' group that I went to occasionally, which Jerry didn't know about. The first time I went there I went with a nervous heart, but they accepted me easily. The group consisted mostly of older men and women, who read each other's writings, criticizing in a supportive way. I was excited because writers were the souls of a region, people who understood the society and still dared to think differently and question. After several sittings, I felt I must read something, otherwise I'd not be considered a member. So I read a few pages from my journey to the source of the Ganges River. There was silence during my reading. The first comment was, "I like it, I like its foreign flavor." A lot of good comments came down how I should make it more tight. There were many queries about my travel. I was happy, they accepted my subject.

As I sat down, the woman next to me asked in a whisper, "Who is Brahma?"

I looked at her pleasant, round face, slightly wrinkled with age, and found her sincere. She was one of the leaders of this group. Should I tell her about the creative force of the universe, symbolized in Brahma, the creator? But I simply told her, "Brahma is the Indian word for God."

"Oh." She handed me back the few pages of my memoir, unmarked.

Jerry was perhaps right, as I pondered further that many writers in the group wouldn't use any curse words as if they didn't exist. Even in the midst of stormy emotions, the characters keep their sanity with the language. When I asked, they simply said, "We don't like those words."

I understood what Jerry was talking about and said, "I know what you mean, Jerry. No foreign films. No alien thoughts. No controversies. And everything is beautiful." My sarcasm came out from my heart.

"Life's good here," he replied. "Can't complain. Good place to raise children."

When I was in Calcutta I loved to see American movies because of the colorful, rich life they portrayed. They were like Alice-in-Wonderland mirrors to go through to a new world; it was like seeing the first color movie when we were only exposed to black-and-white films. We longed for a life that was Hollywood. But longing for richness and other such desires evanesce as one grows older, when life becomes more introspective and the inner questions take a bigger role. Gradually, Idaho then becomes more prominent.

Indeed there is enough space, unspoiled nature, and a simple, good life here—safe and protected—away from unwelcome, urban disturbances. There is no identity crisis here, no apparent individual drive to be an immortal. People's identity comes from the community. The rugged individual, the mountain man, died long ago, but many have acquired that old style of the West, "I can do it myself, I don't need help." Soon the style grows on individuals, and they forget there is a big world outside.

In crowded Calcutta, there is less space—as soon as you get out of the airport, the crowd overwhelms you. The roads are narrow and crooked in most neighborhoods, rooms are small, lights dim, and bathrooms smelly. But people are gentle and hospitable. On her first visit to Calcutta, Catherine admired a shawl in a family she hardly knew, and they gave away their valuable shawl to her. They wouldn't listen to her protests. People in Calcutta, however, wish to live in the mental world; they have to because the physical world is too harsh. So literature, art, music, and politics thrive in Calcutta. Coming from Calcutta, where people bump heads over everything, especially over art and politics, I wonder if the arts and liberal thoughts couldn't flourish a little more here?

The big, old Calcutta is intense. It is strong and definitive and will carry you on by its paradigm. There the aspirations are taller and ambitions higher. The small, young Idaho Falls is simpler and quieter, and life much less hurried. It allows one to live a life unconstrained by others' ideals. Idaho is an open book—a wilderness—you can build your own path, your home, your tipi, whatever.

Chapter Fourteen
AT THE WINDCAVE

Dedicated to Lu Xun (1881-1936), whose story "Upstairs in a Wineshop" greatly inspired the author.

The trail bent to the right and the Windcave was only a short distance away on the western slope of the Teton range. The long scree of large stones that led to the cave's entrance could be seen from this spot. Jagdish could not see a path to the cave. "One would have to go over the boulders," he said. A few cedars and junipers grew in the middle of the rocks as if to add a little variety to the scene. He had reached an altitude of almost 8,000 feet. Jagdish leaned against a large rock and took out a water bottle from his small backpack. Hikers were strung out along the trail below—not crowded, but spread out, some with young children. How green it looked around the ravine and how beautiful was the path that curved along the side of the hill. The red soil and the few boulders on the trail made a rugged contrast to the green landscape. The shimmering light of the afternoon sun cast an orange glow on one side of the canyon. A tingling blue sky covered the expanse. What a different scene it was from Newton, where Jagdish lived. He didn't know of any such place around Boston. How could he? He had never gone hiking.

"I'm glad you insisted we get out of the house," Jagdish told me. "My life's so busy. I spend all my time between lab and home. I've no choice. Research of ATP-myosin complexes has become extremely competitive. Everyone is interested in studying muscle control. Very difficult to find something new, but I've had some success. I work aggressively to stay ahead of the pack."

Jagdish gave me a confident look.

Jagdish, a molecular biologist, worked at the Boston Biomedical Research Institute, a laboratory associated with Harvard University. He had been there for the last twenty-five years. Our acquaintance went a long way back to Calcutta, although we hadn't kept up with each other with regular visits or telephone calls. He stayed on the East Coast while I moved around to several places in the country. I hadn't seen him for the last six years, and before that I saw him in Boston only for a day. We grew up in the same neighborhood in Calcutta. One year ahead of me, he was always a studious fellow and left India as soon as he finished college.

"Did you know I was invited as a guest speaker in Heidelberg?" Jagdish told me. "That was a highlight of my career!"

"Wonderful," I said, "you're becoming internationally known." I looked toward the Windcave and wished I were a devoted scientist like him instead of being a government employee managing scientific projects.

I had been on this day hike before. The trail was about three miles long, and I always felt a sense of accomplishment when I reached the cave. Inside, it was dark and cold. One could stand up at the entrance, but then it tapered to a small hole through which wind gushed in. There was a trail beyond the hole but it required ropes, and I had no intention of going any further. On our way up, when I turned north in Victor and took the East Darby Canyon road, the dusty road littered by cow dung and several cattle guards, I wondered if I was totally wrong in taking Jagdish here. I had known him since elementary school days in Calcutta. He wasn't very athletic. While the rest of us played soccer and cricket, he went to the library in the Science College.

However, Jagdish appeared relaxed. He had gained some weight and middle-age showed its indelible marks; his black hair was gray and the eyebrows were turning color. Lines were developing on his oval face and there was a bulging below the chin. His dark brown skin had faded to a lighter color. But his eyes remained sharp as ever, reflecting, behind his heavy glasses, a readiness to accept academic challenges.

In a slight tongue-in-cheek fashion I said, "You know we don't have much to do here, so we explore the mountains."

Jagdish looked at the top of the mountain and said, "This place reminds me of the Himalayas. I saw big mountains a long, long time back when I visited Karseong. You know, the little town halfway to Darjeeling. That was my first visit to the Himalayas. What a contrast it was from Calcutta. Just like now, how different Idaho is from Boston."

"Truly, life's quite different here," I told him.

A young couple carrying heavy backpacks walked by. Their slim figures and solid leg muscles drew our attention. To two middle-aged Indian men they were the epitome of health and radiated youthful exuberance.

"When I heard you took a job in Idaho," Jagdish resumed, "I was surprised. 'Why go to Idaho?' I wondered. It defeats the whole purpose of coming to the U.S. There are so many research labs in the East. You could have certainly found a position. We thought you had given up."

"Now you tell me," I said in mock surprise.

"Really. I couldn't tell you this before. But I see a different picture now. Just imagine how we live. When I go back, Sobha will have to come early and circle around the airport until I come out. Parking is so difficult, and it is risky to walk alone at night. Imagine the crowded Boston airport. Once, I came out at the upper level, and she was circling at the lower level. It was a mess. Idaho Falls Airport was so easy. At first, though, I thought it so puny I felt a little sorry for you."

"In the beginning I felt the same way," I admitted. "It's such a small place."

I remembered a scene in Calcutta when we were boys. Jagdish was standing in the shallow part of a pond, and we were jumping into the pool from the branch of a tall tree. He didn't know how to swim because when he was very young, his mother wouldn't let him go to the ponds for fear of drowning.

The cement steps in the pond were slippery, so he was always afraid he would fall in the deeper part of the pool.

The remote suburb of Calcutta where we lived was rural in our time. Many large trees—mango, lichi, and neem—grew there, and there were several ponds. Only one rice field, but farmers had many small lots to grow vegetables. I loved watching how two farmers rhythmically pulled two ropes attached to a large vessel to bring water from the pond to the furrows. In late September the ripe rice field glowed with light yellow color, and the paddy swayed back and forth in the wind. Small, white clouds floated in the sky. That was a time of carefree happiness. The potato fields in Idaho were very different when they were ready for harvesting—a dull, brown, dying field. They didn't inspire me as the rice fields did.

I gave Jagdish a bag of trail mix and sat down next to him. A mountain chickadee flew by, and I could see the characteristic narrow white streak on its small head running from the bill over and behind the eyes. These hyperactive birds constantly search for caterpillars and insects among the twigs, foliage, and bark of the trees. The Cheyenne and Blackfeet Indians referred to these birds as "the bird that tells us summer is coming."

"So, how is your research going?" I asked Jagdish.

"It's fine." But his relaxed face quickly became tense. "But, you know, I've to fight at each step. For everything. The SOB's try their best to stop me, but I won't give them an inch. Cliques, cliques are everywhere. You don't know how hard it is. I struggle constantly for funds, for students, for publishing. You have time to go on hikes; we work all the time, Saturdays and Sundays."

He looked at a Douglas fir rising crookedly behind a large rock. It survived in spite of the little space. I knew he was a hard-working man, very devoted to the pursuit of science. In the past, if you weren't involved in scientific research, Jagdish didn't have much to talk about with you. He gave no time to anything but his work. His wife, Sobha, wrote the Christmas cards each year, signing for all of them: Jagdish, Sobha, and Girish, their son.

A ground squirrel came out from under the rock. The always-alert, tiny animal looked up several times and Jagdish threw a peanut. I then knew he was relaxed again. The squirrel ate the peanut standing on its hind legs and scurried back under the rock. A family with a young boy and a girl passed by.

"Did you know my mother passed away two years ago?" Jagdish asked me.

"Sorry, I didn't know."

"She was almost eighty. I hadn't seen her for the last three years. She was not well, but I couldn't go home to visit her. It was contract renewal time when her health took a serious turn. The timing was very bad. I was incred-

Robert Bower

ibly anxious to submit a great proposal for five-year funding. What was I to do? I also needed some good data before I could write the grant. I was awfully involved." He stopped for a few seconds and spoke in a low voice, "I couldn't go for the shraddha ceremony either. She was cremated within twenty-four hours, as you know. So, what was the use? She was gone anyway."

I didn't know what to say, but it seemed he was calm. Was there a way to console a man who had not attended his mother's funeral because he was far away in a foreign country or because he was too busy with his work? With no tall mountains around, the expanse of the sky appeared vast. The sky had been a small crystal blue opening in between the hills when we started. Now it was spacious, but its sharp color had dimmed.

"Last year I went home to perform the annual rites for my mother," Jagdish continued. "But it felt strange, as if I didn't know anyone. Over the years our neighborhood has grown. It seemed I didn't notice it before. I walked around alone. The rice field was gone, replaced by new buildings, and one couldn't see the drug factory behind the field. Then, at the edge of the neighborhood, I saw Aunt Malati's house. It had remained the same—the same one story brick house with flat brown windows. She was very affectionate toward me, you know. I called her aunt, but she wasn't a relative. My mother told me she and her family came from the same village as our family in East Bengal. That is Raipara near Dacca. Our family never talked much about it. I think they tried to blot it out. It was too painful to leave our ancestral house during the '47 riot."

Jagdish's eyes gazed at the stony range next to the Windcave. The solid rocks were arranged in vertical columns, and, below, the pines formed a dense green mass. And the scenery gradually led to the cave in the middle. It was an unusual landscape—rugged and green at the same time. Jagdish looked peaceful, but it appeared to me he had drifted to a different land. He had never taken any time off for himself, and I thought, perhaps he had never sat quietly in a surrounding like this one.

Jagdish turned his head toward me and continued, "You remember Aunt Malati? I knocked at her door. A man came out and when I inquired about her, he gave me a strange look, saying, 'They left long ago. I don't know where they live now.'

"I was surprised. Did she also die? I suddenly felt out of touch with all the people in Calcutta. I was a stranger where I had grown up. Soon a scene from Bangladesh came to my mind, a scene that my mother had described to me. It was a few months before the Independence of India. The Hindu-Muslim riots flared up violently in Dacca before the Partition. In Raipara Hindus and Muslims had lived together in harmony, but now no one knew who was a friend and who was a foe.

My mother told me about a Hindu doctor, who said, 'I treat both the Hindus and the Muslims. Who would harm me?' He went out for a stroll and never came back.

"It was chaos everywhere. Our family had a good size property with farm lands, a large pond, and lots of fruit trees. There was a small Shiva temple on the property where the Hindus came to worship. My parents couldn't decide if it would be safe to stay in the village after the Partition. They delayed their departure, hoping everyday for things to change. But it only got worse. Finally, one day the Muslims surrounded the village and started to destroy property and kill the Hindus. My parents saw the line of torches progressing toward their house. Fires were burning high in several places, smoke rising from distant houses. They were dazed like animals in front of car headlights. It seemed there was no escape. Aunt Malati's family saved them. They had a boat ready, and as the mob was approaching, they sneaked out through the large orchard of mango and jackfruit trees. Without their help my parents would have been killed.

"Aunt Malati and my mother were very close. I used to stop by Aunt Malati's house often on my way back from school. It was very pleasant to visit her. I remember that so well. She used to give me freshly cooked rooti and raw sugar to eat. Simple food, but I enjoyed that very much.

"When I was in India for a conference about seven years ago, my mother told me about Aunt Malati's youngest son, Amit, who was a very good student. 'Could you help him go to America for higher studies?' she asked. 'He is like your little brother.' I wasn't interested, but to appease my mother, and especially because I lived abroad and couldn't really do anything for her, I said, 'Sure, I'll do it for Aunt Malati.' Indeed, I met with them and explained to Amit how to apply for fellowships. And I promised him I'd help. Certainly there would be a school for him in the States. 'Write me when you are ready,' I told him."

Jagdish stopped talking, and our attention shifted to a Western tanager that flew in and sat on the Douglas fir branch. Its small, lemon-yellow body with black wings and tail and a red head looked lively. It was a common bird in Yellowstone and the Teton mountains. How beautiful it was on the bough of the evergreen.

"Life is strange," Jagdish said while watching the restless bird. "You know, that boy, Amit, wrote me a long letter a year later. He had lots of questions, but in the hassle of things I put it aside."

Jagdish was the most studious boy among us, but he was also the most idealistic. The tanager flew away, and Jagdish sighed. "I never wrote him back." He stared at the empty fir branch.

There was no trace of that boyish face now. And as I looked carefully, those enthusiastic eyes were no longer there either. His self-imposed demands and a competitive spirit for research had raised a wall around him. I wondered if we thought of these things only when we came to a place like this —so many things we each wished we had done that were still undone.

I asked if he was in touch with any of our old friends. He was not. He said he used to get a letter or two in the past but hadn't received any in the last few years. He didn't find the urge to write to anyone either. All his correspondence was professional.

"You know, I really feel sorry for not seeing my mother more often," Jagdish said softly. "It's sad. I left home forty years ago, and I saw her only five times after that. Then, when I visited Calcutta, I spent most of my time at the Bose Institute giving seminars. She never complained and only wished I did well. That was my mother! She never asked for anything."

"What happened to Aunt Malati's son?" I asked.

"I have no idea," he said.

"Shall we go further up?" I asked, and got up.

"No, no. Let's stay here for a while. It's very peaceful."

Jagdish searched his pocket and took out a cigarette packet. "I don't smoke often," he said as he lighted one. A blue puff came out of his nose, and he looked at the distant hills. I remembered how in the University canteen he used to blow rings of cigarette smoke, especially when he was in deep thought. They floated out of his mouth in distinct intervals, one after the other, and then he would make an assertive statement. Those were the days long gone.

"I think I should smoke a pipe," Jagdish said and smiled. "I like the image of a scientist with a pipe in his hand."

I thought of my first backpack trip. I went with a few friends to the Moose Creek, not very far from here, east of Victor toward the Teton Pass. It was a serene meadow. What I remembered most was my first view in the morning from a corner of the tent—a light blanket of snow covered the whole area. Then I saw a group of deer grazing near our tents. It was such an uplifting experience to be in the silent wilderness. It would not have been possible if I hadn't got out of the rut I was in. But Jagdish was right about me, I thought. I gave up research because I felt "publish or perish" was not taking me anywhere. Truly good work requires creativity; it does not come simply from hard labor. My papers were forgotten in a short time. The great pleasure of seeing one's name on a technical paper died long ago within me. If it did not last beyond the boundaries of time and the small geography where we lived, what was its use? I accepted the government job and came over here. Idaho? That was a whole new territory, unknown to my Indian friends. Jagdish's words brought me back from my own reminiscences.

"Did I tell you I dropped by my son in Chicago?" Jagdish said. "Since I was coming here for the seminar and I've not seen them for sometime, I arranged to give a seminar in Chicago. Girish is working there at the Heart Institute."

Jagdish looked straight into my eyes and said, "I also had another motive. No harm in telling you. There is this suar-ka-baccha (son of a pig), Don Berger, a member of the National Academy of Science (who works in Chicago). Very well known. I was talking with him for sometime about my work, and I told him all I knew and helped him clarify some intricate concepts. I thought he would endorse my paper for publication in the Proceedings of the Academy—a very prestigious journal like the Proceedings of the Royal Society in England. But when the time came, he simply refused. Bastard! I told this to several of my colleagues, and they said he was like that. He wouldn't help you unless he gained something directly. The SOBs! But I finally found a way. I sent the paper to a well known scientist in Japan, and he immediately communicated it to the Academy. The article was published last month. I wanted to give a seminar in Chicago, at his Institute. to show him we can do it without his help.

"Anyway, Girish and Monica came to receive me at the airport. It was good to see them. When we were in the car, Girish said, 'Dad, we have tickets for the ballgame tonight. You stay home and relax.'

"'Who is playing?' I asked to be courteous. I have no interest in sports or politics, as you know. When Girish was very young, Sobha took him to tee-ball practices. I never went. Not that I didn't want to, but I really had no time. Sobha badgered me often to come home early so I could see him play, but she didn't understand how competitive our work was, especially for a foreigner.

"Once I planned to come to his game and closed the lab early in the afternoon, but then, just as I was walking out, the telephone rang. The call came from the NIH. They fund my work so I had to take it. The NIH guy wanted to know the results of my last experiment. But that was only a pretext. He called to request me to be a member of his team for site visits. That was a great honor. I got delayed by the call, but I still rushed out. It was Girish's first game in the Midget League, you know the Little League they play. As I was driving along Route 30, I thought how surprised and happy they would be to see me. Girish's little round face with a baseball cap came to me. It had a big red A in front, and he was very proud of his cap. The evening before, I threw a few balls to him in the backyard, and he would say, 'Harder, Daddy, harder,' but I couldn't throw hard. I was afraid he would miss it or get hurt. Anyway, as I was passing by the Beacon Street, I swerved by the tram car, but I didn't see a car coming from the side road. I had an accident. It was not serious, but by the time I reached home they had already left, and I didn't know where they were playing."

Jagdish's eyes searched beyond the mountain, but the tall Teton peaks could not be seen from this place. Only the lighted sky stared back at him. He took a drink from the bottle and told me his Chicago trip in a lifelike fashion. I clearly saw him in Chicago:

"It's a home game, Daddy," Girish told his father. "The Blue Jays are playing. Last year they beat the White Sox. It will be exciting to see Roger Clemens play."

"We buy season tickets every year," Monica informed him swinging her head sideways, just doll like. Her dense, black hair, cut short at the neck, made her small face look full, three dimensional. Her eyes also grew bigger with enthusiasm. Jagdish liked his daughter-in-law very much, she had such enthusiasm. It was hard to imagine she taught psychology at Northwestern. "This year it'll be exciting," she said. "Frank Thomas and Al Belle are playing very well, The White Sox might go to the World Series."

"You think they will?" Girish asked her.

"Yes." She was confident.

They were both excited about baseball. Sobha and Jagdish didn't have any common hobby. Sobha liked gardening, and Jagdish enjoyed reading. They both liked to go to Indian parties, but that became boring after a while. They saw the same people at each party and had the same discussions: the engineers talked about how much money people made, others discussed the latest issues in *Newsweek*, and the politics in India. And the same Bengali food, only more oily. Jagdish was excited about his work, but Sobha needed this outlet. So he went along.

"Don't talk much about baseball to Daddy," Girish looked back and told Monica, "He doesn't enjoy the game. Isn't that true, Daddy?" A teasing smile on his face.

"No. I don't mind," Jagdish told them.

"Naah, Dad," Girish patted his dad's hand affectionately, "you never had time to come to my games."

"How is your work going?" Jagdish asked Girish.

"Work? That's fine, Dad. I think I found a new way vitamin E can help reduce cholesterol deposits in the arteries."

"You found a way to enhance the anti-oxidant stimulation of enzymes?" Jagdish was excited about his research. He immediately saw it could open a brand new line of research. But Girish was calm, and said, "Later, Dad. Monica made me promise—no long discussions of work at home. She said if we bring work home, it will eventually take over our life. We'll go to my lab tomorrow and then we can discuss this in detail."

"All right, all right," Jagdish had to say, but he couldn't understand why his son wasn't excited to tell him right away.

"Did Girish tell you we're learning Spanish?" Monica looked at her father-in-law.

"In two decades," Girish added, "twenty-five percent of the U.S. will speak Spanish. Think about it!" "We're planning a trip to Spain next year," Monica said.

"We'll be proficient by then," Girish said confidently. "Que piensas, Monica?"

"Como no. Have you and Mommy gone to Barcelona?" she asked Jagdish.

Spain? Jagdish didn't know any molecular biologist in Spain. So he never thought about that country. Besides, why go to Spain? And learning a language just for a trip to Spain?

"We didn't have the time," he told them.

The car went to a narrow alley and to a single-car garage, near the University of Chicago. It was an old building, but inside was a surprise. A corridor led to the kitchen on one side and the living room at the other end. Two bedrooms in between. A gorgeous, large painting of the Delhi Fort with a procession of people and guards on horses hung on the front wall of the living room. In the painting, light from the setting sun fell on the Red Fort which made it glow and look larger than real—very spectacular. A bright yellow oriental carpet provided a warm feeling. There was a large beige sofa with lots of colorful pillows—matching the red color of the fort—and several Norwegian rosewood chairs. A stereo set was in one corner with four, small Bose speakers almost hidden around the room. A statue of Athena stood on the rosewood bookshelf, simple but very elegant. The coffee table was made of glass with heavy solid glass legs—very modern. The other thing that drew Jagdish's attention away from the Red Fort was a unique plant with soft, light green, long leaves under a recessed light. The room was very beautifully decorated and very cozy. Jagdish felt it must have been designed by a professional decorator.

A small, metallic-bright, red Jaguar sports car lay on the carpet with a tiny antenna sticking out from the end. "That's Girish's toy," Monica told Jagdish with a naughty smile. "It's radio controlled. He plays with it all over the apartment."

The guest bedroom was equally impressive. It was small and lightly furnished—a redwood rollover desk and a writing chair at one corner, a double bed with lace skirts and a simple matching cover, a book shelf and an upholstered chair. The striking thing was how subtly all the colors matched in the room—beige, very light orange, and light green.

When Girish and Monica returned late at night, they were quiet but Jagdish was awake, perhaps the usual parents' worries kept him from falling asleep. Girish said, "Sorry, Dad. Our friends wouldn't let us go home without having a drink. You know the White Sox won by 7 to 5. It was a great game."

They went to bed immediately, but Jagdish kept on thinking how well-adjusted Girish and Monica were. Then he wondered, "If one wasn't born here, could baseball get into one's blood?"

Jagdish's words made me think of the McDermott Field in Idaho Falls. Idaho Falls has a baseball team that plays in the A league and most of the time they lose. The stadium was so small and they played so badly, there was no home field advantage. The fun part was being with the people. I had gone there several times but the game was always an excuse, it was the company that was fun.

From where we were, the front of the cave looked like the tall, rectangular gate of a medieval fort—a fort hidden in the Idaho mountain. The shadow from one side made it look as if its door had closed; we were there too late to get in. The sound of the waterfalls below the cave reverberated in the area.

"How was your talk?" I asked Jagdish, thinking this would give him a chance to tell me about his work.

"Well, I always give a very good talk," Jagdish said without a hint of modesty. "I have a reputation as a good speaker. You know I work on muscle tissue regulation. For example, how calcium gets inside the cell and interacts with the proteins. How the genes work in muscle cells. Very exciting research now."

Jagdish took out another cigarette. I ate dried apricots. A man came by with an Airedale. It was pleasant just to sit there and listen to Jagdish.

The sky changed color from clear blue to a faint, white-blue, but so gradually that I didn't notice it earlier.

"Only one fellow at the seminar was familiar with my work," Jagdish continued. "I was essentially unknown to the audience. I graduated from this university, but everything felt strange. The labs were rearranged and all new people. I walked around the corridors. There was no resemblance to anything when I went to school there. As I came to the restrooms in the third floor, however, I chuckled, remembering what happened to Ramesh, a new graduate student, when he first arrived in the fall.

"You know Chicago is very cold and windy in winter. Not as cold as in Idaho, but that was Ramesh's first winter. He was late for class and walked fast in the bone-chilling cold of the early morning. But suddenly he had to go to bathroom and, in his rush, entered the ladies room. He didn't notice anything special and went to the stall. But as he sat down, a girl came in, and he immediately realized his mistake. What would happen if he was caught? It was not only embarrassing, but people might think he was there with some ill-motive. It was his third month in the country. He thought if he was caught, he would be expelled from the school and sent back to India. Imagine his situation.

"The girl stood in front of the mirror, combing hair and putting on lipstick, but then she noticed that the door of the stall was locked, but no feet showed. Ramesh had lifted his feet up.

"She knocked at his door. 'Is anyone here?'

"He kept silent. Frozen.

"The girl went away saying, 'Strange. I must report this to the janitor.'

"Ramesh ran out as soon as the door closed without wiping his bottom."

Jagdish laughed at this old incident, and his face lit up.

To be invited for a seminar at a prestigious place like the University of Chicago was a great honor, and I was proud of Jagdish. He must be very content although I wasn't sure from his facial expression. Being curious about his encounter with the scientist, I asked, "So, how did Don Berger treat you?"

Jagdish looked at me with a jerk and nodded his head sideways saying, "He wasn't there." He stared at the cave. Two men were coming down, carefully watching their steps.

"You are happy here," Jagdish said, "sometimes I wonder if it's worth what I do. You know, I was kind of sad after the seminar when I returned to Girish's apartment. This had happened to me before. I make all these preparations for a presentation and do give excellent seminars, but in the end, I feel I was only an actor on a stage trying to prove I'm good. It has no permanency. Have you ever put yourself in an actor's shoe? It's very lonely there. I empathize with the middle-aged, not-so-great actor. You were courageous to quit this nonsense and come here."

I thought of the meeting I attended yesterday in the office. The Assistant Manager called for the meeting to broadcast a report prepared by his staff. It was on the role of systems engineering in our work, which is management of a large government laboratory. Near the end of the talk almost everyone agreed that we should have this expertise. Many suggested we needed to hire someone trained in systems engineering.

Dave, an intern, was sitting quietly and looked restless. Finally he said, "I understand what mechanical engineering is and for that matter nuclear engineering and electrical engineering. Would someone explain simply what systems engineering is?"

The presenter babbled for a few minutes and then admitted he didn't know exactly what it was and what qualified one to be considered a systems engineer. He looked at the Assistant Manager for support, but he only said, "You are the expert here." The A.M. then asked, "Who knows it in this room?"

The question went around the table, but no one could clearly define systems engineering or explain it in terms of other engineering. The A.M. finally stood up and pronounced that the other labs had systems engineers. Everyone immediately agreed that we needed it as part of our core competency.

This is what we do in the government. If Jagdish thought what we did was worthwhile, why spoil his image?

Jagdish broke our silence. "At the airport, Girish gave me a hug and said, 'Next time you come I'll have a ticket for you, Daddy.'

"I had pushed him hard to excel in school. I told him often, 'Remember, with brown skin, you will be judged differently. It's all competition, everywhere. You must strive harder.' Recognition was very important to me. My whole life is spent for that. But at that moment I felt I was perhaps wrong. There was more to life than just publishing research papers. Girish and Monica are seeing life from a different perspective. I gave him a hug and silently wished him happiness—a mental peace I didn't have.

"Monica said, 'Bring Mommy along next time.'

"'Sobha is involved in so many things, she hardly has time,' I replied. 'But I'll tell her.'

"The next thing I knew I was in Idaho Falls."

Jagdish stopped and looked at me vacantly. The cigarette burnt brightly in his mouth, stronger than usual, and he slowly released a stream of blue smoke.

"You know, it was good to see Girish and Monica spend time together. When I married Sobha I was so preoccupied, I didn't have any time left for her. But she came as a shy Bengali girl and didn't complain. That was almost thirty years ago."

A young couple in their late twenties hiked by us, and we could hear their conversation. The short girl with bushy, light red hair picked up a wild flower and said, "When I win the lottery, I'll have a cottage in the Alps. And I'll buy a Ferrari for you."

The man gave her a hug sideways. Their smiling faces were those of a couple still in the courting stage.

Jagdish seemed to hesitate a little and said, "You have not visited us for a long time. Our lives are different now-a-days. You'll be surprised to know Sobha's schedule. She is so busy we hardly have any time together. When she came as a new bride, she didn't know anything here. Now I'm left behind."

I wasn't sure what he was hinting at. Jagdish was in this country for almost forty years, and he knew all there was to know. His disheveled hair fluttered in the air. Was he expressing regret at not understanding this society?

"When I come home, she is usually not there," Jagdish went on. "I eat alone. She has meetings to attend. All volunteer work." Jagdish paused for a few moments and stared at the distance. The orange glow of the sunlight had softened to a light pink, and the green hills were doused in the tender color.

"My work was always first. Perhaps, I didn't give her time for so many years, she has grown into her own world. How different it is now from when I first saw her in Sodepur in her parents' house.

"My mother and my uncle, her brother, took me around to interview several prospective brides my mother had selected for me. It was awkward, but that was the way marriages were arranged.

"I remember Sobha's bashful face when her mother brought her to the room for the "showing." She sat there with lowered eyes and answered a few questions from my uncle. He asked her to raise her head so we could get a good view. My uncle even asked Sobha to walk a little. It was a part of the procedure. So there was nothing hidden—no defects of any kind. It was humiliating, but I felt as helpless as her. Then the older folks left one after another with lame excuses. The intent was for us to get acquainted. But the atmosphere was so serious.

"Sobha gazed at the design of the bedspread where she was sitting. The bed cover was probably bought just for this occasion. Her face was so innocent! Long black hair flowed over her back—nicely oiled and combed. Her young, olive-color, small face with a small nose, light eyebrows, and big eyes was charming and attractive. I looked at the unpretentious, white champa flower with a faint yellow tinge on the inside petals that was in her hair, perhaps put there by a cousin, and I felt tender and wanted to take care of her. She was someone I could love and spend the rest of my life with. I didn't know what to say to a candidate to be my bride. How do you interview someone to be your wife?

"I knew she had a B.A. degree in Bengali literature. After a long silence, the only thing I could ask was, "Are you going for an M.A. degree?"

"She kept her head down and nodded, saying, 'Yes,' in a faint voice.

"I looked at the discolored walls in the small room, as it was in most middle-class houses in Calcutta. A built-in concrete shelf contained a large Philips radio and a few books. At one corner stood a statue of Ramakrishna. I remembered going back to Chicago and thinking of my lonely life in the campus. I hadn't socialized much in the U.S. and didn't know what the life of a housewife, especially that of a young Indian wife, was like. I then started to tell her about my daily routine, the cold weather, the traffic, the lab, and my small efficiency apartment. It felt good to talk to her.

"'If it is so cold,' she asked, 'how do people go to work?'

"Well, it was all decided, and we were married in a month. I remember it so well when we came to Chicago a week after our marriage. She was so afraid to go out and talk to an American. My friends threw a party for us. She said 'Hello' when they arrived, and simply bent her head a little without looking into their eyes, then, 'Goodbye,' when they left. That was all she could bring herself to say.

"Within a few months of our marriage, I got an offer of a post-doctoral position at Harvard. It was a great opportunity, and I determined to devote myself fully to research. I realized Sobha's uneasiness in a foreign land. That was natural, but there was nothing I could have done. What alternatives did I have?

"I remember how during the marriage ceremony the old, shriveled priest put her small palm on mine and wrapped both our hands with a thin, red cloth and flowers and durba grass. I felt her soft nervous hand surrendering to my care. Now I wonder did I really take care of her? As you know, the auspicious times for marriage ceremonies are always late at night. We were tired, and in the midst of so much light and onlookers and the elders sitting around the yajna fire on the floor, you feel the responsibility of the marriage. She was given to me to love and cherish and to protect. But I wonder if I have fulfilled that.

"During our first meeting in Sodepur, she wanted to know if one could find Bengali literary magazines in the U.S. I comforted her saying, 'Sure. We get the puja issues of Desh and Ananda Bazaar magazines. We get them as soon as they are available in Calcutta.' But I had no time to read Bengali stories and novellas, and when we came to Chicago, I forgot to order them.

"As soon as we moved to Boston, I got myself very involved in the lab and had no time for her. I didn't help her much in the house either. Well, I didn't neglect her, but she knew what was important to me. Her only recreation was at parties in other Indians' houses. But there I talked and argued with the men and she went to the kitchen to talk with the ladies.

"She asked me once about my work, but it was useless to explain to her. She wouldn't understand it."

Jagdish shifted his legs and looked at a small rock on the trail. How interesting, he thought, one could easily mistake it for a little bird. Truly, he observed, there were so many rocks of varying sizes and shapes along the path. They could make a fascinating border around Sobha's fern-leaved yarrow patch. It was a sudden discovery, and he felt like picking up one to take to Boston.

"Now when I come home," Jagdish continued, "Sobha is usually out—committees and meetings. It all started soon after Girish graduated from high school. She said, 'Now that

I've some time, do you think I could help the Red Cross? Janet from next door has asked me.'

"I was surprised: Sobha doing work for the Red Cross? But I thought it was a good idea, and I had just started a new project, so it was even better. She loved gardening. She and Girish made our flower garden the envy of the neighborhood. Girish was not there to help her, but it was in good shape anyway.

"A couple of years later, one day I came home late and was surprised to see so many cars parked in our driveway and on the road. There was a big party in our house.

"Sobha wore a beautiful light-blue, silk sari and she had a prominent bindi mark on her forehead. She looked young and attractive. 'Remember,' she told me, 'I told you I offered our house for a party to raise money for the homeless? Come, I'll introduce you to the guests.'

"She took me around and they were so friendly and courteous to her. I shook hands and nodded my head. I was unknown and simply the spouse of the hostess. She introduced me to a lady with an expensive silk dress, 'This is my husband, Jagdish. He lives in the lab.' She had a mischievous smile and her eyes glittered. She squeezed my hand in a romantic way. 'I heard so much about you,' the lady replied.

"A man in a blue pin-stripe suit said, 'Your wife has so much enthusiasm, she is an asset for us.' I presumed he must be an important man, perhaps a high ranking executive in a big company. I watched her mingling in the crowd, a happy smile here and a nod there, and I wondered when did she learn all this? I stood at one corner with a drink and overheard the conversations around me, about Oxfam, the Shelter program, the need for money for the Soup Kitchen; the United Way was in trouble and couldn't raise enough money last year, Reagan was of no help.

"A tall man in a tweed jacket came to me and said, 'I'm the mayor of Auburndale. It is very kind of you to offer your house for this occasion. Your garden is wonderful. I wish mine was half as good. I've known Sobha for the last two years. I'll tell you she is such a wonderful person and a great organizer. She has raised $50,000 this year alone for the homeless. Sobha told me you're very busy at the lab. That has given her time to be involved with these projects. I'm talking to her to be the secretary of the United Way Campaign next year. What do you think?'

"I had no idea what people do at the United Way. 'That will keep her busy,' was the only thing I could say.

"Then when I was in the kitchen, I heard her talk to the group in the living room. She spoke so clearly, and so confidently. She told them about an idea based on the Mormon Welfare Program. They could work with the local farmers to receive grains and vegetables that did not satisfy the farmers' quality or grade requirements. The Mormons do it in a very organized fashion. They even have their own farms and canneries, and they store food in big warehouses for eventual distribution. The Mormons have the advantage of a huge volunteer workforce. The question was whether the model could be used in some way in the Boston area. She suggested that if the churches could be mobilized, this was possible. She stressed that they needed to learn how to package food and raise funds to build warehouses for this purpose.

"So many call her every day I have stopped answering the phone. It's not the same Sobha you've seen before. Sometimes she takes me to some of her big gatherings. It's a different world. In several of her meetings I have seen them talk in a way as if they were doing the most important thing in the world. That was the only purpose in their life. I don't understand it.

"She was on the TV twice talking about their work in the Auburndale area and soliciting donations for the needy."

Jagdish gazed at the clump of quaking aspens a little distance away. Their small, almost-round leaves fluttered in the wind. He observed the faint green trunks with some interest – not white like birch trees, and the knots were quite prominent. They added a beautiful distinction to the surrounding.

"You know, we often don't realize the potential a woman has," Jagdish said in his old assertive voice. "It is unknown to me how this happened to Sobha. The thing is she loves it and everyone loves her for that. And you know what? I am fighting every day for thirty years to earn that respect."

A group of young boys came down the slope. Their fast pace and noisy voices demonstrated they hadn't lost a bit of their initial energy. They would probably reach the parking lot in an hour. Jagdish watched them until they vanished at the bend.

I thought how wonderful it was for Sobha to find a role for herself and be happy with it. We sat there quietly. There was nothing to tell Jagdish. I could vividly see our lives from the old, carefree days in Calcutta to now when they were essentially carved in stone—lives driven by our genes. How much power did we really have to mold our lives? Did fate deal a hand when we were born and we simply played that hand for the rest of our lives? Few strove hard and consistently for their ambitions, like Jagdish, but when they came to middle age and saw that the ambitions were illusory and realized what they had lost in life while pursuing their goals, what should they do? Or was there a way to console such a person?

I had no answer and looked fixedly beyond the mountains, wishing the Teton peaks to show up magically in the sky.

The sun dropped behind the hill and the sky looked very pale.

It would take about two hours to get down to the parking lot. "We have hiked enough for today," I told him. "Let's go down now."

"Oh no, no." Jagdish stood up. "I want to see the cave."

Suddenly he had extra energy, as if to make up, in one afternoon, for all the many things he hadn't done. I then saw he was back to himself again.

"Come on." He charged ahead.

Chapter Fifteen
THE RAMAYANA

Although the weatherman predicted the day to be overcast, the morning turned out to be excellent. The sun glowed brilliantly, and only a few little clouds floated in the autumn sky. The Khataks were relieved that the day turned out so well for their daughter's wedding. They had rented the Westbank Hotel for the occasion—the circular highrise on the Snake River with balconies overlooking the waters. Most of their out-of-town guests stayed in this hotel, and it was a first visit to Idaho for many of their guests. They walked around the river, visiting the falls, the ducks and the geese, and the site over the boulders where the first bridge was built 130 years ago. That wooden bridge, the crossing point for goldseekers to the north in Montana, eventually created this little town. Since I lived here and was a friend of the Khataks, I stayed inside and watched the ceremony progressing in the Yellowstone Room. In the bright light of the hotel I actually remained mesmerized and listened to the words of the priest. I had heard the words before, even in my own case, but until now never really listened for their meaning. Perhaps no one does it at the time when it is specifically meant for him or her. Arya heard the words and followed what she was told to do. But she was in a daze.

Arya and Alan were walking around the fire, she behind him. The end of her red, Benarasi-silk sari was tied to one corner of his kurta. She had a veil, but I could see her face beautifully decorated with tiny dots of sandal-wood paste and adorned with earrings and a shiny nose-ring; a tika hung from her hair to her forehead. With an oval, olive-color face and long, black hair braided with little pink and white flowers, she looked very pretty as a bride should, and Alan, dressed in Indian clothes, churidar pyjama and Bengali-kurta, looked like Indra himself—tall, erect, and proud. His shaven, pink face flushed in the shiny light under the yellow canopy with white frills. The solemnity of the occasion had made them serious, especially Arya. Her eyes were downcast, a sign of willing obedience. Any other time, I thought, she would have snickered or protested.

A crowd of well-dressed people watched them in silence. Men in dark suits and women in dresses roamed quietly holding glasses in their hands. The Indian ladies wore the most gorgeous and colorful saris and gold ornaments they owned; they must have taken out the whole stock of gold jewelry they kept in safety deposit boxes. And I knew those were real gold —22 karat. Very rarely does such an exotic gathering take place in Idaho Falls. It is the Intermountain West, and few immigrants, especially those from Asia, think of coming here. The few that were here were because of the excellent nuclear laboratory. Almost all the Indians came here for research work; all were engineers and scientists, many with Ph.D.s.

I remembered little Arya. She was only seven when she came to Idaho Falls. Her father, Sushil, finished a Ph.D. in nuclear engineering from Iowa and accepted a job at the Idaho National Engineering Laboratory. When he was a first year student in Iowa, his mother insisted that he should be married (how could he toil over the cooking fire in a foreign country and study at the same time?), and she found the right girl for him. Sushil went home to satisfy his mother and marry the girl he had never seen before. But that is how it is done in India, and you love the girl you marry. Arya was born a year later.

She was a little older than our children, and the first day she came to visit our house, she took over their games and told them what to do.

"Where is Leia? You don't have Leia? How could you play 'Star Wars' games without her?"

"You can have Yoda," Nikhil told her.

"No. Let's play Nintendo."

Nikhil loved animal crackers and gave her some, but she only made a face, saying, "Babies eat these." She went to where we were having tea.

"I want to drink tea," she told Catherine.

Her mother pulled her and said, "Honey, you are not old enough to have tea."

"But I want to."

She took a sip from her mother and immediately lost interest in drinking. She looked at the painting in front of her and said, "That's silly. How can one have ten heads?"

"That's Ravana," I told her. "He was the King of Lanka, an evil king. He thought of all the bad things he could do with his ten heads. You see the woman in the picture? She is Sita. He stole her to please his sister, but then he fell in love with her."

"Oh!"

She went away to play with the boys.

A column of steady, long smoke rose from the incense-burner in the ceremonial floor. Fresh flowers and leaves were in several vases and strewn all around the small place decorated for this ceremony; the fire burning in the central pot made it very special, sacred. Arya and Alan each had a large, colorful garland hanging from their necks. Alan was touching the heart of Arya with a white carnation, repeating after the priest:

Into my will I take thy heart;
Thy mind shall dwell in my mind;
In my word thou shall rejoice with all thy heart;
May Prajapati (Brahma) join thee to me.

Arya lifted her shy head, and her eyes met his in mutual surrender. I could see a sparkle in her eyes, a glitter for a second, the smile of a teenager, the real Arya, I thought, transforming into the role of a woman. I had seen her grow up in this town and go through the elementary, junior high, and high schools, and was happy witnessing the start of a new phase in her life.

I remembered the evening I took her to the *Pirates of Penzance*. Catherine worked behind the stage, and I didn't want to sit alone. Arya hesitated a little at the beginning, but then the name of the opera attracted her and she agreed to go with me.

"What should I wear?" she had asked me.

"Wear something nice," I told her. "You know you dress up when you go to a concert."

"Do I have to wear a dress?"

"I think so. Ask your mother."

Mrs. Khatak was happy that I offered to take her daughter to the opera. They did not go to operas and, when she brought Arya to our house, she decided to drive me and Arya to the Civic Auditorium. It worked better for us because Catherine could then go ahead of us. Arya wore a long skirt, but ordinary school-going shoes. Mrs. Khatak told me Arya didn't want to dress up.

On the way to the performance, I teased Arya, "You are my date for tonight."

"No, I'm not." She gave me a quick reply and an angry look.

"Don't you want to be my date? We'll be great together."

"You must be kidding."

We saw many cars in the parking lot, and I remembered I didn't buy tickets in advance. "If tickets are sold out," I told Mrs. Khatak, "could you drop us to a movie?"

"I'm not going to a movie with you," Arya said grumpily.

"We can't just go back home." I said.

"Yes, we can."

When the car stopped I got out quickly and opened the door for Arya. Then I extended my hand as if to lead her to the dance floor, but she ignored me and walked up the steps of the auditorium; her facial expression was obvious: "I don't want anyone to know that I'm going to the show with you."

I smiled at Mrs. Khatak, saying, "I guess, she doesn't want to be my date."

"Have a good time," she gave me a broad smile and drove away.

We sat near the front, and Arya stealthily looked around to find known faces. She didn't see any and looked silently at the stage.

"Have you come here before?" I asked her.

"Only once with my school."

"It's nice. Isn't it?"

"I guess."

"Do you know the story?"

"Yes. I read about it before coming."

When the hall became dark and the show started, she said, "I wish I'd worn jeans. It's stupid to dress up to come here."

"You look nice. Don't you see everyone is dressed up?" I wanted to hold her hand in mine and comfort her but a look at her took that thought away instantly.

"You and my mother!" she exclaimed.

"How old are you, Arya?" I asked.

"I'm thirteen." She beamed and sat up.

"Only thirteen?" I spontaneously mumbled; but I should have said, "Oh! You are an adult now." But it was too late. It was a blunder; I was not good in hiding my feelings.

A song from a band of maritime outlaws reverberated the Hall:

Pour, oh, pour the pirate sherry;
Fill, oh, fill the pirate glass.

And watching the pirates toasting the very un-piratical British sherry, I soon forgot my mistake. Arya watched the young man who played Frederic.

In the Intermission we walked out to the lobby. That was where we always went to see who came to the show and announced our presence to each other. Arya found a girl from her school. She was beautifully dressed in a long, white dress and even had her hair done professionally. They talked with each other and I mixed with the adults.

Mrs. Johnson asked me who the gorgeous girl was, and for a second I wondered, "Gorgeous?"and looked at Arya. "Yes, in five years," I thought, "she will be devastating to the boys and some men. This oriental beauty, especially those girls of Asian origin who were growing up here, would have their impact. But for now they are different."

"She is my friend's daughter," I told her.

The new girl sat with us after the intermission and they talked all through the show, but I didn't mind. At least I didn't have to worry: Why did I drag her to this place? I felt she wasn't too conscious about her dress any more.

When we came home I asked Arya, "Did you enjoy the show?"

"It was okay," she shrugged her shoulder. But her face was relaxed and the resentment of the early evening was not there.

Nikhil was home from a camping trip. These two had become friends. "Did you hear?" he told her. "What my dad is planning for the Diwali celebration?"

"No. I hope it's not another drama again." She rolled her eyes.

"Yes. This time it's Ramayana."

"I'm not acting." She walked upstairs.

Ramayana is the legend of a prince in India, Rama. He went on an exile for twelve years to keep his father's promise to his step-mother. Rama's wife, Sita, and his brother, Lakhsman, went with him. During this exile, while they were wandering through unknown forests, Sita was abducted by Ravana, the ten-headed evil. The two brothers searched everywhere and finally found her captive in Lanka, the kingdom of Ravana. It was a difficult task to rescue her. Ravana had become a devil-incarnate and had already terrified the heaven and the earth with his atrocious deeds. He was formidable because he had a boon from Brahma that no Devas, Asuras, or animals could kill him, but in his disdain he didn't ask for protection from the humans. Rama gathered a huge army of monkeys and defeated Ravana after a long struggle. Ravana was killed in the battle, and good won over evil in the end. The Diwali festival, the festival of lights that Indians observe every year, celebrates the victorious return of Rama to his kingdom.

My vision shifted to the bride and the groom performing the shubha-dristi—sacred viewing—part of the ceremony where they see each other—as would-be-lovers—under a cloth placed over their head. In many arranged marriages this is the first time they really see each other. It is such a shy and awkward time, onlookers blatantly gazing at them; there is no romance in seeing your would-be-lover; the bride always has to be coaxed by everyone to open her eyes. In the present case, the situation was different. Alan and Arya had known each other since their college days. But how shy Arya had become. She had become a traditional Indian bride. She slowly raised her head and her mother lifted the veil. Had she become obedient for the sake of the ceremony? I looked for a mischievous smile on her face, but there was none. Alan was looking at her with eyes imbibing her face. Her eyes finally opened and they met. It was like the meeting of the very willing but bashful Sita, the daughter of Mother Earth, with young Rama, the deserving prince who had recently become famous by slaying two ferocious demons. The married Indian ladies uttered a sacred sound in unison to sanctify the moment.

Alan came from a Catholic family. I didn't know if it was Arya's influence, his love for her, or he had really fallen in love with the Indian rituals. He seemed to be quite at ease. I doubted if Arya had changed much during the last few years she was away from Idaho Falls. I had not seen her since she had gone to Oberlin College in Ohio and then to New York City. I heard about her from her parents. She did well in college. Her parents told me she was learning Hindi at school, which she didn't care to learn at home. They said she wanted to understand more of the culture. What a surprise. I thought she avoided me because I was always telling the kids about India. How we grow up and a day comes when we suddenly find our parents and elders not as dumb as we thought they were. And similarly and quite unexpectedly, we start to appreciate our heritage. I remembered how much Arya grudged at Diwali celebrations.

Once Arya came to me to decide on a science-fair experiment, and I told her to think of something that people believe in India and see if that had any value.

"Why India?" she questioned. "I'm doing a science project."

"Hm." I was taken aback. "You don't experiment on India. I meant you to think of something different. Something that others will not think."

"I've an idea," Nikhil spoke up, "Indians think plants have lives. But here we don't consider plants as living objects."

"That's good, Nikhil," I said. "Another example is people in India think animals have feelings; sometimes they even do good things and they can communicate."

"India is full of superstition also," Arya said. She didn't like our chain of thought for her science project.

"How about an experiment with light or sound?" Nikhil suggested, "and see if plants grow faster."

"No. I want to do an experiment with water. Is the Snake River water different in different parts of the city?"

"That's good," I said. "And if you can get a sample from the Ganges River," but before I could finish, she started to walk away toward the kitchen, and I knew she had already made up her mind.

The American guests at the wedding were very interested in the ceremony and were observing the details silently, while several tête-a-tête were going on the side among the Indians. I recognized a man and a woman: Vimala, her aunt, who was visiting from India, and Mr. Sood, who worked at the federal lab.

"The two look so wonderful together," Vimala told him.

"This is the first time I've seen such a wedding here. Whoever has organized it has done a great job."

"She looks so fair," she continued. "If you are born here you become fair. That's what my girls say. They are darker. It'll be difficult to find good husbands for them. How did they meet?"

"I guess in college. You know, no one could find a husband for your niece."

"Yes. I know. She has a mind of her own."

I wondered how she knew that.

"A silly story," she had told me. "The bad guy abducts the princess, and the good guy gathers a big army of monkeys and kills him to recover her. Not very interesting."

"It's one of the two classics from India," I said to the children who had gathered in our house to decide on a play for the upcoming Diwali celebration. "When you perform the Ramayana, you'll understand it better. You know, Vishnu, who protects us, was born on earth as Rama to destroy evil Ravana. That is why Rama is worshiped all over India even today."

"Can't you find another play?" Arya asked.

"What's wrong with the Ramayana?"

"I can't invite any friend to come to the play of a Prince with three mothers."

"It's an old story, they'll understand."

"No. They won't." She walked away from the girls.

"Who wants to be Sita?" I asked. "She is the heroine."

The girls giggled among themselves.

"Since Dipak is Rama and he is tall, Renu seems to be of the right height," I mumbled.

The girls pushed Renu around, saying something to her, and she protested violently, rolling her eyes. "I'm not going to be Sita," she announced to me.

"Well, then Arya will be Sita."

"I don't like Sita," she replied.

"Why not? This is a good part."

"No, I won't. She has no character. She follows her husband everywhere and really does nothing."

Vijaya commented to Renu in a hushed tone , "Hey, Arya will be Dipak's wife! They would be in love with each other," and the girls laughed and almost rolled over each other.

"If you behave like this," I told them, looking especially at Arya because it appeared to me she was the ring-leader, "we won't have a play to perform at the function. Your parents and I will decide which parts will be right for each of you." I was annoyed.

"You don't even know how to pronounce the names correctly," Mala told me obstinately.

She knew the story from her parents, but she didn't know that pronunciations are different in different regions of India because of language differences. How could I explain all this when their world was so confined? I organized a little play each year to instill a sense of the Indian culture in these children. They were growing up in Idaho, disconnected from anything resembling their heritage. In India we didn't have Sunday schools, but we grew up listening to many legends and myths; those provided the moral and ethical basis of the Indians. But the children were not interested. They were here against their wishes, under protest, and only to keep their parents happy. My problem was that there were only a few Indian children in the community and all of them must participate to make it anything at all.

The boys were having a different problem; they wanted to do something else, a more forceful play.

Dipak told me, "We will do the Ramayana, fine, but we'll do a play of our own also."

"What play?" I asked.

"We've not decided yet. It will be a surprise."

"It'll be gory," Anil said, "deaths, but there'll be grand speeches also."

"The Ramayana will be fun. It has lots of fights," Nikhil suddenly said. "I'll be Lakhsman if Rajeev takes the role of Rama."

"Yeah," Anil laughed, "two brothers as in the story."

I heard the Indian music begin. It was time for Mala Badal, exchange of garlands between the bride and the groom. It is like the exchange of rings in a Western wedding, an acceptance of each other as husband and wife. The Indian ritual came from the old times when a princess used to choose her husband from a gathering of princes for her hands; she would put a garland on the neck of her chosen suitor. How willingly Alan took the garland from his neck and put it around Arya's! Then Arya placed her garland on Alan. This was a fun but significant part of the wedding ritual, and the Indians stopped chatting. The priest sprinkled holy water on and around them. The bride and the groom went back to the ceremonial altar.

There are many ways to get married. At the moment, accepting one another with flower-garlands appeared to be a wonderful way to get married. Like cataloging the many forms of love-making in the Kama-Sutra, ancient Indians have defined eight forms of wedding, from marrying one against her wish to eloping. At one time the Gandharva style of marriage was prevalent in which a man and a woman marry each other with mutual consent and without any religious rituals. The present ceremonial wedding is the most common one, in which the father or an uncle gives away the bride to a man of character (as it is the custom in the West). But I seriously wondered if anyone can really give away a daughter, especially some one like Arya, if she didn't wish it?

I remembered Arya acting the role of Savitri in the year before we did the Ramayana. It is a beautiful story illustrating the ideal Hindu wife. Savitri was a princess, and when she grew up, her father sent her to many places to select a husband. After she chose Satyaban, the astrologers told her that Satyaban would die in one year. Once selected, she wouldn't change her mind, as if the marriage had already taken place. A year from the date of the wedding, indeed, Satyaban died while she held him. Although ordinary mortals cannot do so, being a pure and virtuous woman Savitri saw Jamaraj, the God of Death, when he came to take her husband's soul, and she followed him. Jamaraj told her to go back, but Savitri said, "I shall always be with my husband. I go wherever my husband goes."

During the rehearsal Arya balked. She wouldn't say the words, "my husband"; it was too personal. "We can do without these words," she said and went to one corner with a grumpy face. Nikhil acted the role of Satyaban, which was small; he looked the same size as Arya and felt okay with his part. He consoled her, "Just say it, it won't kill you. We know you're not married."

Her mother explained to her, "Honey, it's only acting, like in the movies you see. It doesn't mean Nikhil is your husband."

After much coaxing she agreed to perform the role as written.

In the story, Savitri went on to win over the King of Death by her perseverance and wit, and got back her husband's life and the kingdom he lost.

During the performance, however, Arya gave me a surprise. I heard her telling Jamaraj, "I shall always be with him. I go wherever he goes." This was not what we rehearsed!

That was the last scene and there was nothing I could tell her. She made up lines to suit herself. She didn't change the story; she only didn't say what she didn't feel at ease with. The audience didn't know the difference, and they felt the kids did a great performance. But I knew.

Those days were gone a long time back. I had seen the kids grow up and become young adults and adolescents. They wouldn't perform these dramas any more and went into a world of their own. Arya was no exception. They avoided us, adults, as much as possible. The little conversations I had with her during this period were limited, nothing more than a few formal questions and answers. I kept on directing these dramas each year with younger kids, who still had a dreamy image of India where their parents came from.

Arya went to college and I had seen her only once or twice when she came home. Her parents told me she was doing well in college. They said she faced an interesting problem in her first year. Her friends asked her about the "Temple of Doom," and if that was what the Indians still worshiped. Goddess Kali. She didn't know anything about the goddess and felt embarrassed. She had taken several courses in anthropology and her mother told me she wanted to know more of the Indian culture. Arya had told her, "There is this inside me that is from India, and I want to know it fully."

Once she asked her mother, "Why do Indians dump the ashes of dead bodies in the Ganges River?"

"I see," I exclaimed, "she's exploring her roots."

"She's an American girl," her father told me. "She doesn't want to be viewed as ignorant."

"No, no," her mother said, "she's really interested in our culture. Last year she visited the temple in Pittsburgh with a friend."

Mohan Parikh came over with a glass of scotch and soda in his hand. His face was reddish. "There'll never be an India Town in the U.S.," he seriously proclaimed to me.

"India Town?"

"You know like the China Towns in the big cities?"

"Why do you say that?" I was intrigued. Mohan was new in the country and a strict vegetarian.

"You see our boys and girls are marrying Americans and are being absorbed in the society here."

"Don't you like Alan?"

"No, no. He is fine. He has good qualifications. I'm sure he'll do well in medicine. I mean—think of the future generations. They will be half-Indians, quarter-Indians and soon there will be no Indian culture left."

"I see what you mean."

But I knew Mohan was wrong. Almost forty years ago when my sister got married in Evanston, Illinois, there was no Indian wedding ceremony. In my case, thirty years ago, a rudimentary ceremony was done. Now, the way the Indians are establishing themselves, it will soon reach a stage when the bridegroom will come in the traditional procession of relatives, friends, and musicians escorting him on horseback to the ceremony.

Alan and Arya were performing the Saptapadi, in which the couple take seven steps together symbolizing strength, health and fortune, happiness, progeny, long life, spiritual friendship, and ideals. A scene from the movie *Gandhi* flashed in my mind: an aged Gandhi with his scanty clothes performing the same ritual on the steps of a pond in the village where he was born. This is the final step in the Hindu wedding. After this the bride and the groom would touch the feet of the elders for their blessings; they start with their parents first.

Someone was serving lassi, a yogurt drink. The feast would start soon. But I stood in the corner of the lobby gazing at the Snake River when I heard Arya's voice. The sound of the falls did not reach here, but I enjoyed the scenery. At the end of this beautiful ceremony, I was a little melancholy. I didn't know why, perhaps it is the same reason why women cry in weddings, or perhaps a remembrance of my past life.

"Where is Debu-uncle?" I heard her enquire.

When they came to me I lifted her up, saying, "You don't have to touch my feet. You do that when you're in India," and I looked at her tenderly. What a beautiful bride she was, and although born and brought up in the U.S., she followed her heritage. This was not what I expected from her. I held her hand in mine and said, "I'm proud of you."

She somehow understood what I meant. "Remember the Ramayana we performed?"

"Yes. I do. What trouble you gave me." I laughed.

"But I learned something from you." She squeezed my hand. "Thank you for bearing with me."

For my blessing, however, I couldn't tell her, "Be like Sita," although Sita is the most revered woman in India, Vishnu's wife on earth. Sita's life was sad and really a tragedy, rejected by all the subjects and her husband for her uncertain time spent with Ravana. Sita passed the test of purity by going through a fire and Rama knew she was pure, but he yielded to the pressure of his subjects. She was abandoned in a hermitage in the forest; Rama didn't know at the time she was pregnant with his child. Rama was God-incarnate, but he never knew that. He was a human and fulfilled his life as a true human with human frailties. In the end, Sita had to call her mother to take her. The Earth opened and she jumped into her lap.

I put my hand over Arya's head, saying, "Be like Savitri."

Chapter Sixteen
INDIANS ACROSS THE OCEAN

We are the people of long ago...
We are the blue-green water that runs swiftly in the creek.
We are the flowers which blossom in the spring.
We are the rain that comes pouring down in the mountains.
We are the lightening that streaks in the sky.
We are the cottonwood trees that loom high into the air.
We are the gentle breeze of the many winds.
We are the blood of the mighty warriors.
We are the ancestors of the tribes of Mother Earth.
—Ardith S. Morris,
Shoshone-Bannock Tribes, Fort Hall, Idaho

My niece, Tuli, came to visit us from London. This was her first trip to America, and I could see a nervous look in her eyes. Last time we had seen her, she was going to elementary school in a white and blue jumper suit with a small bag over her shoulder—round, fluffy cheeks, wide black eyes and long black hair—waving at her newly-met uncle from the States; eager to make an acquaintance but too new an uncle to be spontaneous. Now, slim and tall at eighteen, she had a similar hesitation. "Was it the stiff British upbringing or the barrenness of this place?" I wondered. London, the largest city in the world, where she lives, sprawls miles after miles in all directions with buildings, roads, and residents. With centuries of history, London was there when Idaho was not born. It must be a shock to see where her uncle lives.

"This town's quite different, isn't it?" I asked her.

"Of course," she said unabashedly, and looked at the small Navajo rug hanging on the wall. The rug was a gift from a Navajo friend and the only Native American art we have in the house. Nijona gave us the rug from her family treasure and I was very fond of it—five white coyotes, the mythological beings, looking out from four corners and the center, and a large, black one touching them and hovering over the whole picture.

"I expected Idaho Falls to be small," Tuli looked at me, "and I expected it to have American Indian and cowboy motifs, but it has none. This neighborhood looks like any upper middle-class American suburb we see on TV."

"Huh," I told myself, "she is shy, but she speaks her mind." When I came here fifteen years ago, I thought it'd be like a small mining town. The few stray native Indians I saw then were aberrations, of no consequence to this place. American Indians. No one thinks of them anymore.

When we lived on Long Island, I had wanted to visit the Indian reservation, but didn't have the courage to go alone, and no one took me there. "There's nothing to see," a colleague had told me.

Rajeev and Nikhil barged in saying, "We're playing Axis and Allies, come on," and took Tuli away.

But she had thrown a stone in my pool. American Indians roamed in Idaho for centuries, and this was their land; I have come to live here from thousands of miles away but I don't even know one native Indian from here! Our friend, Nijona, and her son, Yazee, who went with us to the source of the Ganges River, were from Arizona; they are Navajo Indians. Several from the local tribes worked at the federal lab, Idaho National Engineering Laboratory located next to the reservation, but I wasn't acquainted with them.

The first encounter of Idaho Indians with Americans took place in 1804 when Lewis and Clark passed through what is now the Idaho Panhandle, 400 miles away from here; Sacajawea's people were the Lehmi (Sheepeater) Shoshone.

Various branches of the Shoshone tribe had lived in Idaho for millennia, perhaps as long as 4,000 years. Lewis and Clark also met with the Nez Perce Indians, who helped them with guides and horses. Later in 1807, a member of the expedition, John Colter, came back closer to this area and met with the Bannocks; he crossed the Teton Range from the east to Pierre's hole near Henry's Fork of the Snake River. Three years later Andrew Henry of the Missouri Fur Company established a fort on the upper Snake River, but it was abandoned after a year. However, this place was not unknown anymore, and a full-scale assault soon started.

The Shoshone and the Bannock are the Native American Indians of this area. Their names and a little of their history and culture are taught in elementary schools. I have talked with many children including my own but found that they learned very little beyond stereotypical images. I cannot, however, blame anyone because only recently have people of native Indian origin begun to write about themselves. In the past there were two portrayals of native Indians: one—the noble one—in which they are "the insightful primitive man, surviving in a hostile environment with verve and color," and the other—the savage one—"as a brute, dangerous to non-Indians and squarely in the way of progress." Since native Indians didn't have a written language and hadn't left behind much about themselves, how could we truly know them?

Young Yazee's face came to me. He looks like a Nepalee, but he is tall and big, and can pass through India without much notice. During our journey to the sources of the Ganges River we came to Joshimath where we had to wait for a long time for the one-way gate to open so we could traverse the narrow mountain path. As the wait stretched into hours, we had walked up and down the road, looking at people and inspecting the goods being sold. One stall owner was loudly playing a rather new American tape. I was naturally curious, and stopped. There sat Yazee, happily ensconced with a few of the locals. He had his sunglasses on.

"They're playing my songs. They dig it!"

"Have you been sitting here all this time?"

"Oh, no. I was at the tea stall before. They're cool. I told them I was from America. They were very friendly. I bought tea for everyone. It cost me only a dollar." Yazee, pleased with himself, smiled, saying, "They told me all about this place. It's cool, man." Collecting his cassette, he walked out with me.

"I really like India. People are nice here. I can jive with them."

"Yazee, you are mingling with the locals so well. How do you do it?"

"It's easy. You just go and talk to them. When I was in New Delhi, a man who drives a three-wheeler took me all over the town at night. I've seen where they live and how they live. I can mix with them. They're good people."

"It must have cost you a lot of money to go all over town?"

"Oh no. I told him I had no money. The driver said he'd show me anyway. I paid him only twenty rupees for gas."

Yazee told me how the man showed him the India Gate and the Parliament area. The streets were wide, lighted and totally empty. Then the driver drove him through a road that took many turns, and he didn't know where he was. He went by neighborhoods where ordinary people lived. Compared to the busily populated city, the night scene was quite different—shrouded in sadness. He saw many sleeping on the sidewalks. Earlier, he had gotten used to large crowds of Indians, but the night scene was strangely quiet and lonely. The three-wheeler stopped in front of a house, and the driver asked him to go inside.

As he entered, he saw a few men drinking beer. They were slightly drunk and appeared to be having a good time. They asked him to go upstairs. A wooden couch and two chairs stood barren in the dim light of the room. A man greeted him, and then said something in Hindi. Soon, several women came out of the adjoining rooms and stood in line in front of him. They were half-naked with bare breasts.

"Like any of them?" the man asked.

Some of them were very young. Teenagers, their breasts were not even fully developed yet, or perhaps, Yazee told me, the Indians look different. Whatever, he realized that the driver had brought him to a whore house. He heard rowdy noises coming up from downstairs. He looked at the women. Rather than excitement, he felt depressed. He simply walked down the stairs.

"I guess the women in America are much better, eh?" the man asked him.

"I'm just not interested." He almost ran out.

What a discovery! Yazee had surprised me throughout the trip. I worried about him all this time, while he had made himself at ease with the Indian people. He had gone out alone and had seen how the Indians lived and had shared their experiences. We were seeing India from the outside, and Yazee was observing India from the inside. He also felt better here because he was not judged by a set standard, as he was judged in the States. He was really happy.

"You know, Debu, I want to come back and live here."

"Yazee, India is good to visit, but very hard to live. Don't think of coming here to live."

"I know how to make American Indian jewelry, and I'm good in hand work. Maybe I can learn Indian jewelry and combine the two forms."

"It is possible, perhaps. But Yazee, I was born here. I know life is not as easy as it seems to you now."

Yazee's face changed and he looked at me calmly, saying nothing. However, I read his mind: "What do you know of an American Indian's life in America?"

Truly, sitting in the living room of my comfortable house in Idaho Falls, I lamented that I have lived here for fifteen years, but haven't made any bona fide effort to know the original inhabitants of this place. We pass by Fort Hall when we go south to Pocatello or to Salt Lake City, but I have entered the reservation only twice in my life.

Three years ago, as part of the federal lab program I was involved with pre-college math and science enhancement programs and I thought I could help the Native American school on the Fort Hall Reservation. I went there—my first real visit

—with a person who worked with them and met the science teacher, an excellent man who was quite aware of science education or lack of it in the country. We talked about how the federal laboratory could help their school. I was excited: I thought this was a chance for the federal government, and particularly for me, to play a small role in helping Native American youth. We could give them laboratory equipment and connect the students with scientists in our laboratory, and I imagined the Indian students becoming the new scientists, the new researchers in this country. The teacher felt my enthusiasm and, after a little time, stared at me with his eyes wide open and said, "The students here are not the same as in regular schools."

"Students are students, how are they different?" I asked, slightly flabbergasted.

"School is not high in most people's life here."

"What do you mean?" I said. "That's the only way they could get out of their predicament in this reservation."

He gave a wry smile. "Most are from broken families. They don't live with their parents, being raised by aunts and grandmothers. Family life in the reservation is not what you are used to. If a Friday is off, very few will come to school the next Monday."

"Really?"

"And little we can do about it."

I suddenly fell off from my lofty ideals. What little he told me was a different world, a world I had no familiarity with. I had no idea of their life, their culture, and I was there to tell them how to educate their children?

So far, only about fifty Shoshone-Bannocks have obtained college degrees. I thought, perhaps their education is still with the outdoors, not with books in the school room.

I was silent on my way home, my tail between my legs.

Yazee's face came to me again. He was standing at the corner and joined Rajeev and me for the hike north toward Mana village, the last village on the Indian side of the India-Tibet border, a few miles further up on the Alaknanda River. Our path went up through the living quarters of Badrinath. Soon we came out to an open space and saw the river on our left and one or two cars on a pitch road leading to Mana.

Because of the last Chinese invasion, the military kept the road in good condition. The Mana Pass, at 18,402 feet elevation, is twenty-eight miles from Badrinath; it is the last pass to Tibet, and one way to go to the sacred Kailash Mountain and the Manos-Sarobar, a lake at 14,950 feet. The sacred Kailash Mountain is 270 miles from Badrinath; we planned to go only three miles.

Slowly, the town of Badrinath became tiny in the distance. We passed by a well-settled military camp. In a nearby, small, tribal village, with only a few huts and small plots for cultivation, we saw some sheep. An older man sold local woolen sweaters, hats and mufflers from his house. The sweaters were heavy, similar to Irish Fisherman-knits, and very appropriate for the cold winter of the Himalayas.

As we walked out, I asked Yazee if he had herded sheep in Arizona.

"Very rarely. I grew up in Tuba City, a big town. My grandmother has sheep on the reservation. I don't like her place."

I knew his parents were divorced. "Did you live with your father in the city?" I asked.

"Sometimes, and sometimes I lived with others. I went to the public school like other boys in the city. I walked or took the regular bus to school, but I didn't like school."

"Didn't your father encourage you to get a good education?"

"He didn't have time for me. I didn't really know my father. He spent all his time drinking and doing drugs."

"You lived in the same house with your father, but you didn't speak much to each other?"

"No. We talked very little . . . I didn't have a great childhood. When I was very young, I was with my parents, but they fought all the time. When I lived with my father, he never took care of me."

"So, what did you do most of the time?"

"I just partied. I loved that."

What Yazee told me was a story not uncommon with many

Indians on the reservation. There is very little hope for the future, and Indian men idle away their time; they have no motivation for anything else. His father even sold drugs. Yazee was on his own until his mother brought him to Idaho Falls. As a young boy he had earned some money by various means, including selling drugs, and partied instead of going to school. No one watched over him.

"Did you lose touch with your father?"

"Yes. I never spoke with him again after I left Tuba City."

"Is he still there?"

"My father died last year."

"Oh! . . . I'm curious, Yazee. Did you go to his funeral? What kind of service did he have?"

"We had a regular ceremony, like the white people. It was a Mormon burial. I found out a surprising thing from my father's girlfriend. She told me my father was proud of me because I was holding a steady job in Idaho. He thought I'd do well in life." Yazee looked at me calmly and said, "My father called me the day before he committed suicide, but I didn't know—I wasn't home."

I glanced at Yazee's face, but he looked away from me and stared off into the distance.

The late afternoon sky was gloomy, and there was a chill in the still air. The path stretched forward to the hills, and the river flowed serenely below us, while we walked silently as the only souls in this desolate mountain road.

Catherine's voice from the kitchen brought me back from the Himalayas, "Why don't you take Tuli to the Public Library? She sure would like to see it."

For a teenager from London, I thought, a small library in Idaho Falls is nothing; but, yes, it is one of the few things people in Idaho Falls are proud of. I could chuckle because when Catherine was in Durgapur, a small town in India, family members proudly guided her to a new dam with decorative gardens around it; but she couldn't find the wonder she was supposed to.

The coyotes stared at me from the wall; the trickster-maker

of the world, did he really put us in the state we are in? The Native Americans certainly had a different vision of life.

I decided I must take Tuli around to show the area. It was nice for her to meet the cousins, but it'd also be nice to know where we lived. It would be even better if she could meet a Native American. But how could I arrange that?

The next day I went to the Tribal Liaison Officer in our office and happily told him, "I have a young visitor who wants to know about the local Indians."

"We don't deal with visitors," he said somewhat sternly. "You should go to the Visitor Center in Fort Hall."

I told him I had gone to Fort Hall several years ago to see the Sho-Ban festival. I had a vivid memory of that: even before we came near the Powwow Arbor I saw the white tee-pees and I was so elated because they were real, made by American Indians who lived there. Then when we came near the ground I saw the place was marked by a line drawn from one tree to another with leaves hanging from the line. It was just like what the Indians do in India during religious events; they hang mango leaves on string over doors and on other entrances to sacred places.

I remembered how I had imagined that the cars were not there, and I went back to the time when the only man-made things in the place were the tee-pees: I saw native Indians leisurely scattered around, women doing household chores and men sharpening their tools for hunting. It was exactly the picture I had in my mind of how American Indians lived; I had it imprinted from my seventh grade book. How real I made it for a few seconds.

Then I went inside and saw the trucks, cars, and trailers, and the crowded ground where people were eagerly buying trinkets: no different from any other fair in the U.S.

"Since you interact with them you probably know them intimately," I stated. "What are they really like?"

"You must be very careful about the Indians," he said. "You know, people generalize about them and they are often wrong. You have to know a lot to understand their culture."

"What can you tell me about them?"

"It's far too complex. I can't tell you in a few minutes."

"Tell me, are they still tribal? Or, they are like us with similar aspirations, only their living conditions are different."

He stared at me for a few seconds; then he said, "Those are serious questions. You've to consult an anthropologist for that."

"Perhaps you can give me some information about them? Their history, culture or anything?"

"I can get you some material. Give me a week, I'll call you when it comes."

Tuli would be gone by then.

I gazed at the buffalo hunting painting behind him: several Indians were riding fast on horses, chasing a herd of buffalo—their sharp, angular facial expressions vividly revealing their intent. How nicely it added to the decoration of his office.

I went to Dennis and told him about Tuli. How could she meet local American Indians?

"Hm. She thinks of this place as the old West. Indians running around."

"Perhaps."

"I have no contact with any Indian. What I know is only from my grandfather. He told me many stories because his father came here in the late 1800s and settled in the Malad area. The Fort Hall Reservation was established in 1867."

"These must be fascinating stories of interactions with the Indians?"

"No. These are stories of how they fought with the Indians and succeeded in putting them in the reservation."

"But they weren't all savages," I responded quickly. "Your grandfather must have known some who were friendly. What was their life at that time?"

"We never talked of their culture, whatever that was."

The green potato field suddenly reminded me that it was not this green merely 100 years ago when the Indians roamed freely in this area. The pioneers like Dennis's great-grandparents have made it fertile from the rugged nature it was, so we are here today in a modern town. I do admire the pioneering spirit of the daring few who came to the West in mid-1800s in search of land and gold, and to establish new life. They fought many adversities, including the Indians. Those are the stories that have survived. The pioneers had left behind the then-civilized world to come here; they were not going to be sent back by the technologically-handicapped Indians, however savage they might have appeared to be. It was a fight for survival, Darwinism at work for the humans.

I thought of Charles Eastman (Ohiyesa), who was born in 1858 and grew up as a true Sioux Indian and later became a medical doctor. He has described what it was to be an Indian. It was to become an expert to live alone in the natural world and be loyal to the culture of the tribe. He was trained thoroughly for an all-round out-door life and for all natural emergencies, alert and alive to everything that came within his senses. He had never known nor expected to know any life but this.

Eastman's father was presumed dead in a war with the Americans; but when Eastman was fifteen, his father came back and took him away from the tribe. His father sent him to the missionary school which he found very foreign. He seriously questioned what these books had "to do with hunting, or even with planting corn?" He obeyed his father as his culture taught him to, but he wondered why his father had deviated from his tribal culture. He took the situation seriously and wrote, "I remember I went with it where all my people go when they want light—into the thick woods." Eastman eventually figured out that the true Indian can no longer exist as a natural and free man.

Dennis's voice brought me back from my ruminations. "There's nothing to see, really," Dennis concluded. "The only thing I can think of is the Sho-Ban festival. It is this weekend."

"Sho-Ban festival this weekend?" My face brightened.

The next Saturday I told Tuli we would go to a festival at

the Indian reservation.

"You are really taking me to see American Indians?" she said with much elation.

"Yes. The Red Indians as we called them in India."

"That'd be super," she said in her British accent and immediately went upstairs to change.

When she came down, she had a red ribbon in her hair, a new white blouse and a light brown skirt.

There was a crowd in the Powwow Arbor. From a distance we could hear the beat of the drums. We saw many Indians—both men and women, some in great costumes—assembled on the ground inside, all dancing together. The loudspeakers relayed the songs. It was the inter-tribal dance where everyone participated. They were dancing with little hand movement. They simply moved in rhythm with the beat. This dance was certainly not for any show.

Soon, the contest dancing started. The place was surrounded by many, primarily by white people. No one dressed up for the occasion, not even those who had strong Native American features. It was simply an outdoor entertainment. I wished someone would explain the dance with some reference to their culture and tradition, but no commentary came over the speakers. The native Indians knew what was going on, but I was quite sure the large audience didn't have a clue about the dances. They came here like us because of curiosity and something interesting to do rather than of any feeling of special attachment with the native Indians. For the native Indians, it was their powwow and the non-natives didn't have a role. The separation between the cultures came out vividly. Even after a hundred years of coexistence, Euro-Americans and the American Indians appeared to be like oil and water, distinct and separate.

Behind the line of the crowd where we were standing, a tall and stout Indian came. He was a dancer with a decorative costume: a single, round, flat bustle of feathers on his back, a porcupine quill roach on his head from which two eagle feathers stuck out, a pair of buckskin leggings, and a breech-clout with feathers hooked onto it. He must be waiting for his turn. Next to him I looked like a thin dwarf. I didn't know what came upon me, but I told him, "I'm the real Indian, you know. I came from India."

Catherine pulled my arm, her face ashen. She was certain I would get a blow from him for my rudeness. But the man looked up and said in clear, crisp English, "I'm from Wisconsin myself."

I struck up a conversation with him about dancing. He explained to me that he was a traditional dancer. Traditional dancers don't wear a whole bunch of feathers as the fancy dancers do, but they often use paint on their face. Older men usually dance the traditional dance, where there is more body movement. They tell a story—hunting or sneaking up on an enemy or some other event. The fancy dancers are more color-ful, they wear two bustles, and they dance expressing their feelings.

There are three types of dances for women's individual com-petition: fancy shawl dance, jingle dress dance with metal cones hanging from their dress, and traditional buckskin dance.

The man told me dancing and singing are primarily for con-tests nowadays. Only in the past it was for social, ceremonial or for victory dances.

A Choctaw fancy dancer with very colorful and intricate cos-tume was dancing. His bustles were large with black, white, red, and yellow long feathers sticking out perpendicularly from his back. His headgear had fine feathers spread out as a crown and he held a large circular fan in his hand matching in color with his bustle, bright red with yellow feathers at the periphery and a blue center piece. He made a wonderful dis-play of color by his movements.

I thought that the dancers had practiced with their songs as they do in ice-skating competitions. But not so here. The drummers come from different tribes and sit in a circle around the arena. The arena director signals the drums to be used for a dance. The dancer does not know in advance the beat that will be played. He must dance to whatever was played and must stop when the drum stops. The Indian from Wisconsin told me that it wasn't often easy to do.

As I watched the dancers I went back to India, to my childhood days. I was seeing the same colorful image of tall, masculine Red Indians decorated with ornaments of beads and feathers. I remembered I didn't think of them as savages like cannibals, but I knew they were different from us, like the tribal people in India, like the Santhals. They lived away from villages in the outskirts of forests and never mixed with the ordinary people. What I knew of the Santhals came from my older sister: they come out and dance in the full-moon night. The women wear mohua flowers of intoxicating fragrance on their hair, the light yellow color contrasting their shiny, smooth, black skin. And their solid, healthy, slim bodies shine in the moonlight. Men come bear-chested with small drums hanging from their necks, and they dance and dance, all through the night in exhilarating mood. One can hear the beat of their drums from nearby villages and can only envy the mad time they are having. I am sure now that my sister secretly wished she could join in their dance, the dance that removes all inhibitions and let one go wild in the true enjoyment of one's free spirits.

Then a strange thing happens each time, my sister told me. They get into a fight. The mohua flower drink does it. Tribal people don't know how to hold back or control their feelings!

I saw Tuli talking to Rajeev. In the house she was quiet and I thought this was her upbringing. "Look at the little girl," she pointed to one standing next to a woman, both costumed for dancing, "she is going to dance with her mother. She's cute with her headdress." Tuli loved the little moccasin she was wearing.

"Didn't your mother teach you dancing?" Rajeev teased her, knowing fully that was not the custom in our family. In Calcutta dancing was only for the stage, for performances, not for social enjoyment.

"You know what I'll do when I go back? I'll learn the sitar."

"Because that's Indian?"

"Yeah. Why not?"

A young American Indian in ordinary clothes was watching Tuli for some time. Finally he came forward and asked her, "Are you or aren't you?"

Tuli didn't know what he was asking and stared curiously at him, the broad-shouldered, stout fellow. A square, solid, brown face with thick lips, he had a masculine appeal.

"Belong to any Indian tribe?"

"I'm from England."

"Is this your first trip to the festival?"

"Yes."

"You like the festival?"

"Yes. I've never seen an American Indian festival before." She had not met an American Indian before, but she felt the Indian man was sincere. "In U.K. the schools don't teach anything about American Indians." She smiled and added, "But we learn a lot of Greek and Roman history."

"You know these dances have changed over time, but they are real," he told her. "I don't dance. It takes too much time. I can show you some steps."

He moved his feet with the beat of the drum with a nice body movement. Rajeev tried to imitate him and gave up soon. Tuli watched with interest. The man was friendly. She asked, "Can you show us the tee-pees?"

"Sure. Come with me."

They walked away toward the tee-pees.

I had never seen Tuli so bouncy as when she and Rajeev came back. She told Catherine what she had seen. The hole on top of a tee-pee with the poles sticking out fascinated her. She asked what happened in winter and the man told them that very little snow comes down the hole, because the smoke from the fire kept a draft going up.

"In the old days they used buffalo hide to make tee-pees," she told Catherine. "Would you believe, *Kaki*, tee-pees were made and maintained by the women? They would get together and sew a tee-pee in one day."

"Like a barn-raising event."

"I guess."

The tee-pee she saw was quite spacious. A trunk was on the floor and many items hanging from the walls. Six people could easily sleep on the floor. She was very pleased meeting the Indian and seeing a real tee-pee.

"How was the Indian boy?" Catherine asked her.

"Dainty." She blushed.

"You know his name?"

"Rick he said, and then when I asked for his American Indian name, he said, 'its too difficult to explain.' How do you translate a name like 'A man whose hunting skill is great'? He told me there is a back-to-tradition movement among the Indians and a child gets an Indian name when he is a few years old." She was bubbly with enthusiasm.

We walked over to the place for food and where many were selling jewelry and other Indian handicrafts.

"Tuli, you want a buffalo burger?" I asked her.

"Do you eat these here?"

"It's okay for a Hindu," Nikhil told her smilingly, "it's not beef."

"And cooked by real Indians," Rajeev added.

She looked at them coldly and said, "Yes, I'd try one."

Catherine spent a long time at the stalls figuring out what earrings Tuli would like most. It turned out she would rather take back moccasins.

Tuli was focussing her camera on an American Indian man. He was dark, thin, and tall and had a very interesting costume with long leggings and a large, very colorful headband and a rosette on the forehead, but the man walked fast to her waiving his hands. "Don't take my picture," he told her firmly.

Tuli was taken aback and only stared at him, frozen.

I explained to him that she was from England and would love to take back a picture of the most wonderful costume she had ever seen.

"No. I don't want my picture taken."

"Okay."

The man looked at Tuli's brown face for a few seconds and said, "Maybe. If you promise to send me a copy."

"Sure, no problem." I wrote down his address. He was not from Idaho. I gave the address, written in a piece of torn paper, to Tuli.

Tuli took the picture and the man walked away.

I wonder now if I did fulfill my responsibility by simply giving the address to a teenager? Another promise to a Native American not kept?

Once I had a discussion with an older lady about the Native American Indians in the federal building cafeteria in Washington, D.C. She was alone and I asked her what she thought of them.

"I feel sorry for them," was her quick reply.

"Don't you feel any guilt for what was done to them?"

"I am a second generation," she told me. "My parents came from Sweden. They worked hard to make it here. People would have to do it individually."

"Come on," I said, "you know the Indians can't do it themselves."

"How did the Blacks do it?"

"A good question. I guess they need a Dr. King."

"They have to put the country to shame," Lilian Munson told me. "When the guilt gets to people, they will get a deal similar to the Affirmative Action plan. We are all in denial so far as the Indians are concerned."

"But they have no power," I exclaimed. "And they are all different tribes. The Blacks were originally many tribes too but the slavery experience has molded them into one. That could not happen for the Indians because of vast distance separating them, different languages, customs and traditions. We spend so much for other countries; billions were spent to save Kuwait. If we spend one-tenth of a percent of our budget per year for the Indians, we can certainly remove a dark side of this history."

"One must find another way than pushing them toward gambling and other addictions," she stated. "You know, countries and companies are run by people who are susceptible to change. Greed and power. They work well. The only thing I can think of is shame. Put them to shame for the Indians. The Blacks succeeded that way."

She stared at the large, bluish-green, metal statue of a muscular man holding the globe in his hand and then walked away.

I sat there a little longer than usual, watching the well-dressed federal employees around me. They are influential people. They deal with millions of dollars in various ways that affect our lives. Whenever I come to the Capital I am overwhelmed by the importance of these people. So powerful they are. And so busy. But I wondered if Native Americans were in anyone's mind.

Is there really a way to help the American Indians?

I often recall the sad words of the Bannock Chief Taghee when I think of the local Indian's final story: "I do not know where to go nor what to do."

When I think of Idaho Indians, I think of small groups of docile, "tribal" people who lived in aboriginal ways with what nature had provided. They moved with the season in search of food and shelter and made a living with what they could dig or pick in the wild, and fish and game they could hunt with simple tools. The Indians had no idea of owning land and not sharing what was available in nature. I think of their style as similar to our camping, you pitch a tent on the best spot you find, and move out when you are done with camping, without thinking that you need to own the spot. The Shoshones and the Bannocks acquired horses in the early 1700s and that changed their life style a little but not much.

However, the third-quarter of the nineteenth century was a disturbed time for them, a sad time. They were helpless in a destiny that was taking shape. It was like a Greek tragedy—there was no way to stop the course of events that were taking place. The settlers were steadily moving up north of the Salt Lake area. They took the grazing land of the Indians and made farms. Their animals dug up the roots the

Shoshones lived on. Their guns considerably diminished the available game, and the buffalo moved away to the east. The Shoshones barely had enough to eat. And the war-like Bannocks were no match against the U.S. Army.

The U.S. government made treaties and did not follow through on their promises. Congress and the federal government have repealed, modified, or abrogated the provisions of nearly every one of the 650 Indian treaties. The promised annuities were not delivered and food not distributed in a timely manner. I wonder if those who were in charge of the native Indians truly had the interest of the Indians in their heart. The Fort Bridger Treaty of 1868 allocated over a million acres for the Fort Hall Reservation, but then the railroad expanded and there was a great need for land for the town of Pocatello. Naturally, the Congress reallocated the reservation reducing their land to 544,000 acres. Eastman, who himself worked for the federal government, wrote in 1919 (after resigning from his medical post): "Never was more ruthless fraud and graft practiced upon a defenseless people than upon poor natives by the politicians! Never was there more worthless "scraps of paper" anywhere in the world than many of the Indian treaties and Government documents!"

The Indian depredations were most of the time due to starvation and extreme destitution.

Sometimes even Mother Nature was not kind to them. Once the Fort Hall Indians cultivated 250 acres of wheat, but the grasshoppers came like flood and destroyed the wheat. The Indians ate the grasshoppers. But even this did not last long, and with no food stored, we can guess what happened when the winter came. Life outside the reservation was worse. Forgotten by the government, they began to starve in the borderlands of Idaho, Utah, and Nevada. Only a few like Chief Pocatello rebelled for a little while but eventually all, including him, were forced to retire to the Fort Hall Reservation.

The value of their culture diminished, so also their self-esteem, and being goal-less and disoriented, the life of the Indians had been in disarray and bitter for a long time. All their attempts to carve their destiny were futile. What could they really have done when they could neither join the victorious race nor hang on to their own culture?

A scene from our journey to the source of the Ganges came to me. When we came down from the high Himalayas to the confluence of the Bhagirathi and the Alaknanda rivers, Yazee was standing alone under the sign-board that described the final *sangam* of the two good-sized rivers that made the mighty Ganges River. He always wore a sunglass, but not now.

I walked over to him. "Yazee, how come you haven't worn your sunglasses for the last two days? Are you okay?"

"When we were in Badrinath, I thought about what I have seen here and made some decisions about my life."

"You decided not to wear sunglasses?"

"Hadn't you realized, Debu, I was high all through the trip?"

"What?"

"I was high on marijuana and hashish."

"Really?" I was surprised, because I hadn't caught on at all.

"What do you think the mendicants do when they sit down and gaze at nothing? They are high on ganja!"

I knew that drugs were a problem on the Indian reservations back in the States, and Yazee had had some encounters with it, but I had no idea that he was smoking all through the trip. One of Yazee's friends sold drugs in the Arizona reservation until he finally died of an overdose, but still Yazee couldn't give it up.

"How did you find marijuana here?"

He took me farther away from our group and told me about his experience. The day we arrived in New Delhi he shared an American cigarette with one of the guards at the hotel. The guard gave him the local biri to try out. The biris are tobacco rolled in dry leaves, about two inches long, and rather harmless. Yazee asked if it was possible to get some real stuff to smoke. Sure, everything was available for a price. When he agreed to pay $10, the guard sent another man to get some marijuana. Within ten minutes he had a large bag of marijuana, an enormous amount for the money. The stuff was also very good. He had been "floating along" since that time.

The other boys knew about it, but did not tell me. None of the boys wanted to smoke marijuana, but he found company among the sadhus and mendicants on the hills. He was also not afraid to go out alone at night, because he was robust compared to the Indians and he could make friends with the street people.

While I could not, he could walk over to an ash-covered, long-haired sadhu and start a conversation with him. The sadhus didn't mind him at all. They would often share their small hand-held clay pipes with him. They took fast, long breaths, holding their pipes with their two hands, until a puff of fire spouted on top of the pipe. "Bohm, " they would say, and be still for a long time. With that deep puff of smoke they had climbed Shiva's mountain, Kailas, and floated there in union with Him.

Sometimes, Yazee enquired why they smoked. Was it helpful to their meditation? Some would tell him, yes, it helped them to travel to a different space, where they felt bliss and achieved a profound perspective about life. Some would not answer.

No wonder Yazee was on his own all this time; he was busy discovering a different world. He liked this world where he was accepted for what he was.

Yazee saw a different India, yet it was as real as the one I experienced. I couldn't help asking, "Was it worth the trip, Yazee?"

"I've learned a lot about myself. I didn't appreciate before what I had in the States. Now I do. You won't believe it, but I have thrown my pack of hashish into the sacred waters of Badrinath."

"You don't need the sunglasses now?"

"Right. No more drugs, no more sunglasses." He stared at the temple of Rama near the confluence and talked to himself, "I wish I could stay here longer."

Tuli left five days later. Before that we had taken her to Yellowstone National Park, the Tetons, and Jackson Hole. She gave us hugs at the airport, saying she would return in a few years.

"Don't forget the moose you saw in Yellowstone," I shouted at her from a distance.

"No. No," she called back, forgetting her quiet demeanor, "The best thing was seeing the Native Americans. I must come back for the Sho-Ban festival."

On my way home, I wondered what Tuli found so fascinating in American Indians. People come here from all over the world for the wonders of the Yellowstone Park, not for American Indians. It was a novelty for her. Perhaps, she was the only one among her friends to visit a festival where American Indians danced. For me, it seemed like going to India and getting a chance to see the Santhals dance in moonlight. Would I similarly value that more than seeing the Taj Mahal? Perhaps, she found something common with them, a sympathy with the people that bear the same heritage name as hers. It is certainly a happy memory for her.

When I see the face of a male American Indian, however, I don't see a happy face. I see a somber face, which always forces me to go back to their glorious days when they were free—free to live their aboriginal ways, believing in the efficacy of dreams, visions, and spirits. Imagine no eight to five work hours, no bosses, no car problems, no house chores, no mortgage to pay, and no taxes of any kind. A backpack trip for the rest of your life! Whenever I am near a serene stream, I think of happy Indians in canoes. I know I have not faced an American Indian on the warpath and have not been here in the old settler-days, but can't I be a little romantic once in a while?

I see detachment on an American Indian woman's face, a face that has no opinion. Perhaps they have seen too much, bore too much, and have forgotten to expect a life of their own.

Indians are destitute in their own land except for a little old pride left in them. Their final assimilation was expedited by a well-orchestrated plan by the government and the missionaries to civilize them into the Judeo-Christian culture. There will likely be no American Indians left in America in 100 years. The word genocide is often used now-a-days. I wonder if "genocide" could include a situation where no blood is shed, no one is killed, but a group or a tribe is slowly wiped out. We call this "survival of the fittest."

How different the fate of the East Indians and the American Indians has turned out to be. Both suffered in the hands of the West. The British captured India during a time when the Indian kingdoms were in disarray; the East India Company used better weaponry and more organized troops, but more importantly they used unethical tactics like violating treaties and double-talking. However, the East Indians kicked the British out in the end. One reason for this is that Indians were numerous and in spite of their many different languages and customs, there was a feeling of one nation among all Indians. And they weren't as isolated as the American Indians were from diseases and new germs from the West. The East Indians were also able to quickly learn the methods and means of the Western world. They resisted violently when their old culture was attacked. At the same time their leaders went to England to be educated. Now they have produced five Nobel Laureates, and India is a nuclear weapons country. The case is so different for the American Indians. And the reasons are many. Their case is similar to the Aborigines of Australia. The American Indians were fewer in numbers, they were never one tribe, and they could not grasp the western methods and their modus operandi. They belonged to a truly different world.

I remembered an old Fort Hall story of a Shoshoni scout who was tracking Crow Indians in the mountainous areas, and took shelter in a cave in the darkness of night. Soon he felt the presence of another person in the cave. In the pitch darkness of night he could do nothing but keep quiet and vigilant. When the morning light came he saw his enemy, a Crow Indian. They saw each other and knew neither of them could escape; it would have to be a fight till death.

They used sign language and agreed to gamble for their scalps. The winner would scalp the loser.

The Crow lost the gamble and submitted himself to the Shoshoni, and was scalped.

I often think of this story and wonder what I would have done in that situation. What courage the Crow had to surrender himself to his fate, to death. Did the Indians honor ethics more than their lives?

I wonder if the modern generation, so eager to save the environment, should feel any guilt for or a responsibility to rectify what had been done to the American Indians; it is not too different from genocide in a broader sense of the term. Is there a way to pay for the deeds of ancestors?

Two summers had passed by since we went to the source of the Ganges River. Yesterday, I got a surprise call from Yazee, "What's happening, my big man?"

Hmm. He had not called me for a long time. "Yazee, you want to get together?"

"I'd like that."

"Let's go for a walk around the green belt. Okay?"

"Great."

When I reached his house, Yazee was on the phone—a new generation warrior movie on the TV—soundless—and loud rock music from a disc player. The few rooms I could see were neat and clean. His mother bought the house many years ago; he lived there alone.

"I am going to jail," he told me when we reached the river.

"I thought you were doing well. What happened?"

"I was caught by the police a month back when I was driving alone, around the neighborhood, at 4 a.m. in the morning. I had alcohol in my blood. They said I was moving like a snake."

"Anything we can do to help you?"

"No. I must do it on my own. I must pay my dues."

"Don't be stupid, Yazee."

"I'm not stupid, Debu. I'm very sad."

He stared at the waterfalls. "This is my favorite place in Idaho Falls. I love it . . . You don't know my life, Debu. I have been involved with drugs, gangs and everything."

"In Arizona?"

"Yes. I have deep sorrows within me. I feel like crying."

We both looked at the ducks playing in the water. I couldn't say anything.

"You know I was not liked by either my father or my mother. In fact, I am not close to anyone in my family. When I go to Arizona, I want to get away from my relatives as soon as I go there. And the friends I associated with before, they'll hold a gun against my head."

"Your mother cares for you. I know that."

"She wanted an abortion—I found out recently. She never really cared for me."

I was surprised because he was always very respectful of his mother. It was more than what I have seen in India. He told me before it was their culture. I have also seen Nijona with her mother and her daughter, what a warm relation they had. The strong female bond of the Navajo society did come across to me very well. Nijona went to Arizona all the time to visit her mother who didn't speak English. Perhaps Yazee's father was a weak link in the chain and Yazee couldn't be brought over to her side of the family. He missed out on the supportive bond of the family.

Nijona had discussed Yazee's situation with me several times. She had brought him to Idaho Falls hoping he would change and finish high school, but Yazee couldn't find interest in studying. For the same reason she took him on the trip to India. She was lost like any other mother who's son wasn't doing well in school and who didn't know what to do. She grew up in Arizona in the comfort of her family, sheep-herding during the summer months and going away to boarding school during the school year. She was always strongly attached to her family, but Yazee didn't grow up like that. And Nijona was unable to guide Yazee in the free western society.

Yazee took out a cigarette, saying, "I won't smoke if you

don't want me to."

"That's fine, Yazee, but are you still on drugs?"

"I'm very good most of the time. I go to exercise regularly at the "Y." I told you this before, there is a cycle within me—it comes and I don't know what happens to me. I can't stop it. I do these crazy things—go on a drinking binge, for example. I can't stop it. Like this time I was caught by the police. I can't control it."

"Are you 22 now?"

"No. I'm 21."

"When is your court date?"

"Wednesday. But I don't want you to do anything. I must pay my dues, and I must clean myself. This is the second time the police caught me. If I have to go to jail, I'll go. It may be for three years, but I'll manage. I'm only afraid that they may send me to Boise. I don't like to be bossed by anybody. It's a boot camp there, and I'm afraid I'll get into more trouble."

"Didn't you learn anything from your trip to India?" I was annoyed.

"Oh. That was wonderful. I thought I'd change when I came back. You know, some of the *sadhus* understood me. They read me like an open book. One *sadhu* told me point blank that I have sadness within me and I'm searching for a way out. Although lots of people think they're goofy, they are very wise. It's amazing, they told me it won't be easy. When I mention karma, nobody understands me here." He looked at the distant mountains, the foothills of the Tetons; the snow had not melted from the top and that reminded him of the Himalayan ranges. "I have to pay my dues. But I'll come out free in the end."

I may be older, but I didn't know how to console one with deep sorrows.

Robert Bower

THE AUTHOR

Marc Giroux

Debu Majumdar, a native of Calcutta, India, came to Philadelphia in 1964 for graduate studies, and after spending several years in three universities and a national laboratory, he settled in Idaho Falls in 1980 with his wife and two sons.

Debu is a Senior Scientific and Technical Advisor with the U.S. Department of Energy and currently represents the United States at the International Atomic Energy Agency in Vienna. He has a Ph.D. in physics from SUNY at Stony Brook. He has completed two full-length manuscripts which are presently with publishers: *Viku and the Elephant* and *A Journey to the Source of the Ganges River*.

THE PHOTOGRAPHER

Robert Bower grew up in the Snake River Country. He has a strong attachment to the region. His great-grandfather hauled freight from the end of the railroad tracks in Utah to the mines in Montana.

Robert graduated from the University of Idaho, Moscow, Idaho, in 1970 and after a short time as an Army officer, ended up back in Idaho Falls working for the *Post Register* as a photographer.

Robert has photographed the Snake River Country from drought to flood, including the Teton Dam Collapse in 1976. At the newspaper he is known as the resident photographer and historian' of the Yellowstone Country.

Acknowledgments

In a non-fiction class, English 324, we were reading essays by E. B. White. White had lived in New York City for many years and had written a wonderful essay about the city. I wondered what he would have written about Idaho Falls and about the locals if he lived here. I wrote up a short article about my first experience of an Idaho winter and gave it to the professor. I had no ulterior motive. He said, "It's nice," and I gave him another. He said, "Write what comes from your soul." So I kept on writing. Thank you, Dante Cantrill, without whose inspiration these articles would not have emerged.

Except for my family, I have used pseudonyms for most of the characters because they are conjured from my impressions and imaginings from a long past. I wish to express my appreciation for the friendship of these people who have touched my life during my years in Idaho.

Thanks are due to several Idaho friends and members of the Idaho Writers' League who taught me the constraints of writing. I have violated many of the rules they told me, but not consciously—my foreign accent just couldn't be avoided. I thank Dawn Anderson, Jerry Bratt, Karen Finnigan, Ralph Hauser, Charlene Johnson, Merle Kearsley, Ken Meyer (now in Pakistan), Earlien Reid and Eric Swisher for their support and friendship. I thank my wife, Catherine, for being my first reader, critic and encourager and for enthusiastically bringing home stories from the New Yorker, Atlantic Monthly, and Granta for me to read, and for bearing with our unconventional lives together.

Last, but not least, I thank Robert Bower, longtime photographer for the *Post Register* in Idaho Falls, for providing the pictures of southern Idaho for this collection.

Other Books About Idaho
From CAXTON PRESS

Snake River Country

ISBN 0-87004-215-7

12x15, 195 pages, cloth, boxed $39.95

River Tales of Idaho

ISBN 0-87004-378-1

6x9, 50 maps, 12 illustrations, 14 maps, 344 pages, paper

$17.95

A Cabin on Sawmill Creek

ISBN 0-87004-380-3

6x9, photographs, 228 pages, paper

$12.95

Gem Minerals of Idaho

ISBN 0-87004-228-9

6x9, 14 maps, 23 illustrations, 129 pages, paper

$18.95

Southern Idaho Ghost Towns

ISBN 0-87004-229-7

6x9, 14 maps, 95 illustrations, 135 pages, paper

$12.95

For a free Caxton catalog write to:

CAXTON PRESS
312 Main Street
Caldwell, ID 83605-3299

or

Visit our Internet Website:

www.caxtonprinters.com

Caxton Press is a division of The CAXTON PRINTERS, Ltd.

WC